'Undoubtedly a comprehensive review of all things creative in primary science. Uniquely drawing on his findings from across the UK and New Zealand, Dan Davies provides both theoretical and practical support to teachers and students looking to learn about the key issues associated with adopting a creative approach to teaching creatively and for creativity. The authors' interest and passion for this area is demonstrated through the wealth of relevant references which coupled with his own insights stimulate a thought-provoking attitude in the reader. A text for all seasons – to inspire, to question and to kick-start one's own creative explorations in science teaching.'

Dr Lynne Bianchi, Senior Research Fellow, Centre for Science Education, Sheffield Hallam University, UK

'With dialogic teaching and collaborative activity firmly at its core, Davies sets out a clear rationale for the importance and value of exploring creativity within science and teaching science creatively while at the same time drawing our attention to the tensions and limitations of an education system driven to obsession with targets, standards and league tables. Drawing upon his experiences of working in the primary classrooms of both England and New Zealand, he captures and conveys something of the essence of creativity in science and how the excitement and sense of awe and wonder generated through it can be captured and put to good use. His passion and enthusiasm for creative science is particularly evident throughout this book, an essential purchase for all working in the primary sector as well as for those currently enrolled on courses of initial teacher training.'

Professor John G. Sharp, Bishop Grosseteste University College Lincoln, UK

TEACHING SCIENCE CREATIVELY

How can you unlock your own creativity to help children learn science creatively?

How do you bring the world of 'real science' into the classroom?

Where does science fit in a creative curriculum?

Teaching Science Creatively explores how creative teaching can harness primary-aged children's sense of wonder about the world around them. It offers innovative starting points to enhance your teaching and highlights curiosity, observation, exploration and enquiry as central components of children's creative learning in science.

Illustrated throughout with examples from the classroom and beyond, this book explores the core elements of creative practice supporting both teacher and children to develop their knowledge and skills. Key themes include:

- the importance of science in a creative primary curriculum
- the role of play in early scientific learning
- developing children's own interests and ideas into creative enquiry
- how theories of learning can help you understand children's creative development
- teaching science topics in innovative and creative ways – games, drama, role-play, puppets, mini-safaris and welly walks!
- using new technologies to enhance your science teaching in the classroom and outdoors.

Stimulating and accessible, with contemporary and cutting-edge practice at the forefront, *Teaching Science Creatively* introduces new ideas to support and motivate new and experienced primary teachers. It is an essential purchase for any professional who wishes to incorporate creative approaches to teaching science in their classroom.

Dan Davies is Head of Applied Research and Consultancy in the School of Education, Bath Spa University, UK.

LEARNING TO TEACH IN THE PRIMARY SCHOOL SERIES

Series Editor: Teresa Cremin, the Open University

Teaching is an art form. It demands not only knowledge and understanding of the core areas of learning, but also the ability to teach these creatively and effectively and foster learner creativity in the process. *The Learning to Teach in the Primary School Series* draws upon recent research, which indicates the rich potential of creative teaching and learning, and explores what it means to teach creatively in the primary phase. It also responds to the evolving nature of subject teaching in a wider, more imaginatively framed twenty-first century-primary curriculum.

Designed to complement the textbook *Learning to Teach in the Primary School*, the well-informed, lively texts offer support for students and practising teachers who want to develop more flexible and responsive creative approaches to teaching and learning. The books highlight the importance of teachers' own creative engagement and share a wealth of innovative ideas to enrich pedagogy and practice.

Titles in the series:

Teaching English Creatively
Teresa Cremin

Teaching Maths Creatively
Linda Pound and Trisha Lee

Teaching Science Creatively
Dan Davies

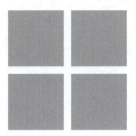

TEACHING SCIENCE CREATIVELY

Dan Davies

Routledge
Taylor & Francis Group

LONDON AND NEW YORK

First edition published 2011
by Routledge
2 Park Square, Milton Park, Abingdon, Oxon OX14 4RN

Simultaneously published in the USA and Canada
by Routledge
270 Madison Avenue, New York, NY 10016

Routledge is an imprint of the Taylor & Francis Group, an informa business

Typeset in Times New Roman and Helvetica Neue
by Wearset Ltd, Boldon, Tyne and Wear
Printed and bound in Great Britain
by TJ International Ltd, Padstow, Cornwall

British Library Cataloguing in Publication Data
A catalogue record for this book is available from the British Library

Library of Congress Cataloging-in-Publication Data
Davies, Dan (Daniel John), 1962–
Teaching science creatively / Dan Davies.
p. cm. – (Learning to teach in the primary school series)
Includes bibliographical references.
1. Science–Study and teaching (Primary)–Activity programs. I. Title.
LB1532.D48 2011
372.3'5–dc22   2010025056

ISBN13: 978-0-415-56131-0 (hbk)
ISBN13: 978-0-415-56132-7 (pbk)
ISBN13: 978-0-203-83998-0 (ebk)

CONTENTS

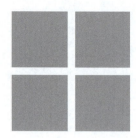

FIGURES

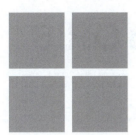

TABLES

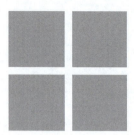

SERIES EDITOR'S PREFACE

Over the last two decades, teachers in England, working in a culture of accountability and target setting, have been required to introduce both the National Curriculum and the literacy and numeracy strategies; both content and pedagogy have been specified. Positioned as passive recipients of the prescribed agenda, practitioners, it could be argued, have had their hands tied, their voices quietened and their professional autonomy threatened and constrained. In order to conform to expectations and deliver the imposed curriculum, research reveals that some teachers short-changed their principles and their knowledge and understanding of pedagogy and practice (English *et al.* 2002; Burns and Myhill 2003). The relentless quest for higher standards and curriculum coverage which dominated this period may well have obscured the personal and affective dimensions of teaching and learning and fostered a mindset characterised more by compliance and conformity than by curiosity and creativity.

Recently, however, creativity and creative policies and practices have become prominent in government policy alongside the standards agenda, and a focus on creative teaching and learning has been in evidence. Heralded by the publication *All Our Futures: Creativity, Culture and Education* (NACCCE 1999), this shift is exemplified in the Creative Partnerships initiative, in the Qualifications and Curriculum Authority's creativity framework (QCA 2005) and in a plethora of reports (e.g. OFSTED 2003; DfES 2003; CAPEUK 2006; OFSTED 2006; Roberts 2006; DCMS 2006). The definition of creativity employed by most of these documents is that coined in *All Our Futures*: namely that creativity is 'imaginative activity fashioned so as to produce outcomes that are both original and of value' (NACCCE 1999: 30). As a new decade commences, schools continue to be exhorted to be more innovative in curriculum construction, and the coalition government plans to introduce primary phase academies, which will apparently be formally afforded increased freedom and the opportunity to shape their own curricula. Yet for primary educators, tensions persist, not only because the dual policies of performativity and creativity appear contradictory, but also because in recent years they have been positioned more as technically competent curriculum deliverers, rather than artistically engaged, research-informed curriculum developers. I believe, alongside Eisner (2003) and others, that teaching is an art form and that teachers benefit from viewing themselves as versatile artists in the classroom, drawing on their personal passions and creativity as they research their practice. As Joubert observes:

> Creative teaching is an art. One cannot teach teachers didactically how to be creative; there is no fail safe recipe or routines. Some strategies may help to promote creative thinking, but teachers need to develop a full repertoire of skills which they can adapt to different situations.
>
> (2001: 21)

However, creative teaching is only part of the picture, since teaching for creativity also needs to be acknowledged and their mutual dependency recognised. The former focuses more on teachers using imaginative approaches in the classroom in order to make learning more interesting and effective, the latter more on the development of children's creativity (NACCCE 1999). Both rely upon an understanding of the notion of creativity and demand that professionals confront the myths and mantras which surround the word. These include the commonly held misconceptions that creativity is connected only to participation in the arts and that it is confined to particular individuals; a competence of a few specially gifted children.

Creativity is an elusive concept which has been multiply defined by educationalists, psychologists and neurologists, as well as by policy makers, in different countries and cultural contexts. Debates resound about its individual and/or collaborative nature, the degree to which it is generic or domain specific, and the difference between the 'Big C' creativity of genius and the 'little c' creativity of the everyday. Notwithstanding these issues, most scholars in the field perceive it as involving the capacity to generate, reason and critically evaluate novel ideas and/or imaginary scenarios. As such, I perceive it encompasses thinking through and solving problems, making connections, inventing and reinventing and flexing one's imaginative muscles in all aspects of learning and life.

In the primary classroom, creative teaching and learning have been associated with innovation, originality, ownership and control (Woods and Jeffrey 1996; Jeffrey 2006), and creative teachers have been seen, in their planning and teaching and in the ethos which they create, to afford high value to curiosity and risk taking, to ownership, autonomy and making connections (Cremin 2009; Cremin *et al.* 2010). Such teachers, it has been posited, often work in partnership with others: with children, other teachers and experts from beyond the school gates (Cochrane and Cockett 2007). Additionally, in research exploring possibility thinking, which it is argued is at the heart of creativity in education (Craft 2000), an intriguing interplay between teachers and children has been observed; both were involved in possibility thinking their ways forward and in immersing themselves in playful contexts, posing questions, being imaginative, showing determination, taking risks and innovating (Burnard *et al.* 2006; Cremin *et al.* 2006). A new pedagogy of possibility beckons.

This series, *Learning to Teach in the Primary School*, which accompanies and complements the edited textbook *Learning to Teach in the Primary School* (Arthur and Cremin 2010), seeks to support teachers in developing as creative practitioners, assisting them in exploring the synergies and potential of teaching creatively and teaching for creativity. The series does not merely offer practical strategies for use in the classroom, though these abound, but more importantly seeks to widen teachers' and student teachers' knowledge and understanding of the principles underpinning a creative approach to teaching, principles based on research. It seeks to mediate the wealth of research evidence and make accessible and engaging the diverse theoretical perspectives and scholarly arguments available, demonstrating their practical relevance and value to the profession. Those who aspire to develop further as creative and curious educators will, I trust, find much of value in the series to support their own professional learning journeys and markedly enrich their pedagogy and practice right across the curriculum.

TERESA CREMIN

Teresa Cremin (Grainger) is a Professor of Education (Literacy) at the Open University and a past President of UKRA (2001–2002) and UKLA (2007–2009). She is currently co-convenor of the BERA Creativity SIG and a trustee of Booktrust, The Poetry Archive and UKLA. Her work involves research, publication and consultancy in literacy and creativity.

Her current projects seek to explore children's everyday lives and literacy practices, teachers' identities as readers and writers and the characteristics and associated pedagogy that fosters possibility thinking within creative learning in the primary years. Teresa has published widely, writing and co-editing a variety of books including: *Teaching English Creatively* (Routledge 2009); *Learning to Teach in the Primary School* (Routledge 2010); *Jumpstart Drama* (David Fulton 2009); *Documenting Creative Learning 5–11* (Trentham 2007), *Creativity and Writing: Developing Voice and Verve* (Routledge 2005); *Teaching English in Higher Education* (NATE and UKLA 2007); *Creative Activities for Character, Setting and Plot, 5–7, 7–9, 9–11* (Scholastic 2004); and *Language and Literacy: A Routledge Reader* (Routledge 2001).

REFERENCES

Burnard, P., Craft, A. and Cremin, T. (2006) 'Possibility thinking', *International Journal of Early Years Education* 14 (3): 243–262.

Burns, C. and Myhill, D. (2004) 'Interactive or inactive? A consideration of the nature of interaction in whole class teaching', *Cambridge Journal of Education* 34: 35–49.

CapeUK (2006) *Building Creative Futures: the Story of Creative Action Research Awards, 2004–2005*, London: Arts Council.

Cochrane, P. and Cockett, M. (2007) *Building a Creative School: a Dynamic Approach to School Development*, London: Trentham.

Craft, A. (2000) *Creativity Across the Primary Curriculum*, London: Routledge.

Cremin, T. (2009) 'Creative teaching and creative teachers', in A. Wilson (ed.) *Creativity in Primary Education*, Exeter: Learning Matters, pp. 36–46.

Cremin, T., Burnard, P. and Craft, A. (2006) 'Pedagogy and possibility thinking in the early years', *International Journal of Thinking Skills and Creativity* 1(2): 108–119.

Cremin, T., Barnes, J. and Scoffham, S. (2009) *Creative Teaching for Tomorrow: Fostering a Creative State of Mind*, Deal: Future Creative.

Department for Culture, Media and Sport (2006) *Government Response to Paul Roberts' Report on Nurturing Creativity in Young People*, London: DCMS.

Department for Education and Skills (2003) *Excellence and Enjoyment: A Strategy for Primary Schools*, Nottingham: DfES.

Eisner, E. (2003) 'Artistry in education', *Scandinavian Journal of Educational Research* 47(3): 373–384.

English, E., Hargreaves, L. and Hislam, J. (2002) 'Pedagogical dilemmas in the National Literacy Strategy: primary teachers' perceptions, reflections and classroom behaviour', *Cambridge Journal of Education* 32(1): 9–26.

Jeffrey, B. (ed.) (2006) *Creative Learning Practices: European Experiences*, London: Tufnell Press.

Joubert, M.M. (2001) 'The art of creative teaching: NACCCE and beyond', in A. Craft, B. Jeffrey and M. Liebling (eds) *Creativity in Education*, London: Continuum.

National Advisory Committee on Creative and Cultural Education (NACCCE) (1999) *All our Futures: Creativity, Culture and Education*, London: Department for Education and Employment.

OFSTED (2003) *Expecting the Unexpected: Developing Creativity in Primary and Secondary Schools*, HMI 1612. E-publication. Available online: www.ofsted.gov.uk.

—— (2006) Ofsted inspection of creative partnerships. www.creative-partnerships.com/aboutcp/businessevidence (May 2007).

Qualifications and Curriculum Authority (QCA) (2005) *Creativity: Find it, Promote it! Promoting Pupils' Creative Thinking and Behaviour across the Curriculum at Key Stages 1, 2 and 3 – Practical Materials for Schools*, London: QCA.

Roberts, P. (2006) *Nurturing Creativity in Young People. A Report to Government to Inform Future Policy*, London: DCMS.

Woods, P. and Jeffrey, B. (1996) *Teachable Moments: the Art of Creative Teaching in Primary Schools*, Buckingham: Open University Press.

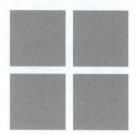

PREFACE

In 2009 I was granted three months' study leave from Bath Spa University to travel to New Zealand with my family and work with Ian Milne at the University of Auckland Faculty of Education. Ian, the Chair of the New Zealand Association of Science Educators (NZASE), introduced me to a number of inspirational primary teachers in the Auckland area, with whom he had been working on his concept of 'creative enquiry' (see Chapter 5). The opportunity to observe these teachers in action gave me some of the material for this book, together with talking to primary practitioners at four regional conferences across New Zealand which Ian organised. The rest of the book has come from my experiences of running a number of research projects over recent years on different aspects of primary science and children's creativity. I am also a national judge for the annual Rolls-Royce Science Prize, which has enabled me to see a number of exciting and innovative school-based curriculum development projects, some of which are highlighted in this book.

ACKNOWLEDGEMENTS

I would like to thank the following people who have made this book possible:

Ian Milne and his colleagues at the Faculty of Education, University of Auckland.

Professor Stephen Ward, Dean of Education at Bath Spa University, for reading the manuscript.

Teachers and children at the following schools featured as examples:

Mount Eden Normal Primary School, Auckland
Russell Primary School, Bay of Islands, New Zealand
Point Chevalier Primary School, Auckland
King's School, Remuera, Auckland
Remuera Primary School, Auckland
Red Beach Primary School, Auckland
Botany Downs School, Auckland
City Impact School, Auckland
Batheaston Primary School, Bath and North East Somerset
Redfield Edge Primary School, South Gloucestershire
Hawksley Primary School, Birmingham
Shoscombe Primary School, Somerset
Twerton Infant School, Bath
Pensford Primary School, near Bristol
Beckfoot School, Leeds
Hillfields Primary School, Bristol
Summerhill Junior School, Bristol
Northleaze Primary School, near Bristol
Neston Primary School, Wiltshire
La Sagesse Primary School, Newcastle upon Tyne
Wribbenhall Middle School, Worcestershire
Maybury Primary School, Hull
Elmlea Junior School, Bristol
Moorlands Infant School, Bath
Saltford Primary School, Bath and North East Somerset
Bishop Sutton Primary School, Bath and North East Somerset
Nancledra Primary School, Cornwall
Marsden School, Lancashire
Caerau Nursery School, Cardiff

ACKNOWLEDGEMENTS ▨ ▨ ▨ ■

St Stephen and All Martyrs Primary School, Bolton
Cherry Gardens Primary School, South Gloucestershire
Combe Down Primary School, Bath
Freshford Primary School, Bath and North East Somerset
Upton Noble Primary School, Somerset
St Anne's Primary School, near Ballymena, Northern Ireland
Kells Lane Primary School, Gateshead
Exeter House School, Salisbury
Grove Primary School in Romford

AstraZeneca Science Teaching Trust for funding the *Improving Science Together, Eco-monitoring at Key Stage 2* and *e-scape Primary Assessment of Scientific and Technological Understanding* projects.

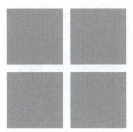

INTRODUCTION

At first glance, science teaching and creativity might seem to be strange bedfellows. For many of us, our experiences of being taught science at school – and for many of the new teachers I work with it is usually secondary science lessons that stick in the mind – were anything but creative. We think back on experiments to 'prove' scientific truths; of information to be memorised; of mathematical algorithms to be replicated. Even in the upper years of primary education in England, the pressures of national testing in science up to 2009 have tended to squeeze creativity out of teachers' practice and children's learning, in favour of revision. Yet we also know that science education need not be like this. The growth and relative success of primary-led approaches to science teaching and learning over the past 20 years – with their emphasis upon curiosity, observation, exploration and enquiry – have inspired many children and have even begun to influence the secondary curriculum. It is my argument in this book that we can no longer leave children's creative development to the arts; science needs to have just as strong an emphasis in the creative curricula being adopted by so many primary schools.

In Chapter 1 I examine the threats to primary science education reflected in continuous curriculum change over recent years and resulting in concerns over international comparisons of scientific attainment. This chapter reviews the rationales for including science in children's education and develops the case for science to be considered as a creative component of the primary curriculum. In Chapter 2 I consider what it might look like to be a creative teacher of science in the primary school, and some of the reasons why it can be difficult to achieve this ideal without support. Chapter 2 also takes a closer look at children's creative learning and development, exploring some of the models that have been developed over the past decade and how science fits in. Chapter 3 turns our attention to the early years of education, drawing out the scientific and technological dimensions of children's play and how an exploration-based curriculum can develop specific creative dispositions. I consider the role of the adult in supporting children's scientific thinking and creativity; how practitioners might establish the social and physical environment necessary for creative science to flourish; and how adopting a narrative approach involving the use of picture books can help children to explore phenomena around them in a new way.

Chapter 4 again turns the attention back to the teacher, in thinking about how we contextualise science for children through relevant and stimulating starting points. While achieving the 'wow factor' in our teaching can engage children's enthusiasm at the beginning of a topic, we need to remember that our role is not to produce conjuring tricks but to bring about creative learning, so it is worth thinking about how we encourage children to explore further. Cross-curricular links can also enhance the creative potential of science lessons and help children to make the unexpected connections which are a hallmark of creative thinking. In Chapter 5, Ian Milne outlines the process of 'creative enquiry' which he has been developing with primary schools in New Zealand. Starting with children's own interests and concerns, this process aims to build on their sense of wonder at the world around them, developing different kinds of 'wondering' into scientific enquiry which is spontaneous and less rule-bound than that prescribed by national curricula. The theme of scientific enquiry is further developed in Chapter 6, where I bring the idea of social creativity – that which emerges in the space between children's minds as they collaborate on a shared task – to the processes of investigation in science. It is possible to exercise the individual process skills of enquiry more creatively without losing sight of the whole, as is demonstrated by case studies of children using creative thinking to design experiments, solve problems and present their findings in new ways.

Using language to communicate ideas is at the heart of science education, so Chapter 7 considers how children might use different literary genres to break out of the formal, impersonal ways that we often assume are needed to report scientific findings. Chapter 7 also emphasises the central role of questions in science; I argue that asking questions is more important to creative scientific learning than answering them. Yet as teachers, the kinds of questions we ask can make the difference between a routine or a thoughtful response, so it is worth examining our own questioning skills to bring out children's creativity. Chapter 8 turns our attention to the vast potential of new technologies to be used by children and teachers as creative learning tools in science. Through case studies of innovative projects, I explore some of the affordances of e-learning for promoting creative thinking while removing some of the more routine elements of scientific enquiry. Another resource with enormous potential for enhancing children's firsthand experience of scientific phenomena is the outdoor environment, which many primary schools are rediscovering. Chapter 9 considers how a 'welly walk', working in the school garden or building dens in the wood might help children understand more about the interdependence of the living world, while developing their creativity in shaping natural materials. Finally, in Chapter 10 I challenge the reader to think about their role as a creative teacher of primary science more broadly. What are the wider support mechanisms that can feed teachers' own creativity and help them to lead curriculum change across the school? How might we engage in the big scientific debates that will affect the future of the planet, given that we carry the awesome responsibility of educating the generations whose creativity could make the difference between sustainability and destruction? I hope this book will motivate and inspire you to bring a greater element of creativity to your classroom practice while recognising and supporting the creative thinking of the young scientists with whom you work.

CHAPTER 1

CAN SCIENCE BE CREATIVE?

INTRODUCTION: THE PROBLEM WITH PRIMARY SCIENCE

There is an uneasy relationship between science and the public in many Western cultures. We are drawn to its amazing discoveries – black holes, the human genome – and appreciate the many benefits science and technology provide in our everyday lives, but we are turned off by its seemingly cold logic and impersonal nature. With its insistence on evidence and rational thought, science seems to try and explain away all the mystery in our universe. We are distrustful of its lack of human emotion, and tend to blame scientists for many of the things that have gone wrong in our world: pollution, nuclear weapons, 'Frankenstein foods', 'superbugs', etc. If only they had 'switched their feelings on' when they were splitting the atom or engineering the genes of our crops, surely we wouldn't be in the mess we are now?

Of course, this is a gross caricature of science and scientists, but unfortunately it seems to be the view that many of us have come away with from our school science education and subsequent exposure to the media. Working with successive cohorts of primary student teachers, I have repeatedly come up against negative attitudes towards science, many of which stem directly from students' experience in their own science education. Typically, my student teachers tend not to remember very much about their primary science education (unfortunately!) but often have vivid tales of crushing experiences in secondary science laboratories, where they have received the impression that science is hard, boring and irrelevant to their lives. I need to note here that there are many inspiring secondary teachers of science and that the secondary science curriculum has undergone many changes over the last decade to make it more human and personal. Nevertheless, there is evidence stretching back over many years that children's positive attitudes to science decline as they get older, and that this is related to the types of science courses they experience and the science self-concept they develop as part of these courses (George 2000).

However, this book isn't about secondary science education. Surely primary science can't be blamed for public antipathy and dwindling numbers of pupils going on to study science at university? After all, primary science is fun! It is human and personal, it engages children's emotions and could even be described as 'magic' – not in the supernatural Harry Potter sense but in the same way that a conjuring trick is magic; it engages our curiosity and we want to know how it works. Primary science is also 'magic' in the sense that the word was used by young people in the 1970s and 1980s to mean 'brilliant' or 'fantastic'. Since its emergence from nature study in the middle years of the twentieth century and its incorporation into the statutory curricula of many countries around two decades ago, primary science has gone from strength to strength. According to the fourth Trends in International Mathematics and Science Study (TIMMS), 2007, children at fourth grade (9–10 years old) have an overwhelmingly positive attitude towards science, with an average of 77 per cent responding at the highest of three levels of the index of Positive Affect Toward Science (PAT) across 36 countries (Martin *et al.* 2008). Martin *et al.* (2008) also cite shows a steady upward trend in children's attainment in science across the majority of participating countries, as measured by the standardised TIMMS assessment. For example, scores for participating 10-year-olds in England, which lies seventh out of 23 countries which have participated in the study more than once, show a 2.7 per cent increase since 1995, while those in the top-performing country, Singapore, have increased by 12 per cent. Generally, TIMMS shows improvement at fourth grade ahead of the equivalent eighth grade (14–15-year-olds) assessment, lending further weight to the impression that primary science is doing better than its secondary counterpart. It also seems to be outperforming mathematics and English, the other 'core' primary curriculum subjects in England, showing a 15 percentage point rise in the number of children reaching the benchmark Level 4 at age 11 between 1995 and 2007. This has led the recent Cambridge Primary Review to conclude that 'primary science represents something of a success story for England' (Whetton *et al.* 2007).

However, there are some disturbing signs that not everything is lovely in the primary science garden. Hidden within the generally encouraging statistics of Martin *et al.* (2008) are some worrying indicators. Only 59 per cent of 10-year-olds in English schools responded at the top level of PAT, considerably below the average, and 13 per cent down from 1995 levels, though interestingly the UK-based Performance Indicators in Primary Schools (PIPS) Project shows Year 6 pupils' attitudes to science to be remarkably stable and quite positive over time (Tymms *et al.* 2008). If it is true that children are not enjoying primary science as much as they used to, does it matter as long as they are still achieving well? TIMMS is unequivocal that those with more positive attitudes had higher average science achievement than students with less positive attitudes (Martin *et al.* 2008) and found, unsurprisingly, a positive association between level of self-confidence in learning science and science achievement. In England, neither TIMMS results nor standardised national test scores at age 11 have increased since 2003 (Tymms *et al.* 2008). We could of course argue that such tests don't really measure children's understanding of scientific concepts. With this in mind, Shayer *et al.* (2007) have used one of Piaget's standard tasks to compare 11-year-old British children's developmental understanding of the scientific concepts of mass and volume over a period of 30 years. They found that the performance of both boys and girls on the Piagetian Volume and Heaviness Task declined significantly between 1976 and 2002, and used this to suggest that since the introduction of science as a 'core' subject in the primary National Curriculum, its teaching has become more formal and beyond the developmental level of many pupils (Shayer *et al.* 2007).

Many primary teachers in England would no doubt blame the decline in children's enjoyment and achievement in science on national testing at age 11: high-stakes testing and league tables put pressure on schools to restrict the Year 6 science curriculum to a revision programme. Wynne Harlen, in her recent review of primary science education in England, claims that there is unequivocal research evidence that testing in science has had a detrimental impact on learning and teaching (Harlen 2008), while other research suggests that the recent abolition of such tests in Wales is having a beneficial effect on the development of Year 6 children's knowledge and understanding of science (Collins *et al.* 2008). However, New Zealand does not have national testing at age 11 and has suffered worse drops in science attainment, while the only country out of 36 to rank lower than England in terms of 10-year-old children's attitudes towards science in TIMMS 2007 was Denmark, which is known for its liberal approach to education with minimal testing. Perhaps we need to look beyond the tests to find the root of some of the problems primary science seems to be experiencing.

One obvious culprit is the amount of science children are actually doing in primary classrooms. Science curriculum time in English primary schools was reduced from around 20 per cent to 10 per cent over the 1990s (OFSTED 1999) and the introduction of National Literacy and Numeracy Strategies further relegated it to an 'afternoon' subject in many schools (Boyle and Bragg 2005). By 2007 science represented just 7 per cent of curriculum time in England. So where has primary science gone? What are teachers doing instead? What will happen in England when, as seems likely under recent proposals, science loses its supposed 'core' status in the curriculum? Could it even lose its identity as a subject, being subsumed into the learning area of scientific and technological understanding? Would that matter?

I believe that it does matter how much science children experience at primary school, for reasons I outline in the following section. However, I also believe that it matters what *kind* of science teaching they receive. Here again the TIMMS 2007 results suggest that there may be a problem: fourth grade pupils report that their most frequent science investigation activities were writing or giving an explanation for something being studied and watching the teacher do a science experiment (Martin *et al.* 2008). This kind of passive observation with an emphasis on recording in a written form does not seem to fit with what we know makes teaching effective: engaging learners in hands-on activities and stressing the relevance of science through issues-based experiences (Koballa and Glynn 2007). Whether because of a restrictive curriculum, national testing or low teacher confidence, primary science doesn't seem to inspire many children. What can be done to spice it up a bit? Is creativity in teaching and learning the answer to the problem? This is the question which I hope to address in this book; but before we consider the arguments for creativity in primary science, we need briefly to revisit the rationale for including science in the primary curriculum in the first place.

WHY DO WE WANT CHILDREN TO LEARN SCIENCE?

Since 1989, science has enjoyed 'core' status in the primary National Curriculum in England, though arguably it has remained a 'core subject' in name only since the late 1990s, and even that is now under threat in the current review (Rose 2009). Clearly, core status has entailed pros and cons for science; it has resulted in a broader science curriculum for children and – certainly in the 1990s – much more teaching time, together with better preparation for student teachers. But it has also brought with it a heavy assessment and inspection burden. Nevertheless, the original architects of the National Curriculum must have been convinced of the importance of science to young children's education when they took that radical decision in the first place. I believe there are plenty of compelling reasons for children to learn science, and it is worth examining them briefly before going on to consider whether creativity has a place in that scientific learning. These reasons tend to fall into several broad categories.

The 'scientific literacy' argument

As early as 1962, Isaacs (cited in Harlen 2008) was stressing the need for everyone to be able to relate to the rapid changes that science and technology were bringing to the world around them. Science has become such a dominant part of our culture that, regardless of whether or not we go on to study science at a higher level or go into a science-related career, we all need to have some awareness of 'how science works' – who funds it, what scientists do, how their findings are communicated – to be able to participate as citizens in our society. We need to be able to interpret scientific information coming at us from the media in order to make everyday decisions that affect our lives – whether to vaccinate our children, which toothpaste to buy, etc. The case is summarised well in the influential *Beyond 2000* report:

> It is our view that the enormous impact of the products of science on our everyday lives, and of scientific ideas on our common culture, justify the place of science as a core subject of the school curriculum, studied by all young people from 5 to 16.
>
> (Millar and Osborne 1998: 4)

The 'saving the world' argument

This is closely related to the scientific literacy argument, but is more sharply focused on environmental considerations. We need our children to know enough science and enough about how science works to avoid perpetuating our throwaway, energy-wasting, planet-polluting society. Clearly this involves understanding of concepts such as biodiversity, greenhouse gas emissions and material recycling, but the emphasis is on developing scientific *attitudes* such as respect for living things in the environment. We need to build on children's natural emotional responses to animals and plants – remembering to switch our feelings on as teachers and help them to do something positive to protect what they care about.

The 'big ideas' argument

If we see education, as Lev Vygotsky did, as 'cultural reproduction', then there are some ideas which have been so influential in shaping our culture that to deny children access to them is to exclude them from cultural life. One of these is Darwin's theory of species change through natural selection, which enjoyed its 150th anniversary in 2009. Because it challenges ideas and beliefs about our identity as humans it continues to be as controversial today as it was in 1859. The phrase 'big ideas' (so called because they explain a range of related phenomena) was introduced in the *Beyond 2000* report (Millar and Osborne 1998). Their relevance to primary science is that 'big' ideas have to be created from 'small' ones, developed through understanding specific events familiar to the children (Harlen 2008). And whether we introduce these ideas to them or not, children's ideas about the world are developing throughout the primary years anyway. Without intervention to introduce a scientific approach in their exploration, many of the ideas they develop are non-scientific and may obstruct later learning (Harlen 2008). Just as children's responses to the richness of the world around them can be full of awe and wonder, so also the joy of arriving at a new understanding that seems to make sense of a puzzling phenomenon is a pretty compelling reason for learning science.

The 'transferable skills' argument

When children are engaged in scientific enquiry they are learning a systematic approach to problem-solving that they can apply in other parts of their lives. Although other curriculum areas employ many of the same skills – hypothesising, planning, gathering and interpreting evidence, evaluating – the subject matter in these domains does not lend itself to the kind of thinking and manipulation that can be conducted in relation to the subject matter of science. The difference between generic and scientific enquiry lies in the kind of reasoning about evidence that is possible (Harlen 2008). However, science's claim to special 'ownership' of enquiry skills seems to be going unheeded. Furthermore, it is quite hard to find evidence for claims of transferability of scientific enquiry skills to other parts of children's school work, let alone their wider lives beyond school. So even though as teachers we might want to emphasise 'process' over 'content' in primary science education, we need to beware of overselling the benefits of the skills children will learn.

The four arguments for the inclusion of science education as an important – if not 'core' – component of the primary curriculum I have outlined above are all represented in the official statements of the UK government. Interestingly, the scientific literacy argument is probably the most prominent, as in the following extract from the 'importance of science' statement in the National Curriculum for England (DfEE/QCA 1999a: 1): '[Pupils] learn to question and discuss science-based issues that may affect their own lives, the direction of society and the future of the world.'

This represents something of a shift from earlier government justifications for science, which have tended to emphasise a fifth, 'economic' argument: that we need as a society to provide enough new graduates in science and technology to ensure that we maintain industrial competitiveness. I have not included this argument in the above list, partly because it represents an elitist view of the purpose of education – the preparation of a specialist subgroup rather than science for all – and partly because there is little evidence of a direct link between healthy science education and a healthy economy (Millar and Osborne 1998). Also, twenty-first century economies appear to require more than just specialist skills and knowledge. We are frequently told that flexibility and creativity are the keys to success in the globalised world, both for individuals and societies. Without wishing to rehash another version of the economic justification for science education, perhaps we do need a new fifth argument for its inclusion in the primary curriculum: that science promotes creativity, and so benefits the economy.

IS CREATIVITY THE SOLUTION?

Creativity is big business in the primary curriculum of the twenty-first century. This surge of popularity among teachers, inspectors and governments has been described by Anna Craft as the 'second wave' of creativity in education (Craft 2005). The first wave, sparked off in England by the *Plowden Report* (Central Advisory Council for Education 1967), can be said to have fizzled out in the 1980s and 1990s after criticisms of 'laissez-faire' discovery learning and increasing concern about 'the basics'. However, interest was rekindled by the influential report, *All Our Futures* (NACCCE 1999), championing creative and cultural education. While definitions of the problematic terms 'creativity' and 'culture' were framed in broad, cross-curricular terms, this report can be regarded as a lobby for the arts, which it was argued had been marginalised by the increased emphasis on literacy and numeracy. The report's recommendations were picked up in a number of UK government initiatives, including the incorporation of *creative development* – to include art, music, movement and dance activities – as one of six areas of learning within the early years curriculum (QCA/DfEE 2000); an emphasis on flexibility in teachers' cross-curricular planning in the *Excellence and Enjoyment* strategy (DfES 2003); and the establishment of a national Creative Partnerships programme in 2005. Creative Partnerships, involving schools working in most cases with arts professionals, illustrates the general characteristic of the above initiatives to equate notions of creativity principally with participation in the arts (Sharp *et al.* 2006). But what has all this got to do with science?

Part of the problem with creativity is defining what we mean by it. Neurologists tend to define it differently from psychologists, while the growing educational literature on creative teaching and learning largely avoids precise definitions, preferring simply to extol its virtues. To capture this slippery concept and its possible relationship to science we need to combine several definitions of creativity – for example, imaginativeness or ingenuity manifested in any valued pursuit (Elliot 1975); a process leading to cultural production (Sefton-Green and Sinker 2000); a function of intelligence (Robinson 2000); or going beyond the 'conventionally agreed' (Craft 2000) – all of which refer to a domain-independent attribute or activity. However, Kaufman and Baer (1998) claim that, on the contrary, there is evidence from a variety of sources that creativity is very domain-specific, with poor correlations between an individual's creativity ratings in different areas. Being a creative poet, they suggest, offers no indication that an individual would show creativity in collage making. Yet Koestler (1964) defined creativity as the ability to make connections between previously unconnected ideas, which suggests that activities which bring different domains or curriculum areas together are likely to yield creative opportunities. On the other hand, Craft (2005) refers to the notion of life-wide creativity, which brings together the imaginative acts of an individual across a range of domains. Craft (2008) also points to the importance of collaborative activity in fostering 'middle c' creativity, lying between the 'Big C' creativity of genius and the 'little c' creativity in which originality is unique to the individual. Looking at some of the definitions above, we can begin to see how children learning science might exhibit creativity. For example, if we accept that science is a valued pursuit, children might show 'imaginativeness' in their scientific ideas or ingenuity in the way that they approach an investigation. Similarly they might make connections between ideas they had never connected before, such as boiling and evaporation – not the 'Big C' creativity of ideas nobody had ever connected before, but the 'little c' creativity of their own personal learning journey. I aim in this book to show many such examples of children's creativity in scientific learning. But surely first there is a deeper question to be asked – why do we want children to be creative anyway?

The current obsession with creativity in education appears to assume that it is, by its very nature, a 'good thing', like motherhood and apple pie. As a society, we appear to believe that the development of individuals' creativity offers them 'agency' in responding to and shaping change (Craft 2005). However, this view of the autonomous individual contributing to the knowledge economy seems to be based on Western assumptions about liberal individualism and our abilities to form our own identities and make decisions about our lives. It is a market-driven, product-oriented, non-sustainable view of creativity, which may not be shared by people from different socio-economic, religious, political, cultural or gender backgrounds (Craft 2005). Indeed, there seem to be differences in the way creativity is defined and valued in more collectivist, Eastern societies (Ng cited in Craft 2005). This is illustrated by comparing an 'Eastern' model of creative process (Maduro cited in Craft 2005), based on observations of Indian artists, with the 'Western' one synthesised by Dust (1999) from reports of creativity across a number of professions (see Table 1.1).

■ **Table 1.1** Comparing eastern and western views of creative processes

'Eastern' view of creative process	'Western' view of creative process
Preparation (in terms of making contact with one's inner self and removing oneself from the external and everyday world)	Preparation – investigating the problem and gathering data
Achievement of personal identification with the subject matter	Incubation – usually an unconscious/subconscious phase
Insight (focused more on the personal than on a product)	Illumination/revelation – the insight, the moment of creation
Social communications of personal realisations	Verification/reframing – the 'testing' of the idea, usually through communicating the outcome to peers or 'gatekeepers' or 'field' of the domain

The Eastern view of creativity seems less product-oriented and more concerned with personal growth. In this way it appears more connected with values and morality; one of the criticisms of creativity in the primary curriculum in the West is that it pretends to be value-neutral. In theory a child could be praised either for coming up with a particularly ingenious design for a new gun or for displaying creativity in experimenting on frogs. Creativity, like science, needs to 'switch its feelings on' and be concerned with ethics in its outcomes, otherwise we risk alienating children with 'creative science' just as much as they've been turned off the more traditional versions.

We need to remember too that creativity in science is not necessarily associated with educational success as currently measured. The countries whose 10-year-olds performed better than those of England in TIMMS 2007 – Singapore, Chinese Taipei, Hong Kong, Japan, Russian Federation, Latvia (Martin *et al.* 2008) – are not necessarily renowned for their creative approaches to education, and in many cases could be described as 'collectivist' rather than 'individualist' societies. The UK government has attempted to sustain the tension between creativity and 'high standards', arguing that the one can lead to the other (DfES 2003), but in reality few primary schools have had the luxury of being able to focus upon both. The key to resolving this conflict may lie in the growing emphasis on learner self-efficacy – 'learning how to learn' – which has been promoted by Guy Claxton (2002) and has been picked up in the recommendations of the *Independent Review of the Primary Curriculum* (Rose 2009). In primary science education, this approach is exemplified by *Smart Science* (Bianchi and Barnett 2006), which aims to develop the following core personal capabilities:

- ■ teamwork: working well in groups and teams;
- ■ creativity: thinking of, sharing and playing with new or unusual ideas;
- ■ communication: communicating opinions and feelings appropriately;
- ■ self-management: taking charge of your learning;
- ■ problem solving: working towards a solution by analysing a problem and forming strategies.

While creativity features as one of these capabilities, its setting within a broader framework of elements which research suggests can be developed through science (Bianchi 2002) gives greater weight to the arguments for a creative approach to scientific teaching and learning. So our fifth argument for the inclusion of science as a core element of the primary curriculum rests on its potential for 'creative learning' (Craft 2005) – an idea I will explore further in Chapter 2 – and through this to other components of what Claxton (2002) described as 'learnacy': effectiveness in learning.

'REAL' SCIENCE VERSUS 'SCHOOL' SCIENCE

So if primary science has all this potential for creativity, why don't we often see it realised in the classroom? Part of this, I suspect, is how the nature of science – what scientists actually do – has been represented in primary curricula and how teachers have interpreted it. Despite noble words about the tentative, changing nature of science in the introductions to curriculum statements, the overwhelming impression given to the nonspecialist primary teaching force over the past two decades has been one of a body of facts, together with a 'scientific method' – investigation, experiment, enquiry – through which this knowledge has allegedly been 'discovered' or proved correct. There is a tension between the conceptual content and the development of process skills which originated in curriculum development projects during the 1960s. This was identified by Ros Driver (cited in Harlen 2008) as teachers wanting children to plan their own investigations, but also wanting them to conduct specific enquiries to illustrate a conceptual point. It can also be traced in different emphases in the published schemes primary teachers have used to support their planning. For, example *Nuffield Primary Science* (Wadsworth 1993), drawing upon the *Science Processes and Concept Exploration (SPACE)* research project (Russell *et al.* 1991), has emphasised children's conceptual development. By contrast, *New Star Science* (Feasey *et al.* 2003) has focused on the development of investigative skills following the findings of the *ASE–King's College School Investigations in Science* (*AKSIS*) project (Goldsworthy *et al.* 2000b). While the process–content debate is important – I would argue that children can be creative in both their scientific ideas and the way they go about enquiry – it has not really fostered creative approaches to the science curriculum by teachers. Primary practitioners, particularly in England, have perhaps been too concerned with getting children to know the 'right answers' and being able to conduct a 'fair test', rather than considering how scientific phenomena can engage children's emotions, and to elicit that sense of awe, wonder or 'magic' that can lead to a creative response.

By contrast, science in the real world is done by people who have a passion for it, for whom the universe really is a source of awe and wonder. While not denying that science, like creativity, is, in Einstein's words, '99 per cent perspiration and one per cent inspiration', there have to be very human reasons why scientists choose to do it. Although the enthusiasm of the fanatic can be off-putting, most scientists are ordinary people with extraordinary curiosity. In this way they're a little like children: they enjoy playing with ideas and seem to have managed to avoid having their curiosity crushed by the education system. It probably helps that most of them have enjoyed considerable educational success. They notice the little things that most of us overlook, and use their considerable background knowledge and ability to link apparently unrelated ideas to turn these observations into powerful theories. For example, the physicist Richard Feynman used observations of a wobbly spinning plate in the cafeteria to work out spins of electrons that ultimately won him the Nobel prize (cited in Wickman 2006). Another example of Koestler's definition of creativity – 'the ability to make connections between previously unconnected ideas' – is provided by Einstein himself. Faced with the conundrum that the speed of light is the same wherever it is measured – on a speeding train or standing 'still' – Einstein postulated that it is actually time and space (those qualities of the universe previously regarded as separate and immutable) that are really part of the same essence and must change, depending on where you look at them from (your 'frame of reference'). Of course, these are examples of 'Big C' creativity – originality on a global scale – whereas the scientific thinking that children engage with is more likely to be of 'little c' significance: original to themselves at their particular stage of development (Craft 2000).

Scientists often choose their areas of study for very personal reasons; for example, biologists might choose particular habitats or species because they find them

aesthetically pleasing (Wickman 2006). In this way, we can see that science is profoundly culturally situated; it is done by particular people in particular places for particular reasons, which may have a lot to do with what funding is available. Thus science
can also be seen as the servant of power – political or economic. It is also historically
situated; ideas change over time and an idea which makes sense today only does so
because it builds upon successive generations of earlier thinking. The more we can help
children see the real people behind the science, the more they will realise that science is
to do with feelings and magic, that scientists can be creative, and that they themselves
can be scientists.

For example, the context 'You, me and UV' provides a link to work by a team
of researchers across several universities, funded by the Cancer Society, to find out
about New Zealand children's exposure to ultra-violet (UV) radiation from the sun. This
is a particular issue for New Zealand, where clear skies and seasonal thinning of ozone
can lead to much higher doses of UV than in countries in equivalent latitudes in the
Northern Hemisphere. In the summer of 2004–2005, 491 school children (Year 4 and
Year 8 students from 27 schools throughout New Zealand) took part in a study where
physicists from the National Institute of Water and Atmospheric Research (NIWA) and
social scientists from the University of Otago measured each child's personal exposure
to UV as well as their activity during the day and how they were protected from UV.
The results surprised the scientists. They found that the average daily personal UV
exposure was relatively low, but some children did experience enough UV exposure to
be sunburnt. Boys experienced a higher exposure rate than girls, and Year 8 students
experienced higher UV exposure than Year 4 students. The site contains links to other
related research on UV, such as monitoring levels of UVA (just beyond the visible spectrum) UVB (higher energy, responsible for burning) and UVC (very high energy,
absorbed in the atmosphere) at different heights in the atmosphere using 'exploding'
weather balloons, finding out about beneficial levels required to manufacture vitamin D
in our skin (yes, we do photosynthesise) and the use of UVC to treat waste water. As
well as being 'subjects' and collaborators in this research, children in primary schools
around Hamilton in the North Island have made use of the data on the website to undertake their own classroom topics on ultra-violet light using 'UV beads' which change
colour on exposure to different intensities for varying periods. By placing the beads in
different places around the school buildings and grounds for fixed periods at different
times of the day children were able to build up a 'sunburn risk' map, while also using
the beads to design and make science-themed jewellery.

SUMMARY OF CHAPTER 1

In this first chapter I have reviewed what appears to be something of a crisis for primary
science, which seemed to be such a success story in the 1980s and 1990s. The combined
impact of negative pupil attitudes spreading downwards from secondary science – associated with high-stakes testing and a perceived lack of affective content – unfavourable
international comparisons and the increasing marginalisation of science in the primary
curriculum appear to be eroding its status with teachers and children. However, as I
have argued, there are many good reasons for children to continue to learn science and,

contrary to popular opinion, being scientific can also involve considerable creativity. We have looked at different ideas about creativity in relation to the differences between 'real world' science and that which tends to go on in schools, while acknowledging that the most creative scientific studies may involve children working directly with scientists.

TEACHING CREATIVELY AND FOR CREATIVITY

INTRODUCTION

In Chapter 1 I argued that creativity – although a buzz word used rather loosely in educational circles and closely associated with Western, individualistic cultures – is probably worth cultivating in primary classrooms, since it can help children gain a sense of 'agency' in their lives. I also introduced the idea that science can be creative, both for scientists who engage in the 'Big C' creativity of global originality and for children who may develop original ideas in their own terms ('little c' creativity) or go about scientific activity in novel or unusual ways. I challenged the accepted wisdom that creativity is more closely associated with the arts than with science, and introduced the idea that science is a worthwhile element in the primary curriculum because its content fosters enquiry approaches and the development of what Claxton (2002) calls 'learnacy' in children. This chapter looks in more detail at what creativity in learning science might look like, and what we as teachers can do to help foster it. However, the title of this book is *Teaching Science Creatively*, so we must first consider our own creativity as teachers, what creative teaching in science might look like and how we support each other in developing and maintaining a creative approach in the classroom. Teaching is – or should be – one of the 'creative professions': every time we plan a lesson or consider how to enthuse or engage children in learning we need to come up with new solutions to unique problems. Cremin *et al.* (2006) have proposed a model highlighting three inter-related dimensions of creative practice, summarised in Table 2.1.

It may be helpful to think of our pedagogy as composed of two distinct elements: 'teaching creatively', where the focus is on *me the teacher* (or perhaps more helpfully *us as a team of teachers*) and our ability to communicate science in as creative a way as possible, and 'teaching for creativity' where the focus is on the *creativity of the learners* and our role is to teach in such a way as to enable the children to express and develop their creativity (Craft 2000). Having introduced these terms, Craft acknowledges that the

■ **Table 2.1** Dimensions of creative practice

Personal qualities	Pedagogy	School ethos
• Commitment to children • Desire to learn • Flexibility and enthusiasm • Risk-taking and curiosity • Understanding children's needs and interests • Using humour • Secure knowledge base	• Using diverse teaching methods • Identifying entry points for individuals • Linking ideas • Connecting with pupils' lives • Using ICT • Adopting a questioning stance • Encouraging pupils to ask questions • Encouraging independence • Working together	• Environment reflects positive values • Environment promotes emotional engagement • Pupils feel safe, valued and trusted • Pupils encouraged to speculate and take risks • Appropriate resources provided • Links with the wider community • Supportive leadership

Source: Adapted from from Grainger *et al.* (2006).

dichotomy between them may be false and unhelpful, since one so clearly depends on the other: 'a pedagogy which fosters creativity depends on practitioners being creative to provide the ethos for enabling children's creativity' (Craft 2005: 44). I have divided this chapter into two, with the focus on fostering the creative professional in the first half and an exploration of children's creative learning in science in the second half. But I need to state at the outset that I value both equally and regard them as mutually dependent.

WHAT DOES IT LOOK LIKE TO TEACH SCIENCE CREATIVELY?

'There may be a high level of correlation between ability to be creative and ability to teach.'

(John Faire, Principal of Mount Eden Normal Primary School, Auckland)

Several authors have offered useful checklists that primary teachers can use to recognise when they are teaching science creatively. For example, Jane Johnston (2005: 88) argues that: 'creative science educational experiences have three essential elements: they should be practical, memorable and interactive'. She goes on to recommend that practitioners with subject and pedagogical knowledge need to adapt their teaching to suit the learning objectives, the children and the context, and that they should make their own decisions about teaching styles and learning experiences, producing novel ideas for achieving objectives for the benefit of the children's learning. While this advice is certainly helpful, it doesn't seem to readily distinguish 'creative' science teaching from 'good' or 'effective' teaching. This reflects findings of a survey by OFSTED that whereas primary teachers tended to assume that creative teaching was associated with some radical new pedagogy, in practice it turned out to be very little different from what many would consider to be effective primary practice (OFSTED 2003).

Be that as it may, the effective teacher can become a 'creative teacher' of science by rethinking some elements of his or her practice. The first of these is the subject content. Teaching science in the primary school requires us to understand some very basic things at a very deep level. Rather than take these ideas for granted, we need continually to question our understanding of them and come to new insights. The physicist Richard Feynman, widely regarded as a brilliant and creative teacher of science, put it this way: 'If you're teaching a class, you can think about the elementary things that you know very well.… It doesn't do any harm to think them over again' (cited in Wickman 2006).

An example of this was provided for me recently by a challenging conundrum in relation to floating and sinking (Archimedes' principle) – a concept I thought I understood very well. The puzzle goes like this: Archimedes was playing with a toy boat in the bath. The boat was filled with stones, but was still floating. Accidentally, he tipped it over and the stones fell out, but without letting any water into the boat. The stones fell to the bottom of the bath. Did the water level go up, stay the same, or go down? While you're thinking about this (answer at the end of the chapter) it is worth noting that just because we're talking about creativity it doesn't mean that there are no right or wrong answers! It's usually the case that the 'wrong' answers (i.e. those that don't seem to fit with the evidence or with what we thought we knew previously) are the ones that lead to the most creative thought. Creative teachers are risk takers, and this applies just as much to their own subject knowledge as to other aspects of their practice. It's probably a truism to say that 'less is more' in terms of subject content for creative teachers.

As well as rethinking our ideas on subject content, creative teachers need to take a fresh perspective on the learners in our classrooms. This may involve a move away from a 'cognitive' view of teaching and learning to a more 'sociocultural' one. What do I mean by this? Well, primary science education over recent decades has tended to focus on children's individual ideas – their cognitive constructions – in relation to the accepted scientific ideas. We have typically elicited these 'misconceptions' (or, as Ros Driver (1983) more kindly puts it, 'alternative frameworks') with a view to challenging and developing the individual children's scientific understanding, maybe through social interaction but certainly by focusing on their cognitive abilities. What a sociocultural view of science education acknowledges is that there is a close relationship between cognition, identity and cultural values (Aikenhead 1996). Children in a classroom will each bring a set of cultural ways of knowing and relating to one another, which will affect their perceptions of what happens in that cultural space. For example, in Maori culture it is considered offensive to sit on tables, since these are what we eat our food from. Therefore, the teacher who seeks to encourage an informal sharing of ideas by perching on the edge of a table in a New Zealand primary classroom actually closes down communication by violating a cultural taboo. There are also specific cultural ways of understanding the natural world, which we need to be aware of as teachers, particularly in diverse school settings. By our ways of teaching science we may include meanings of one gender, ethnic group or social class while excluding those of others (Aikenhead 1996). What count are *shared understandings* developed on the 'social plane' of the classroom, which may themselves be specific to the culture of openness and negotiation the teacher has created in that classroom. For more on the way we can use discussion to create a community of inquiry in science, please see Chapter 7.

An example of how schools can include different cultural interpretations of natural phenomena is provided by Russell Primary School, in the Bay of Islands, New Zealand. As part of their celebrations of Matariki, the Maori New Year, in June, the school holds special science lessons planned around stars and gardening. There is an evening for the parents, with a video of the Maori perspective on time. Matariki is the Maori name for the small cluster of stars also known as the Pleiades or the Seven Sisters in the Taurus constellation. In New Zealand it comes into view low on the north-eastern horizon, appearing in the tail of the Milky Way in the last days of May or in early June, just before dawn. This heralds the Maori New Year, and is also associated with the winter solstice when the sun, drifting north on the shortest day in winter, reaches the north-eastern end of the horizon. The sun then turns around and begins its journey south (Meredith 2009). Another example of Maori science is provided by Joanne Hobson, a teacher of 5–6-year-olds at Point Chevalier Primary School, teaching a lesson on 'night and day'. She started with a number of beautiful photographs with questions for children to discuss in pairs. One of these was a representation of the Maori story of Maui throwing a net over the sun to slow it down, so that the people could have long enough days to accomplish all they had to do. Asked what they thought about this, one child said:

'They wanted to catch it so they can learn to do maths and have time to do other things.'

Another child, looking at a photograph of the sun shining through a window and asked what might happen later in the day, answered:

'It's because the sun moves and it's how you tell the time if you've got no watch, you stand with your back towards it and then if you look on the ground you see your shadow, and you know when it's lunch time.'

Both children were making connections between the apparent movement of the sun across the sky and our notions of time; both scientific ideas which are inherent in the Maui story although it does not claim to be a scientific explanation. The children also related the story to the culture of the classroom – we need daylight hours so that we have time to learn maths! The use of a range of photographs in this lesson is an example of making the ordinary fascinating, one of several characteristics of creative teaching in science identified by Ann Oliver (2006) from her observations of and participation in science lessons which have fired children's imagination. You may find this list useful as an audit of your own practice.

1 Turning predictable outcomes into something better

One of the regrettable consequences of the introduction of a national *Scheme of Work* for primary science in England (QCA/DfEE 1998) – although the scheme itself included many worthwhile activities – was that practice in many schools began to have a 'sameness' about it. This is a danger with any national scheme. To be creative teachers we need to 'tweak' some of these tried and tested activities to give them a freshness and unpredictability that will fire us with new enthusiasm and communicate the message to the children that science isn't just about following safe procedures.

For example, probably the most predictable science activity in primary schools is that children will grow cress or broad beans in containers. McMahon (2006) suggests as an alternative that children try growing potatoes or rice, or that they could even plant a bed of vegetables outside. Batheaston Primary School, near Bath, allots each of its classes a section of the school field for growing fresh produce which is then harvested, washed and used in the school kitchen to cook the children's lunches. What better rationale for trying to optimise the conditions for growth? When studying the human body, our senses or how we see, a predictable activity in upper primary is to draw a diagram of the human eye, showing how rays of light pass through the pupil and form an image on the retina. However, since this rather passive activity is unlikely to challenge children's ideas about how we see, Davies (2006) suggests we involve the children in making pinhole cameras. A pinhole camera works in a similar way to the eyeball and can be made using a cereal box – make a pinhole in the front, cut a window in the back and cover it with a tracing paper 'screen'. Shield the screen with a 'visor' of black paper. With some experimentation, an upside-down image will be visible. If you're feeling particularly adventurous, why not replace the tracing paper with a piece of photographic paper. This has to be done in dark conditions. Then the camera must be held in place looking at a strong light source such as the window for a period of five minutes, before developing. If this is too technical, simple 'sun prints' can be made using sugar paper. Place objects with strong shapes onto the paper and leave on a surface in strong light for up to a week. The exposed paper will fade, leaving a silhouette of the object. Children could experiment with different papers and discuss how this idea is used in photography and to bleach clothes in some countries.

2 Making the ordinary fascinating

For many young children the everyday world around them is a source of constant fascination – the shiny, smooth brown surface of a conker, the pink spirals in a shell from the beach. However, either the deadening effect of formal education or the over-stimulation of our visual culture tends to erode this sense of wonder, so that the ordinary becomes

mundane and they forget how to 'look'. Creative teachers try to convey a sense of fascination with the ordinary by valuing children's explorations of commonplace materials,
but first we need to stimulate their interest and help them to see things they take for
granted with fresh eyes. For example, Collier (2006) suggests that when studying the
optical properties of materials we make a collection of glass objects, possibly as a table-
top display, so that the variety and splendour of glass are revealed. Paperweights, magnifying lenses, tumblers, mirrors, opaque glass, coloured glass and objects with fibre
optics as part of them will serve as a reminder to the teacher of glass's versatility and as
a stimulus for children. Changing the lighting of the display, maybe by altering its
colour or direction, stimulates further interest. Soil seems less promising yet even a
scoop of this can be fascinating if stirred into water in a large, clear jar and allowed to
settle over the space of a few hours. Magically the variety and colour of different grain
sizes are revealed as the soil sinks to form graded beds. Another beautiful example of
layering – liquids this time – is to stir different amounts of salt into water with different
food colourings added. If you're careful you can get the different colours to float on one
another, an effect which is more easily achieved with oil and water.

3 Sharing a sense of wonder

Stuart Naylor and Brenda Keogh (2009) exhort all primary teachers to exclaim 'Wow!'
to their classes every day. Our wonder at the amazing things we have noticed or discovered about how the world works can be infectious, and you may just catch the children
saying 'Wow!' to each other as well. For example, the way that sunlight casts shadows
and bright or colourful patches on the classroom wall – particularly if children are able
to move these reflections by altering the angle of objects such as spoons or watches that
are reflecting the light – can create a sense of wonder if the teacher expresses amaze-
ment rather than treating it as a distraction from the real business of the lesson. Spectra
or rainbows can be created in the classroom by using a strong light source and a prism –
a glass bowl of water, for example, or water mist and some plastics. The 'playing
surface' of a CD makes a particularly effective spectrum, as can a thin film of bicycle
oil on water or a bubble. The colours in bubbles can be a source of great fascination and
wonder, modelled by the teacher in 'wondering questions', such as: 'I wonder where the
colours come from … I wonder why the colours change … I wonder why the colours
disappear just before the bubble bursts.'

4 Seeing differently

In order to make the ordinary fascinating to children or help them to express wonder at
the everyday scientific phenomena around them, the creative teacher has first to help
them see the world differently – through a scientist's eyes perhaps, but maybe also as an
artist might see it, expressing some of the commonality between science and art. Children enjoy looking at optical illusions and these are a good way of demonstrating how
the brain decodes what we see. As teachers we can share our own perceptions of these
images; children may be able to decode them better than adults. If you can bring in a
'Magic Eye' book, see whether anyone can defocus their eyes sufficiently to see the

hidden three-dimensional images in the pictures; it's quite spectacular when you suddenly see in the 'right' way.

5 Maximising opportune moments

'Much of the artistry in being a successful teacher involves holding on to the notion of possibility in what may seem to be adverse situations' (Craft 2000: 3). When an investigation 'goes wrong' or throws up unexpected phenomena, such as the discovery that in a circuit containing a lamp and buzzer wired in series the buzzer will sound but the lamp won't light, it's tempting to blame faulty equipment or seek to sweep the inconvenient science under the proverbial carpet. However, the creative teacher of science will use such moments to spark new ideas for enquiry, demonstrating along the way some of the scientific attitudes referred to above. We could respond as follows: 'Wow! That's interesting. I wonder if any other combinations of two different components in a circuit will do the same thing? What if we put a buzzer and motor together? Anyone got any other ideas?' This should spark children's creativity to come up with new investigations and novel explanations of the surprising result. (It's actually the high internal resistance of the buzzer which reduces the current all around the circuit to such a low level that, although it flows through the lamp, it doesn't make the filament hot enough to glow.) McMahon (2006) suggests that changing weather and seasons provide opportunities to look at habitats in different conditions; a dewy autumn morning might be a good time to go spotting spiders' webs. When the early morning dew on the playground is being 'burnt off' by the sun would be an appropriate time to discuss the way water changes from liquid to gas. After a fall of snow overnight we could look at how humans keep warm, and the thermal insulation properties of cold-weather clothing. Taking topical news items as a stimulus for science work also makes children feel their lessons have a point. One way to find out the news which children are listening to is to watch *Newsround*, the BBC television programme aimed specifically at children, or its website at www.bbc.co.uk/cbbcnews. The Association for Science Education (ASE) resource *Primary Upd8* (www.primaryupd8.org.uk) takes current news stories and turns them into science lessons, a useful way to keep your practice fresh and relevant.

6 Humanising science

As I suggested above, creative teachers adopt a 'sociocultural' perspective on the learners in their classroom and always look for the human angle in any science topic that can help children to relate it to their own lives. For example, during a topic on 'forces' – perhaps the area of science children find it hardest to relate to – Liz Ireland, a teacher at Redfield Edge Primary School near Bristol, asked children to make short animation films using plasticine figures, similar to the Wallace and Gromit films made by nearby Aardman Animations. The children related their understanding of forces to a series of everyday situations involving a range of fictional characters with whom they could engage in a much more human way than they could with abstract ideas. Their short stop-frame animations involved characters getting pushed over, stuck in mud or falling out of aeroplanes as the result of forces acting on them, which the children showed by means of arrows added on the computer as they put the films together. McMahon (2006) suggests that when studying 'habitats' we could invite children to share their favourite places in the playground, e.g. sunny spots, places out of the wind, places where you see people, places where you don't. Children could create a picture of an imaginary habitat they would like to live in, and insert a photograph of themselves being there.

7 Valuing questions

In science education we claim to value questions more than answers, but this is sometimes belied by our actions as teachers! Because in our planning we have usually identified beforehand the enquiry activity we wish children to undertake and resourced it accordingly, it is sometimes difficult to know what to do with children's unusual or surprising questions. Having a 'questions board' in the classroom, or even a 'wonder wall' (to borrow the title of a well-known Oasis song) to which the teacher or children can add the ones that don't seem immediately answerable helps to value them and may support our planning for future activities. If it is a 'Q and A' board children can be encouraged to go away and come up with answers to each other's questions or suggest investigations for the class or a group to undertake. Building a creative exploration phase into our classroom practice (see Chapter 5) is more likely to generate children's questions than diving straight into investigation. For example, while exploring a collection of toys, children might initially ask 'Which toy is the best?' With guidance, this could become 'Which toy goes the furthest?' With further guidance an *investigable* question such as 'Does the size of wheels (or weight of vehicle, or shape of vehicle) affect the distance a toy rolls?' can be developed. When studying living things or materials, McMahon (2006) suggests that opportunities for children to generate their own questions can come from making collections; for example, asking groups to collect natural items on a theme of spirals, holes, shells, stripes or spots. The collections can then be sorted and ordered using questions such as, 'Can you find some big differences? What about some tiny differences?' If children are unused to raising questions they may need some question stems to get them going such as 'How many…?', 'Where did…?', 'How did…?', 'Which is…?'

8 Modelling explanations

Much emphasis in primary schools in recent years has been given to children's different learning styles (Cassidy 2004). Although the term 'learning style' tends to be used rather loosely and I have some scepticism as to whether children can be classified into one style or another, the creative teacher clearly needs to find ways of presenting science that children can access in as many ways as possible. To engage children's visual, auditory and kinaesthetic learning, it is always useful to have physical resources with which to explain difficult concepts. For example, Sandy Jackson helped children in her Year 5 class experience the relationship between the pitch (frequency) of a sound and the length of vibrating objects by inviting them to bring in musical instruments from home to demonstrate how they could make different notes. After looking at how a trumpet, saxophone and flute could change the length of the column of vibrating air she challenged the class to make a paper straw 'clarinet' by cutting one end into a v, flattening it and blowing through. It took a bit of practice for some children to get the lip position and force of breath right, but they all eventually managed to produce a 'toot', a little like the sound some people can make by blowing over a blade of grass held between their thumbs. Making their 'clarinets' different lengths by cutting pieces off the other end of the straw as they blew very clearly demonstrated pitch rising as the length shortened. Sandy then challenged the children to make more than one note from the same straw, which produced some ingenious solutions such as changing how hard you blow, compressing the lips, adding a sliding section like a trombone or holes like a recorder. Other examples of modelling activities include pulling the bristles of two hairbrushes against each other to help children understand friction – the microscopic unevenness of any two surfaces rubbing against each other; acting out the process of pollination in which children take on the roles of different parts of a flower, an insect or the wind; or becoming a food web by giving each child a photograph of an animal or plant to hang around their neck, and then creating a web of links of wool between the eaten and the eater. The movement of particles in solids, liquids and gases or the relative movements of Earth, moon, sun and planets are also best experienced through role-play, though these activities require lots of space and are therefore often best carried out in the playground or school hall.

9 Encouraging autonomy

Creative teachers take risks and begin to 'let go' of activities once children have developed the skills – both social and scientific – they need to pursue their own enquiries. If our science activities are too tightly controlled – for example by prespecifying the question to be investigated, variables to be changed, resources to be used, or format for communicating findings – we limit children's opportunity for demonstrating their creativity. For example, Feasey (2005) reports on a class of 6- and 7-year-olds who were given a selection of magnets and different materials. Their open-ended instructions were to find out as much about the magnets as they could and also to think about what they would like to find out about them; their result was a rich floor book of ideas. One primary school has developed a whole-school policy for progressive autonomy in scientific enquiry. Children in Years 1 and 2 undertake whole-class investigations which they plan collectively with their teacher; those in Years 3 and 4 work in groups to plan and carry out activities within a whole-class theme; while children in Years 5 and 6 work on individual enquiries in areas that interest them with support from both home and school. On a smaller scale, creative teachers offer children *choices* – of means of recording, of media to draw with, of scale of observations. A structured starting point can then open out with opportunities to diversify and respond to children's ideas.

WHY DO WE FIND IT SO DIFFICULT TO TEACH SCIENCE CREATIVELY?

While Ann Oliver's list of characteristics of creative science teaching outlined above is probably not exhaustive, many primary teachers will recognise them as aspects of self-evidently good practice to which we aspire. So why is so much teaching of science in primary schools pedestrian, mundane or lacking in spark? Johnston (2005) reports on a study of 10 primary science specialists in training, who viewed science as a creative subject, but when observed in the classroom exhibited little correlation between these espoused views, their planning and practice. So the problem with this group was not their perceptions of the subject, which can be an inhibiting factor for non-specialists. For example, surveys of general populations of student teachers by Davies *et al.* (2004b) and Johnston (2005) revealed that they viewed science as less creative than every other subject in the primary curriculum except mathematics. That these perceptions were often challenged by comparing their observations of science lessons with those they expected to be more creative (Davies *et al.* 2004b) is little compensation if this is the starting point for the overwhelming majority of students entering primary teacher education. Unfortunately, this impression of lack of scope for creativity in science may well have been formed by students' own experiences of their science education, as discussed in Chapter 1.

Nevertheless, even if we are able to overcome science's 'image problem' with primary teachers, there still seem to be barriers to overcome. Johnston (2005) identifies these as the difficulty of covering the knowledge curriculum in science, the understandable fears of the management issues involved in whole-class practical activities, and many teachers' lack of confidence in their own subject knowledge in science. Many teachers, she argues, tend to play safe with demonstrations or worksheets in tightly confined knowledge areas because of the fear of being asked a question they don't know the answer to or because they are unclear of how the children's ideas relate to or can be built towards the scientific ones. However, research by Davies *et al.* (2004b) has suggested that primary student teachers lack confidence in their own creativity and that some head teachers of primary schools consider new teachers lack the flexibility required to plan for a more cross-curricular approach by comparison with more experienced colleagues, who may have started their careers before the introduction of a National Curriculum and are therefore more comfortable with the idea of 'topic work'. Bore (2006) has suggested that student teachers' exposure to school culture, with its high levels of accountability through inspection, testing and league tables, appeared to inhibit their ability to plan imaginatively. This fearfulness, together with the tendency for teacher education providers to continue to focus on preparation for teaching numeracy and literacy, has arguably left a generation of new primary teachers ill-equipped to teach science creatively. More experienced teachers, while perhaps less fearful of stepping outside prescribed boundaries, may lack the flexibility to change their practice. In a study of creative approaches by secondary biology teachers, Haigh (2007) found that the role of the teacher and his or her attitude to change, or difference, were significant. Some of the teachers in the study found it easier than others to adapt their approaches to give pupils more control over their activities.

In a study on barriers to creative learning within the Creative Partnerships scheme, Spendlove and Wyse (2008) identify three kinds: barriers attributed to statutory requirements such as national testing, imposed curricula and strategies; organisational barriers associated with competing demands and parental influence; and pedagogical barriers to taking risks. To these we might add a fourth: teachers' orientation towards their own learning. According to headteacher John Faire, too many teachers switch off too early on learning, preferring to 'stick to what they know'. Gender may also be significant here; a study for the Wellcome Trust found that: 'female teachers tended to use creative contexts such as role-playing and drama in science teaching more often than male teachers' (Murphy and Beggs 2005: 20). Men in primary teaching have faced an increasingly uphill struggle as their numbers have dwindled and classroom discourse has become increasingly feminised. Their need to find masculine ways of relating to creative identities in classrooms may need particular support from school leadership.

How we can support each other: social creativity for teachers

I believe passionately that every teacher has the potential for creativity, in the same way that every child has. However, in an age when pressures on teachers are increasing exponentially, we need to recognise that the creative practitioner requires nurturing. One of the ways to start is by recognising that creativity is not just the property of individuals; it can reside in the space between people when they collaborate together and spark ideas off each other. We need to recognise a creativity between the 'Big C' of genius and the 'small c' of personal originality: perhaps the 'middle c' of collaborative creativity – a new idea or product emerging from a small community or from within a single organisation (Craft 2008). Initiatives which seek to develop partnership between educators and those beyond the classroom – university scientists or engineers perhaps – may nurture such co-production of possibilities, but studies of reflective practice designed to do just this acknowledge that this does not automatically happen but rather emerges from intentional, mindful effort (Craft 2008).

Collaboration with people outside education can be useful, but the creative school can also draw upon its own resources to support the creativity of its teachers. For example, one primary school decided to start developing an educational direction for itself in 2004–2005 under a new headteacher. All staff, teaching and ancillary, started by collectively establishing a set of principles to work by, and articulated a vision of what the key characteristics of their pupils would be by the time their left the school. They then looked at all the existing practices in the school and asked, 'What needs to continue and what needs to change?' They gave careful consideration to the 'hidden curriculum' – being aware of the principles underlying the learning dispositions they wanted to create. They also did away with written overviews of the taught curriculum since, in the headteacher's words: 'We can't cover everything, but we do need to justify our choices so that the children can meet the "big ideas" in a topic. Once teachers are clear on what the "big idea" is behind a topic, they don't have to write it all down.' Deputy heads monitor the gaps and balance in the curriculum, while teaching teams analyse the results of 'assessment *in situ*', so that children can be given another go at what they have not yet grasped. The headteacher believes that there may be a high level of correlation between our ability to be creative and our ability to teach. Maintaining the creativity of staff depends on their orientation to learning – teachers need to be prepared to learn alongside their pupils and each other. Planning collaboratively in year groups pools the ideas and expertise of the teachers, enabling them to learn from each other. When they are released from teaching duties for a morning to plan the following term's science topic, the ideas flow thick and fast.

TEACHING FOR CREATIVITY

We now turn our attention away from teachers' creativity in communicating science in an accessible and stimulating way to their role in fostering children's creativity through science. There are strong assertions in England's science curriculum statement that students should participate in science education as a creative activity in order to understand that there is a place for creative conjecture in the construction of scientific knowledge (Haigh 2007). However, in a recent talk to schools, the educational commentator Kelvin Smythe claimed that: 'science is suffering from children not being given enough space for their emotions to be engaged, their curiosity to be aroused; and divergent, imaginative thinking to emerge' (Smythe 2009: 4).

Although this statement does not mention creativity explicitly, it does use the phrase 'imaginative thinking' which many people would recognise as being closely related to creativity. But are creativity and imagination the same thing? According to Craft (2005), creativity involves being imaginative, and may at times involve the mental activity of imagining something, but to be creative we need to go further than this and apply our imagination to the accomplishment of a goal. This need not be a physical product – it could be a new idea or theory – but it will always require some degree of effort or action, which merely 'being imaginative' doesn't necessarily entail. It is probably worth also distinguishing creativity from its other near neighbour, innovation, which Craft (2005: 20) defines as 'the implementation of new ideas to create something of value, proven through its uptake in the marketplace'. Thus innovation takes creativity one step further, providing us with the following model of the relationship between these terms: 'Creativity may be seen as encompassing imagination, and innovation may be seen as encompassing both creativity and imagination' (Craft 2005: 21). While industry and government may be keen to foster pupils' innovation through the science curriculum, most primary teachers might consider creativity a more appropriate aim within the framework of scientific literacy for all. So why does our teaching of science in primary schools appear not to be achieving this? One answer might lie in the relationship between models of science education and teaching for creativity.

Creativity and models of science education

We can think of science education as being composed of three main traditions (Anderson 2007). The dominant model is probably that of *conceptual change* – pupils learn with understanding only if they modify their own 'alternative frameworks' (Driver 1983) to accommodate the more sophisticated scientific conceptions. The teacher's role is to provide *conceptual conflicts* between pupils' ideas and scientific evidence (e.g. by showing that the current is the same in all parts of a simple circuit, or that objects of different weights but the same shape fall at the same rate), supposedly like those that have driven historical advances in scientific communities. This process is predicated on *rationality* (Anderson 2007) and leaves little room for creativity. Children's alternative frameworks (e.g. 'all living things move, therefore fire is living but plants aren't') may be regarded as ingenious or quaint, but ultimately they are wrong and need to be replaced by logical inferences from first-hand experience. The emphasis here is on 'thinking' (cognition) – creativity is described as a 'thinking skill' in the National Curriculum.

Creativity has a lot to do with thinking, but it is also about feeling. The affective dimension to learning has been much emphasised in the curricula of both England and New Zealand – indeed one could almost argue that the hidden curriculum has become the visible and vice versa – but a model of science education that appears to ignore the emotional component of learning is clearly limited in its potential for fostering creativity.

A second tradition in science education which has grown up in the last few years is the *sociocultural* model introduced earlier in this chapter. This is associated with 'dialogic' teaching (see Chapter 7) and the development of children's imaginative reasoning in science. In this tradition, science education can be seen as composed of several intersecting discourses. Children can only learn science when they are able to adopt scientific language, values and social norms for the purposes of participating in scientific practices, such as enquiry and application of scientific concepts. Rational argument is not sufficient for children to learn this new language – they have to deal with hidden cultural conflicts as well as hidden conceptual conflicts (Anderson 2007). To understand why some socio-economic and ethnic groups seem to take to science more readily than others we need to ask how close their home languages and practices are to the scientific ones we are introducing in the classroom. A sociocultural view of science education appears to have more room for creativity within it. For example, Wickman (2006) has argued for the role of aesthetics in cognition: objects, phenomena or ideas to which our emotions respond positively (the 'Wow' factor) we also find easier to understand. Children's imaginative ideas in science can be regarded as alternative cultural ways of knowing rather than simply 'misconceptions', while not denying the cultural power of science's 'big ideas'.

A third and more radical tradition of science education is the *critical* perspective, which draws on the sociocultural model in recognising that science is part of a dominant culture of power within society, which disadvantages minority groups and relegates their cultural ways of knowing to the margins. In the New Zealand context McKinley (2007) relates this to what she calls 'ecological imperialism' – the importation of European species which have decimated the country's flora and fauna. In her view, science education up to the 1970s was based on 'exotic' plants which had been introduced around school playgrounds. This undermined Maori empirical knowledge of the world, replacing indigenous knowledge (IK) of native plants with Western Modern Science (WMS). She argues for a stronger role for IK in the New Zealand science curriculum, since it shares with WMS an empirical database, with observations of the natural world having provided information that has been accumulated over time, systematised, stored, and transmitted either orally or in written form. Both share an ability to construct theories (models) and make predictions, and are subject to verification over time. This model also allows for creativity in children's interpretation of the world around them, as in the child's response to the story of Maui netting the sun, on p. 17.

Recognising and fostering children's creativity in science

Whichever model of science education we subscribe to, in order to teach for creativity we need to be able to spot it in the classroom. Craft (2005) has coined the term 'creative learning' to express children's development of new insights into the subject matter of their own learning. We could argue that, from a constructivist perspective, all learning is creative in that children are continuously building 'new' knowledge. However, the phrase 'creative learning' expresses something about the depth and generative potential of that learning, something about the way in which the learning occurs. Typically, a child engaged in creative learning might express 'possibility thinking' (Craft 2000), characterised by the question 'What if...?' Craft conjectures that this might offer a 'lens for understanding the middle ground' between creative teaching and teaching for creativity, if teachers also engage in possibility thinking alongside the children. For example, Sandy Jackson, working with a Year 6 class at King's School, presented them with the following imaginary scenario:

> New Zealand's pine forest has a new pest – the Siberian hamsters have escaped and are attacking the pine trees. They know that the Barcelonian fly, in native Siberia, kills off the hamsters by biting them. They want to introduce the fly to NZ. Unfortunately the fly also attacks native birds like the Tui, bellbird and Fantail. What do you think?

The children were invited to record their possibility thinking on a 'PMI' (plus, minus, interesting) grid. Here are some of their ideas:

'A plus is the Siberian hamster is destroying our pine forests which may cripple our industry, so it might be better for our native wildlife if the pines are destroyed rather than our native fauna and flora.'

'We could put out poison traps for the Siberian hamster to feed on instead.'

'I think we should make a machine that sucks the Siberian hamsters out of the forest and puts them into people's houses.'

'One of the interesting things is that they have deadly bites against animals, and another interesting fact is that they don't bite humans.'

There is evidence that primary teachers sometimes find it difficult to identify creative learners. When asked to propose children with creative potential for an out-of-school design experience, Davies *et al.* (2004a) found that teachers tended to choose children they viewed as 'quirky' or who found social interaction difficult. In a survey of primary student teachers, Rogers *et al.* (2005) found that many took the view that since creativity is seen as a desirable personality trait, the idea of making a judgement about a child's personality is anathema, for 'what was a creative act for me, may be mundane for you'. Nevertheless, the Qualifications and Curriculum Authority (QCA) asserts in *Creativity: Find it, Promote it* (2003) that it is possible to identify when pupils are thinking and behaving creatively in the classroom by noting occurrence of the following behaviours:

- questioning and challenging;
- making connections and seeing relationships (echoing Koestler (1964));
- envisaging what might be (like Craft's 'possibility thinking');
- exploring ideas; keeping options open;
- reflecting critically on ideas, actions and outcomes.

The comments above from children at King's School exemplify the 'envisaging' point in this list; they are also weighing up the pros and cons of different courses of action ('exploring ideas'). Creative thought may also be exhibited when children *make connections* between two different aspects of science using analogy, for example the 'push' of a battery in driving electricity around a circuit. Children's own analogies are powerful learning tools in science (Yanowitz 2001) and valuable indicators of their creativity. Feasey (2005) reports on a lesson in which the teacher introduced two cans of cola, one diet and one ordinary, asking for the children's predictions as to what would happen when they were placed in a tank of water. To their surprise, the diet cola floated higher in the water than the other, promoting a great deal of speculative hypothesis, e.g. 'There are more bubbles inside the diet cola so it will be lighter and float higher. Diet cola is always fizzier.' Regardless of whether they were 'right' or not, children here were drawing upon previous experience and *seeing relationships* between, say, gas and density.

But what does creativity look like at different stages of children's development? While we can recognise clear lines of progression in children's scientific concepts and process skills, little thought has yet been given to how they might progress in terms of creative thinking in science. In the field of art education, Rosenblatt and Winner (1988) distinguish three phases of children's creativity: the *pre-conventional phase* (up to the age of about 6–8 years, when children are unaware of the conventions of drawing), the *conventional phase* (from age 6–8 to about 10–12, when they try to make their drawings 'lifelike') and the *post-conventional phase* from about 12 years of age and extending into adulthood, when those who have not decided that they 'can't draw' are more prepared to experiment with the medium. Do children's drawings have anything to do with science? Well, drawing our scientific ideas may help us to understand them. Edens and Potter (2003) found that children who drew their own ideas from an explanatory science text showed better conceptual understanding than those who copied diagrams or summarised the text in writing. If we apply this framework to science it might suggest that young children will become *less* creative as they move into the 'conventional phase' during the primary years. A pre-conventional idea, such as the following expressed by a child at Point Chevalier Primary School in response to a photograph of the moon in the daytime – 'in the morning time it's time for the sun to come up, but the moon needs to go down' – might become more conventional as the child draws on a wider range of evidence and the ideas of others, such as:

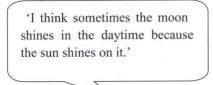

'I think sometimes the moon shines in the daytime because the sun shines on it.'

Some children, however, having attained a degree of confidence in their scientific skills and knowledge, may begin to challenge us as teachers from a *post-conventional* level of development. It can be profoundly uncomfortable as a teacher to respond to statements beginning, 'But I thought you said…' when a child has discovered that light passing through glass or water doesn't always travel in straight lines. These challenges are qualitatively different from those of a pre-conventional child whose reluctance to accept evidence is rooted in their own highly imaginative take on the world.

So what are the kinds of teaching which children view as helpful in developing their creativity? The Europe-wide *Creative Learning and Student Perspectives Project* (Jeffrey 2006: 401) identified the following characteristics of teaching *for* creativity from the pupils' perspective:

1   Relevance. Learning should be meaningful to the immediate needs and interests of pupils and to the group as a whole.
2   Ownership of knowledge. The pupil learns for herself – not for the teacher, examiner or society. Creative learning is internalised and makes a difference to the pupil's self.
3   Control of learning processes. The pupil is self-motivated, not governed by extrinsic factors or purely task-oriented exercises.
4   Innovation. Something new is created. A major change has taken place – a new skill has been mastered, new insight gained, new understanding realised, new, meaningful knowledge acquired. A radical shift is indicated, as opposed to more gradual, cumulative learning, to which it is complementary.

Social creativity for children

As teachers, we want to be able to recognise and support individual creativity in children, but just as our creativity can be shared with our colleagues in a team planning situation, so children can be part of a creative community in the classroom. Our role as teachers often ends up being that of *gatekeeper* (Csikszentmihalyi 2002) in making judgements about the value of children's work and the creativity they have expressed. In a democratic classroom it is better for children and their peers to make judgements about their outcomes based on shared values. Harrington (1990) explores this notion of social or *distributed* creativity by using the biological analogy of an ecosystem. Just as a biological ecosystem consists of a complex interrelationship of organisms, habitats and environmental conditions, he argues that: 'social creativity does not "reside" in any single cognitive or personality process, does not "occur" at any single point in time, does not "happen" at any particular place, and is not the product of a single individual' (Harrington 1990: 149).

Through analysing descriptions of creative episodes, Harrington identifies common process features and argues that in the same way that life processes make biochemical demands upon organisms and their ecosystems, these creative processes make psychosocial demands upon individuals and their support networks, which must provide sufficient resources to enable creativity ('life') to be sustained. These are represented in Table 2.2.

Applying this to the primary science classroom, we could think of the left-hand column representing the creative dispositions that children and their teacher bring to the learning environment, and the right-hand column as the conditions the teacher needs to put in place for an 'ecosystem' of social creativity to flourish. Using an adapted version of this framework, a group of primary student teachers analysed their observations of science lessons against other areas of the curriculum (Davies *et al.* 2004d). They found that science lessons generally provided a non-threatening atmosphere in which pupils are encouraged to take risks. Similarly, science activities appeared more likely to be presented in exciting or unusual contexts than other subject areas and ideas were more likely to be greeted openly:

> Ideas received were welcomed and accepted. Even those that were less relevant were written on the board so as to encourage further input from the children.
>
> (student teacher)

Table 2.2 Personal and ecosystem resources to meet psychosocial demands of creative processes

Personal resources	Ecosystem resources
• Strong motivation • Courage • Curiosity and willingness to explore • Confidence in own abilities • Awareness that creativity often involves substantial periods of discouraging and fumbling work • Willingness to take risks and persevere • Tolerance of ambiguity	• High ambient levels of creative activity • Norms and rewards for task engagement and for 'hands-on' work with project materials • Norms that encourage 'playing around' with ideas and materials • Quick and easy access to materials, space and time • Explicit or implicit expressions of confidence in the creative abilities of those within the environment • 'Loose' assignment to projects and deadlines • Prevalence of accurate information about creative processes and episodes • Known history of creative people and activities • Sufficient environmental wealth to permit slow and risky work • Roles that permit some long-term projects • Rewards for successful creative activity

Source: Adapted from Harrington (1990).

Another child suggests that an even fairer test would be to time the drops. . . . Teacher acknowledges and praises the originality of the child's idea.

(student teacher)

However, in other respects science fared less well. For example, the student teachers observed relatively few opportunities for critical reflection in science or engagement and ownership of tasks in other curriculum areas. There is clearly room for primary science education to provide more of the elements of an ecosystem that might encourage children's creativity to flourish, and this will be the focus of succeeding chapters.

SUMMARY OF CHAPTER 2

In this chapter I have drawn the distinction between how as teachers we can make science more exciting and engaging for children by adopting creative strategies, and how we can recognise and foster children's own creativity through their scientific learning. The chapter has reviewed some of the characteristics of creative teaching in science with examples, then asked why it is sometimes so difficult for teachers to adopt such strategies, before making some suggestions for how teachers' creativity can be sustained through collaboration. In relation to identifying and promoting children's creativity, we have reviewed some of the different educational understandings of the term in relation to imagination, innovation and learning. I have explored how creativity might fit within different understandings of science pedagogy and proposed strategies for recognising and developing children's creative learning in science, introducing the notion of the 'creative ecosystem' which provides the conditions for creativity to flourish.

Answer to the Archimedes puzzle on p. 16

The water level goes down. This is because while they're in the boat (floating), the stones are displacing their own weight of water. Once they've fallen out of the boat they only displace their own volume, which, since they're more dense than water, is less than the water displaced when they're in the boat.

CHAPTER 3

TEACHING SCIENCE CREATIVELY IN THE EARLY YEARS

INTRODUCTION

By 'early years' in this book I mean children aged between 3 and 5 years, though the principles will be relevant both to children younger than this – the *Early Years Foundation Stage* in England starts from birth – and to teachers working with children up to age 7, who are included in the *Foundation Stage* in Wales. Because early years education tends to be holistic and play-based it readily lends itself to creativity, so there is perhaps less tension for practitioners between policy and practice than there might be for teachers in primary schools. Indeed, the UK government has actively encouraged creativity in early years settings: 'We will ensure that creativity continues to be of fundamental importance in the Early Years Foundation Stage. We will also examine ways of recognising and rewarding practitioners and settings which demonstrate particularly effective creative practice' (DCMS/DfES 2006: 6). Nevertheless, the challenge to managers of early years settings is to find ways to support practitioners' creativity through 'giving permission' to innovate and take risks with their practice. There may also be a challenge in recognising where scientific learning is going on in the setting, since it does not form part of official early years curricula. Yet I believe that children can and do learn science from a very early age – whether or not it is identified as such – and that therefore early years practitioners need to make this scientific learning experience as creative as possible.

YOUNG CHILDREN AS CREATIVE SCIENTISTS

We have all been surprised and charmed by the unexpected ideas young children come up with, and describe them as imaginative when they become engrossed in role-play activities or indulge in flights of whimsical fancy. But is what we are admiring really creativity or just immature thought processes? Are young children really more creative than the rest of us and do they just need to be left alone, or are there things we can do as educators to help them develop as creative individuals? At a neurological level young children's apparent creativity may correspond to greater plasticity and capacity for making connections between neurons in an infant's brain by comparison with the more rigid structures present in later life (Greenfield 2000). This 'brain-based' model of creativity may also be relevant to learning science. As children explore materials and physical or biological phenomena through play, physical changes are actually occurring in their brains as neurons connect to each other, forming networks which can help them to think and solve problems. The more of the right kinds of experience they have, the more complex their neural networks will become, so there is a role for practitioners in supporting both scientific and creative learning. It may even be that particular parts of children's brains are associated with science; Howard Gardner's theory of multiple intelligences (Gardner 1983) locates different types of thinking in specific areas of the brain. For example, the ability to transform or rotate objects in the 'mind's eye' (Gardner's 'spatial intelligence') is crucial to science, but so is a systematic approach to tackling problems which he names 'logical-mathematical intelligence'. Every time children pick up, squash, slide or roll objects, arrange them in lines or build them into towers, they are exercising those parts of their brains concerned with logical-mathematical thought; they are being scientists. Some may be better at it than others – aspects of our brains concerned with space and logic may be 'pre-programmed' to an extent – but the remarkable plasticity of young children's nervous systems means that all can improve. The role of 'emotional encoding' (Gardner 1999) is crucial; children need to feel good about themselves in order to learn and the emotions are just as fundamental to the functioning of the brain as is 'logical' thought.

One of the problems with neurological models of creativity is that they tend to focus on the individual rather than the community. As I argued in Chapter 2 above, social or collaborative creativity is at least as important to young children as their individual ideas, particularly if we take a socio-cultural view of learning in the classroom or setting. Another limitation of the brain-based model is that it tends to focus on only one part of the creative process: 'illumination'. For example, one measure of creativity popular among psychologists is 'ideational fluency' (Moran 1988). Ideational fluency tasks require children to generate as many responses as they can to a particular stimulus, such as different uses for a simple object or examples with a common characteristic: 'all the things you can think of that are red'. While measures such as this may provide some indication of children's abilities to generate ideas, they fail to capture or even acknowledge the other phases of creative processes (see Table 1.1 in Chapter 1). For example, 'preparation' involves accumulating knowledge, skills, wisdom and research to underpin the value of the idea proposed and is part of what separates 'pre-conventional' or naive creativity from more mature versions. Perhaps practitioners have a role here in providing children with access to information and experiences that will help them sustain longer periods of engagement, increasing the richness and depth of their learning. Often the times when children are most involved in an activity – what Csikszentmihalyi (2002) describes as 'in the flow' – are when they are playing, which leads us to make a close connection between play and creativity.

PLAY, CREATIVITY AND SCIENCE

Certain kinds of play seem to be strongly associated with the development of children's creativity. For example, Bruner *et al.* (1976) made links between the playfulness with which children interacted with a specially designed toy and their 'originality' scores four years later. The more exploratory children were at play, the more creative they seemed to become, outperforming children who had been 'taught' to perform well in the originality tasks. The low-risk nature of exploratory play seems to give children the confidence to be inventive and make mistakes when the situation becomes more structured. Exploration, which Hutt (1979) calls 'epistemic' play, is also closely associated with young children's scientific learning (Johnston 1996). Johnston (2008) uses the term 'emergent science' to describe the informal version of scientific enquiry which helps children develop the skills of questioning, predicting and trying out things they will later need during investigations. However, there may be different kinds of exploration. For example, Moyles (1989) identifies 'specific exploration' as being that kind of play which looks at what a material is and what it can do – which sounds like science – and 'diversive exploration' as leading a child to explore what they can personally do with the material – perhaps more technological. For example, a child might manipulate play-dough for some time, exploring its properties (specific exploration), then later start to make an animal out of it (diversive exploration). At first glance, diversive exploration might look more creative, but we could equally see both stages as parts of a creative process in which children's specific exploration acts as 'preparation'.

Other play behaviours can also help develop both children's scientific understanding and their creativity. For example, Hutt *et al.* (1989) defines 'ludic' play as that which is symbolic, repetitive, set in imaginative fantasy contexts and concerned with innovation. Ludic play can help develop what Bruner (1996) calls a 'concept of mind' – an awareness of our own and others' thinking and an ability to play with our own mental images in a 'fuzzy' reality where objects and ideas can stand for other things:

> the child who plays at pretending is finding out that many things that sort of look like others can be manipulated and played with, and eventually learns that many things can be played with in the privacy of the mind.
>
> (Singer 1994: 13)

This idea of 'meta-representational' thought (Leslie 1987) is an important one in cognitive psychology, since it involves a shift from 'embedded' thinking (Donaldson 1978) – characteristic of young children who find it difficult to transfer an idea from one context to another – to more generalised concepts such as weight or time. Activities that demand representation, such as symbolic play, help in providing this access to abstract thinking, provided that children are able constantly to refer back to the concrete situation. Bruce (1994: 93) goes as far as to claim that play, 'when in full flow, helps us to function in advance of what we can actually do in our real lives'. We can be superheroes in our imaginations, but we can also be Einsteins, conducting thought experiments with our own private versions of the universe. So the symbolic aspects of ludic play can help children become more scientific, but the fantasy elements can also help develop divergent thinking (Russ 2003), an essential dimension of creativity. Russ argues that it is the emotional engagement children achieve through fantasy play, as much as its cognitive content, which facilitates creativity. The more emotion children feel during play, the more original their responses.

One feature of ludic play that could raise doubts about its creative potential is the presence of schemas: patterns of 'repeatable behaviour into which experiences are assimilated and that are gradually co-ordinated' (Athey 1990). For example, a child may be fascinated by putting objects into bags or wrapping them up, while repeatedly drawing enclosed shapes (an envelopment schema). Schemas tend not to be isolated patterns of behaviour – they develop in clusters and are part of whole networks of senses, actions and thinking, characteristic of Piaget's 'sensori-motor' stage of development between the approximate ages of 2 and 4 (Piaget 1929). They may be important stages in the development of key scientific and technological concepts: for example, a 'circle' schema may be laying the foundations for understanding wheels, axles and electrical circuits. However, repetitive behaviour as observed by Hutt *et al.* (1989) in sand and water play may lack cognitive challenge and limit children's potential. Rennie and McClafferty (1998) found that children whose play with exhibits in a hands-on science centre was exploratory and investigative demonstrated higher levels of cognitive understanding than those whose play was repetitive or involved fantasy or pretence. The key to getting the most out of ludic play appears to lie in the nature of adult interventions; in Hutt's study these were predominantly monitorial and did not involve sustained conversations, whereas activities where an adult was present (commonly collage and 'junk modelling') produced more sustained engagement and lively discussions. A consistent theme running through these studies is that as educators we need to be active and promote the conditions for creative development through play, as discussed in the section below.

INTERVENING IN PLAY TO MAXIMISE CREATIVITY AND SCIENTIFIC LEARNING

Gura (1992) argues that a number of conditions are necessary to support high-quality play. These include:

- enabling children to take risks and be creative and playful in their ideas;
- organising the physical setting to maximise learning opportunities;
- adult involvement;
- allowing children to share the initiative about what is to be learnt;
- developing effective systems for observation and record keeping, and using these to inform curriculum planning.

It is interesting to relate these to Harrington's 'creative ecosystem' outlined in Chapter 2 above (Harrington 1990); it appears that facilitating high-quality play should also develop creativity. The Effective Provision of Pre-School Education (EPPE) Project (Sylva *et al.* 2003) found that, in early years settings, freely chosen play activities often provided the best opportunities for adults to extend children's thinking. By engaging thoughtfully with children's play, skilful practitioners can extend its scope and involve the children in 'sustained shared thinking' which the team found was most likely to occur when children were interacting one to one with an adult or with a single peer partner. Achieving sustained shared thinking in play is hard – it requires an adult who is sensitive to the direction in which the child wishes to take the play, who listens carefully and waits for the ideal moment to join in (often when invited by the child). Developing such sensitivity requires a common approach among the staff team along with shared knowledge about individual children's interests and levels of cognitive development. Intervening in children's play can have several purposes (Edgington 1998):

- ▨ to encourage imitation (e.g. to demonstrate appropriate use of equipment);
- ▨ to broaden knowledge (e.g. sitting in the dentist's chair and asking: 'can you look at my filling?')
- ▨ to challenge and extend thinking (e.g. by introducing incongruity such as the teacher in role as a crying police officer who is afraid of the dark).

Sigel (1993) suggests that certain types of talk, referred to as 'distancing strategies', are better at challenging thinking, by producing mental conflict or 'disequilibrium'. For example, a child playing with model farm animals who has grouped them into two fields – 'animals' and 'ducks' – may have to redefine their classification when the participating adult asks, 'Can my hen join your animals?' Of course, the child may spontaneously have to rethink her classification of animals through the play, but the adult as a 'more knowledgeable other' can scaffold this step through a deliberate action within the play scenario, potentially leading to sustained shared thinking about whether a hen is an animal, a duck or some new category of living creature. Of course, children may talk about their play even without anyone else present. This is what Vygotsky (1986) called 'egocentric speech', which children use as an aid to solve 'internal' problems. He believed that as children move from 'thinking out loud' to thinking internally, adults have the opportunity to support and develop speech, through talking to them about what they are doing, feeling, seeing and thinking. As well as developing their scientific vocabulary, this can help children engage in 'possibility thinking': 'a continuum of thinking strategies from "What does this do?" to "What can I do with this?"' (Craft 2002: 113). This kind of thinking can be promoted without the adult doing any talking. For example, when playing alongside a group of children with a display of magnets she had set up, one practitioner noticed a child making the following observations:

'When I stuck a magnet to another magnet they stuck really hard.'

'The can has metal on the back.'

Yet most of his utterances were questions:

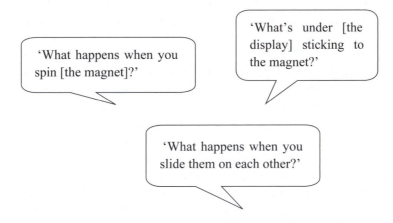

'What happens when you spin [the magnet]?'

'What's under [the display] sticking to the magnet?'

'What happens when you slide them on each other?'

She recorded these examples of possibility thinking in a 'floorbook' – a large-format 'home-made' book of plain pages, made of 'sugar paper' or 'flip-chart' paper in which an adult or the children write and draw ideas, observations, predictions, questions and explanations. With young children the book is compiled on the floor so the group can all have a good view and opportunity to contribute. It can be completed during one session or revisited on a number of occasions.

Children can be prompted into new patterns of play by presenting them with materials in new ways, for example by changing the contents of the water tray to promote new thinking. A 'sparkly water tray' contains a range of objects small and large, some of which float, some sink, some reflect and some refract the light creating changing colours, leading to a range of questions and observations such as: what do these things do when they get wet? This wet mirror is a bit like the one in our bathroom that gets 'steamy'. Is this the same tinsel that was on the Christmas tree? Can I stick the wet sequins to my arm? Why do some sequins float and some sink? Perhaps the best materials for encouraging possibility thinking are those gathered from nature. Natural materials are of infinite variety and therefore more capable of provoking original responses than manufactured, uniform resources. For example, children can be challenged to think about what they could do with a pile of autumn leaves. They may provide a 'habitat' for the toy dinosaurs; they can be scrunched to make a satisfying noise; torn to create confetti; gathered together or scattered apart; sorted by colour, size, shape, veins, etc.

The provision of interesting resources in the setting role-play area can make all the difference to the scientific and creative potential of ludic play. Broadhead and English (2005) suggest that pre-themed role-play areas may actually have less potential for stimulating cooperative play and higher-order learning than practitioners assume. Their research has focused on the setting up in reception classes of open-ended role-play areas or 'whatever you want it to be places'. Two key features of these are:

■ play resources that can be used for a variety of purposes;
■ extended play periods with regular access so children can become 'expert players'.

However, children cannot easily create play in contexts they haven't experienced. They need to be provided with knowledge on which to base their creativity. A key ingredient in the above research is the provocation of a theatre performance where the actors 'suggest' ways in which the play props might be used. Children will mimic adult behaviour whether it is in the context of a play or of 'real life'. Visitors to the classroom or visits to workplaces can be used to provide new knowledge and ideas about how adults interact and behave. These experiences can in turn stimulate play. For example, a visit to a local garden centre can subsequently involve children in setting up a 'garden centre' area where they can play the adult roles they witnessed during the trip.

The role-play area tends to be used differently by girls and boys, as they establish their gender identities through ludic play (Epstein 1995), which may have implications for the scientific concepts they can develop. For example, through their re-creation of domestic and medical scenarios in the role-play area, girls may be learning more about biological and – to an extent – chemical concepts (e.g. mixing, drying, changing through heat). In this respect boys may be disadvantaged. However, since early years practitioners may not recognise the role-play activities as 'science' there is, conversely, the risk that girls feel disengaged from scientific learning. Boys, on the other hand, may be developing more understanding of forces and movement through their epistemic play construction activities and wheeled toys in the outdoor area. Because this physical and constructional play is perhaps more obviously 'scientific', practitioners may inadvertently convey the message that science is a boys' area of the curriculum. In order to introduce greater gender equality into children's scientific play, we need a two-pronged approach. For girls, we need both to validate the science content of their existing play, and enable them to access those areas of play which may tend to have been dominated by boys. So, once girls have learned to recognise themselves as scientists when playing 'doctors and nurses' they can be encouraged to 'be scientific' in areas such as construction play. By thinking carefully about the scientific potential of ludic play, we can help boys to engage with it. For example, the theme of 'Looking After Animals' gave one reception teacher, John, scope for combining the knowledge and understanding of scientific ideas (the needs of living things, their external features, their life cycle) with personal, social and emotional development. John set up a role-play opportunity where children could 'be' an animal of their choice and think through how that animal would behave and how it should be looked after. In another class, teacher Louise used 'Ourselves' as a theme to generate interest and opportunities for role-play in 'the hospital' and provided for mathematical development by playing sorting and classifying games with snack foods.

There is a third type of play which Hutt (1979) includes in her classification: this is 'games-play' where the focus is on rule making and following. Playing games with rules might not seem to offer much scope for creativity. Rules that are open to interpretation or allow for creative responses, however, offer a clear structure within which creative thinking can be developed. For example, Davies and Howe (2003) suggest 'playing the scientist game' with young children, including a set of 'rules' or steps to be followed. The rules are expressed in terms of questions that guide the process of scientific enquiry:

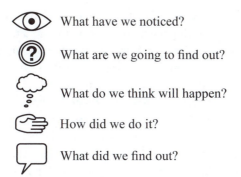

What have we noticed?

What are we going to find out?

What do we think will happen?

How did we do it?

What did we find out?

The shapes used for each stage in the game are intended to convey something of what that particular step involves. Some teachers make a display or mobile of the shapes for the classroom, or even use giant versions on the floor for children to move between when playing the scientist game. 'I've moved to the think cloud so now I'm predicting what will happen' is a kinaesthetic way of remembering the process. Armed with magnifying aids and note-pads, children can be encouraged to be scientists as they make observations, perform 'investigations' and report back their findings. This is an example of 'guided exploration' by practitioners who are modelling scientific behaviour themselves. Expert practitioners are able to see the everyday through a child's eyes – the shape of a snail trail, the flow of sand, the smell of an apple – and these 'commonplace' observations can promote questions: 'Where is the snail now?' 'Does the sand feel wet?' 'Does an apple core smell different to a whole apple?' By modelling questions, we can show children how to put their natural curiosity into words, which can then form the basis of the rules for the scientist game. This kind of structured games-play is moving children towards the kinds of scientific activity they will experience as they move into the statutory years of schooling. However, first we need to examine how current early years curricula can promote science and creativity.

RECOGNISING SCIENCE AND CREATIVITY IN EARLY CHILDHOOD CURRICULA

Internationally, science and creativity have been at the heart of influential models of early years education. For example, the 'Montessori Method' – derived from the work of Maria Montessori (1869–1952) and followed by Montessori schools and nurseries worldwide – emphasises 'scientific creativity' which she argues is based in first-hand experimentation, enabling children's subsequent 'flights of imagination' to start from a 'higher plane' and their intelligence to be 'directed into its natural channel of creation' (Montessori 1917). Montessori emphasises the value of exploration – 'epistemic play' – over ludic or imaginative play in offering children knowledge and experiences based on reality rather than fantasy. By contrast, schools and settings following the educational philosophy of Rudolf Steiner (1861–1925) place greater emphasis on children's spiritual and cultural development, involving self-initiated imaginative play in fantasy contexts which are seen as providing the foundations of flexibility and creativity (Nicol 2007). Steiner regards creativity as a spiritual attribute, capable of establishing harmony between science and art, and religion and morality; this is consistent with my belief that a creative approach to science can free it from its curriculum 'box' and help it to make a more holistic contribution to children's development. In Reggio Emilia and the surrounding villages in northern Italy, a model of early childhood education has developed which has attracted worldwide attention and admiration. Running through the practice of a network of pre-schools and infant-toddler centres in the city, serving the needs of children from three months to 6 years of age, is the concept of a child rich in potential and competence and closely connected to the adults and children around (Mortimer 2001). This leads to practice in which activities are built around individual children's interests, focusing on relationships between adults and children while playing. Creative skills and expression are seen as part of the 'hundred languages' of children in Reggio practice (Malaguzzi 1998) and are primarily associated with the arts; however, the focus on 'sustained shared thinking' (Sylva *et al.* 2003) between child and adult is consistent with the development of scientific argument.

While the above examples are not government-sponsored curricula, *Te Whariki*, the New Zealand curriculum for early childhood education (New Zealand Ministry of Education 1996), embodies many of the values of these influential approaches to early years education. *Te Whariki* (literally, 'the mat') is 'woven' from four principles – empowerment, holistic development, family and community, relationships – and five curriculum strands: exploration – *Mana Aoturoa*, communication – *Mana Reo*, well-being – *Mana Atua*, contribution – *Mana Tangata* and belonging – *Mana Whenua*. Each of these strands can be linked to both scientific and creative development. For example, the well-being strand includes the learning outcomes of 'increasing understanding of their bodies and how they function' and 'knowledge about how to keep themselves healthy' (1996: 48) – both of which involve explicit science content – together with 'a growing capacity to tolerate and enjoy a moderate degree of change, surprises, uncertainty, and puzzling events' (1996: 50), which seems to me a prerequisite for a creative response to the world. The communication strand appears to offer the richest opportunities for developing creativity (albeit in a rather arts-based fashion) through its championing of 'non-verbal ways of expressing and communicating imaginative ideas' and its requirement that children develop 'an ability to be creative and expressive through a variety of activities, such as pretend play, carpentry, story-telling, drama, and making music' (1996: 74). However, it is in the strand of exploration – *Mana Aoturoa* – that the greatest potential for science and creativity lies. The value of epistemic or exploratory play is championed in the acknowledgement that: 'trying things out, exploration, and curiosity are important and valued ways of learning' and that 'playing with ideas and materials, with no objective in mind, can be an enjoyable, creative, and valid approach to learning' (1996: 84). The structured exploration and enquiry skills of the 'scientist game' (see section above) are embodied in the following statement:

> using a variety of strategies for exploring and making sense of the world, such as in setting and solving problems, looking for patterns, classifying things for a purpose, guessing, using trial and error, thinking logically and making comparisons, asking questions, explaining to others, listening to others, participating in reflective discussion, planning, observing, and listening to stories.
>
> (NZME 1996: 88)

Children's conceptual understanding in science is also present in the requirement to 'generate and modify their own working theories about the natural, social, physical, and material worlds'. This requirement appears to have a Piagetian, discovery-learning flavour about it – implying learning through direct interaction between the child and her environment – unless it is seen in relation to the previous requirement where the value of social interaction in children's exploration is emphasised. Overall, *Te Whariki* offers early years practitioners plenty of opportunities to support children's 'working theories' about the world and to engage them in play – both ludic and epistemic – to foster their creative capabilities in different disciplines.

By contrast, the UK government's *Statutory Framework for the Early Years Foundation Stage* (Department for Children, Schools and Families (DCSF) 2008), by including a Learning Area of *Creative Development* linked to 'art, music, dance, role-play and imaginative play', risks reinforcing the widespread perception that in order to develop children's creativity we need to involve them in arts-based activities (Davies *et al.* 2004b). Another unfortunate feature of the framework is the apparent 'owner-ship' of science by the learning area *Knowledge and Understanding of the World*, which is said to form the foundation for later work in science, design and technology, history, geography and ICT, a message reinforced by the progression outlined in the *Independent Review of the Primary Curriculum* (Rose 2009). Howe and Davies (2005) have emphasised the relevance of scientific activities to each of the six learning areas in the framework, including *communication, language and literacy*, through which children can be encouraged to tell the story of what they have done, what they have found out or what they plan to do. They can play with new language that they learn (the names of dinosaurs or trees) or invent vocabulary to describe the properties of materials. Science and *mathematical development* can be combined by using the learn-ing potential from collections of objects that lend themselves to description and classi-fication. This mathematical sorting can also be used to develop questioning skills and as a way of introducing children to concept areas of science such as the properties of materials where children are encouraged to test for the criterion they suggest. Chil-dren's *physical development* can be developed by using scientific equipment such as magnifying glasses, 'bug boxes', liquid droppers and beakers. And, of course, science is at the heart of *creative development* through its emphasis on epistemic play and 'pos-sibility thinking'. Although statutory frameworks do not always make it easy to identify the potential for science and creativity in early years practice, it is only neces-sary for the observant practitioner to look around the setting at what children are doing to realise the huge scope for these dimensions to be made more explicit across the cur-riculum. We can then begin to make creative development through scientific activity more visible in our planning.

PLANNING FOR CREATIVITY AND SCIENTIFIC LEARNING IN EARLY YEARS SETTINGS

Planning in early years settings tends to be qualitatively different from that in primary schools in that, since children frequently have some freedom of choice in moving between different activities, the focus needs to be on creating the conditions, stimuli and social support for specific kinds of learning, rather than specifying aspects of the curriculum to be covered. Therefore the main consideration in planning for science and creativity in the early years should normally be the physical environment of the setting. For example, nursery teacher Debbie Bateman at Hawksley Primary School, Birmingham, set up with her class a beautiful sensory space both to engage their aesthetic appreciation and to provide scientific phenomena for them to puzzle over, thus supporting both ludic and epistemic play (see p. 34). Some items – such as fibre optic lights and hanging mobiles – were donated, and the school purchased a 'light table' specifically designed for young children to work at, selecting, sorting and arranging transparent, translucent and opaque materials. Children and their parents were involved as much as possible in planning and resourcing the space, making decisions about where the different elements should be placed, what theme the room should have and how it should be used. Debbie noted that the children have subsequently shown more confidence in making choices about their environment. The room has a theme that changes from time to time – the surface of the moon, a rainforest jungle, a circus. Staff have noticed children's imaginative talk and play developing dramatically in response to the themes, together with motivation to investigate the objects on the light table. They begin to ask questions such as 'What if…?', 'How does it work?' They also cooperate and play well together in the space and are keen to share their experiences and discoveries with others.

A word of caution is needed here. The notion that if simply provided with a set of resources within a stimulating environment, children will spontaneously 'discover' scientific principles has been discredited (Harlen 2000). Even non-directed, child-initiated activities need to be part of a carefully planned sequence, and the value of any experience we set up should be judged on the basis of its potential future pathways. For example, a water tray activity in which carefully chosen objects float at different levels may be more productive than one in which all have equal buoyancy, depending on the prior experience and observation skills of the children. We need also to remember that it is not just the indoor environment that we need to plan for. Our outdoor spaces need to include resources that children can use to explore physical phenomena such as the flow of water, perhaps by providing a range of containers, pipes, tubes and funnels. Children could use collaborative creativity to assemble the components into a giant 'water machine'. We also need to plan for a regular time when children are taken outside to explore an aspect of the environment: for example, visiting a local park during autumn to play in the leaves and collect conkers and seeds. On return to the setting the sand tray could be filled with some of the natural materials collected, offering scope for children to use the sticks and leaves to make shelters for toy animals, exploring the concept of camouflage. At times, we should endeavour to 'bring the outside in' by providing a range of natural materials for children to explore. In Reggio Emilia settings, one principle is that children have access to real materials at all times. Children are not given miniature, sanitised versions of the real world, but are immersed in the real world just as it is. A collection of pebbles or shells or sticks carefully selected to include a range of shapes, sizes, textures or colours will lend themselves to individual and small group play. This way of guiding play could be seen as an extension of the 'heuristic play' approach of providing 'treasure baskets' of natural objects – stones, bones, fruits, feathers, etc. At times it is more difficult to bring the outside in. ICT can offer additional possibilities for exploring the outside world – for example, pictures taken by children before it rained, a video of the class when they were playing outside, live links to web cams such as those provided by parks and zoos, simulations of day and night, summer and winter.

The first step in planning for young children's conceptual development in science is to consider the potential of existing, everyday activities. Recognising where science is already happening needs to be shared between teaching staff, nursery nurses and classroom assistants, who need to meet as a team to identify the scientific potential of various types of play in the setting, as suggested by Howe and Davies (2005). For example, water play could provide opportunities for learning about forces, density, flow, capacity, surface tension, light, colour and reflection; sand play could focus upon properties of materials, mixtures or evaporation. We also need to plan for children's development of scientific enquiry skills (exploration, observation, asking questions, trying things out). The younger the child, the more emphasis we should place on the procedural ('doing') aspect, in comparison with the conceptual ('understanding') components of scientific learning. Not that we would wish to separate these elements; for young children, doing is intimately bound up with knowing, and both depend fundamentally upon the development of scientific attitudes. Children's emotional disposition towards learning, and their responses to natural phenomena can serve as the starting points for developing the attitudes of curiosity, open-mindedness and respect for evidence. These scientific skills and attitudes can be developed through exploratory (epistemic) play; however, we should acknowledge that a smooth transition from scientific exploration to enquiry is desirable, provided children do not lose their playfulness in the process. One way to plan for this is to provide activities that focus on developing particular skills, such as observing a spider carefully as it spins a web or lies in wait for its prey. Observation has always been a central component of early years science, enabling children to focus on colour, texture, outline, shape, form, pattern, length, capacity and mass of interesting objects or living things. As children get older, measurement can play an increasing role in observation, starting with direct comparisons ('heavier', 'longer'), moving on to non-standard units (e.g. handspans) and gradually introducing equipment such as scales and rulers. In developing young children's scientific observation skills we need to remember that observing has a strong cognitive element (Nicholls 1999) – what we see is determined by what we know. Children may differ from adults in which aspects of an observed object they consider to be important (e.g. focus on a part of a flower that 'looks like a face' rather than the anther and stigma) or bring in other information (e.g. pictures from storybooks). While we may wish to draw children's attention to particular features that we consider of interest, we need to acknowledge the creative potential in what they choose to observe, how they choose to observe (perhaps using a range of senses) and the interpretation they put on what they see.

Another approach to planning for science and creativity in the early years is to explore the potential of a thematic starting point such as a story. Stories are particularly relevant to science, since many scientists communicate their ideas by telling us stories: for example, about how the world began or how the mountains and seas, animals and plants came to be the way they are now. They tell us about how they have carried out their research and what they found as they delved, dissected and deliberated over the universe. Many of their stories claim to be 'true', but usually only until better stories take their place. Black and Hughes (2003) suggest that the construction and use of narrative is a vital part of coming to understand the world. This approach is ideally suited to foundation stage practice, where children encounter stories, songs, rhymes, fantasy and scientific phenomena daily. Children can be encouraged to tell the story of what they have done, what they have found out or what they plan to do. They can play with new language that they learn (the names of dinosaurs or trees) or invent vocabulary to describe the properties of materials. In turn, they can be told stories about how things came to be as they are. Practitioners need not worry if the stories are 'correct' or fantasy; there is still plenty of debate about 'How The Zebra Got Its Stripes' among biologists. More importantly, children may wish to follow up stories with their own questions or play around with their own ideas – this is the beginning of the scientific skill of hypothesising.

A narrative approach to science in the early years is supported by a socio-cultural understanding of children's learning (see Chapter 2). Talking about what we have found out is probably the most important phase of the 'scientist game' (see above) yet is sometimes neglected through lack of time or the stress of tidying up. Harlen (2000) places great importance on speech as reflection upon what we have learned; we often understand better when we try to explain to others. Some children may lack confidence in verbalising their ideas; this is where a prop such as a puppet can be invaluable, since it does not have the status or authority of the teacher and so may be seen as more approachable and less judgemental. Simon *et al.* (2008: 1231) found that the use of puppets to tell stories and initiate scientific discussion could 'legitimise certain kinds of talk that do not normally feature within a teacher's repertoire, such as claiming to be confused or ignorant about a situation'. This resulted in an increase in the time that children used talk involving reasoning and a decrease in the time that they talked about practical and procedural matters; an increase in the teacher's use of argumentation and a decrease in the extent to which he or she gave information to children; and, perhaps most importantly, an increase in the teacher's use of story and narrative and an increase in the extent to which he or she offered encouragement. These findings give strong support to any early years practitioner planning to use puppets to initiate and sustain children's scientific exploration around a story. Many lists of suitable stories exist; one such is provided by Lewisham Education and Culture (1999), which includes suggestions to use Jill Murphy's *Peace at Last* to explore our sense of hearing; Verna Aardema's *Bringing the Rain to Kapiti Plain* to investigate grass growth in the playground; and Mick Inkpen's *The Blue Balloon* to initiate purposeful sorting and classification of materials. Of course, the creative practitioner will soon think of their own story starting points, and the imagination of the children can be engaged by wondering 'What would happen next in the story if...?'

SUMMARY OF CHAPTER 3

In this chapter I have argued that science and creativity are 'natural' parts of young children's neurological, physical, social and emotional development, and that both can be fostered by certain kinds of play. I have considered how different types of exploration, or 'epistemic' play can involve scientific reasoning and possibility thinking, and how 'ludic' or fantasy play can engage children's imaginations and develop flexibility in their thought patterns. I have recommended ways in which practitioners can intervene in different kinds of play to bring out their scientific and creative potential, and have also examined how these attributes are represented and supported within international models of early years practice and government-sponsored curricula. Lastly, I have suggested ways in which early years practitioners might plan to use the indoor and outdoor environments to support children's scientific and creative development, as well as using 'games-play' activities such as 'the scientist game', stories and puppets to get children thinking and talking about science in creative ways.

Practical resources for creative science in the early years

- A 'light table' with lots of coloured and translucent materials, toys, feathers, etc.
- Thick fabrics to make a 'dark cave'
- A shadow puppet screen, overhead projector and materials for making shadow puppets
- A range of kaleidoscopes, convex and concave mirrors
- Water tray with a range of sparkling, reflective objects (sequins, baubles, glitter), objects that float at different levels or surprisingly
- Collections of different kinds of balls, shoes, wind-up toys
- Selection of musical instruments, blindfold, card for making 'ear trumpets'
- Sound pots – shake and match the sound with the contents
- Play-dough, 'feely bags', 'feely boxes', 'feely feet' (foot shapes cut from different materials for children to touch with bare feet)
- Depending on the season, flowers, leaves, twigs, 'scrunchy' brown leaves, seeds, fruit
- Toy animals
- Digital camera, digital microscope
- Range of storybooks (see examples in text above)

CROSS-CURRICULAR STARTING POINTS

INTRODUCTION – WHY CROSS-CURRICULAR?

The idea of a 'creative curriculum', which seems so popular in primary schools at the present, appears to be closely associated with a cross-curricular approach. Increasing numbers of schools are basing learning experiences around a 'big bang' – a highly engaging starting point (or 'provocation' to use the Reggio Emilia term) which is designed to stimulate children's curiosity and imagination – leading off into a range of work in each classroom, transcending subject boundaries and following children's interests. Alternatively, primary school curricula are being built around 'thinking skills', 'enquiry approaches', 'multiple intelligences', 'accelerated learning', 'philosophy for children', 'creative dispositions' or 'habits of mind': all indicators of a dissatisfaction with a traditional knowledge-based curriculum and a concern to reflect a holistic ethos concerned with the development of the whole child. Subjects can occasionally be dismissed as artificial human constructs which bear little relation to the ways in which children view the world and act as a constraint on their creativity. This movement has been supported to some extent by government reforms; in England the policy document *Excellence and Enjoyment – the Primary National Strategy* (DfES 2003) gave permission to innovate by freeing schools from the constraints of the National Curriculum for part of the week and exhorting them to make links between subjects in their planning. More recently, both the influential *Cambridge Primary Review* (Alexander 2009) and the UK government's own *Independent Review of the Primary Curriculum* (Rose 2009) have proposed primary curricula based around learning areas or domains rather than subject disciplines. It is almost as if what was previously the 'hidden curriculum' – the affective domain which schools sought to inculcate by 'osmosis' – has become the overt curriculum, while the more traditional subject-bound, knowledge-based curriculum is now 'hidden'.

To those of us who were teaching in primary schools during the 1980s, this trend has a curious sense of *déjà vu* about it. We were trained to plan from 'topic webs' in which the various components of the primary curriculum were subsumed under broad themes and we were encouraged to follow individual children's interests as far as possible within the constraints of class size. The backlash against this liberal, developmental approach to the primary curriculum deriving from the Piagetian ideas in the *Plowden Report* (Central Advisory Council for Education 1967) was sudden and devastating. The publication of a statutory, subject-based National Curriculum (DES 1987) was followed by a radical critique of primary pedagogy by the 'three wise men' Alexander *et al.* (1992) in which they suggested that cross-curricular topic work risked diluting children's understanding of important concept areas and compromising their literacy and numeracy skills in favour of 'contrived' links to broad themes. An increasing focus on teachers' subject knowledge and children's standards of attainment through the 1990s virtually drove topic work to extinction in English primary schools. Of course, its re-emergence is set against a very different cultural and legal background from that of the 1980s: schools still have to 'deliver' the National Curriculum, necessitating regular audits of curriculum coverage, and children's literacy and numeracy skills continue to be tested and reported upon nationally. The outcome of this is that, in many primary schools, English and mathematics are considered too 'important' to be fully integrated into the cross-curricular mix, retaining their special status of 'morning subjects'. However, science is not so fortunate, particularly since the abandonment of national testing at the end of primary school in 2010. As in the 1980s, science is everywhere being subsumed into topic work, losing its identity within more general 'enquiry' approaches which may tend to skate over its conceptual difficulties. In some ways, the high water mark for primary science was in the 'bad old days' of the 1990s, where it had a clear curriculum status as a 'core subject' and its own designated space in the timetable!

This is not to suggest that science cannot combine effectively with other aspects of the curriculum to enhance learning. As suggested by the title of this chapter (and introduced in Chapter 2), it is one of the characteristics of creative teachers that they make links between 'previously unrelated ideas' (Koestler 1964) and begin to rethink subject content to make it more meaningful and accessible to children. But it is not cross-curricularity per se that makes science teaching creative; it is perfectly possible to teach a scientific concept creatively while remaining firmly within subject boundaries. For example, in teaching the unit *Gases all around us* (QCA/DfEE 1998) to pupils aged 9–11 at Shoscombe Primary School, Somerset, teacher David Young surprised the class by setting up a series of 'engage activities' on their tables while they were out at break. These consisted of a candle burning; a series of plastic cups containing different numbers of marbles; and pairs of inflated and deflated balls. Although there were question cards explaining the activities – e.g. 'Watch the candle as it burns, what do you notice?', 'Look at how the marbles are arranged, shake them, what is happening?', 'Squeeze the two rugby balls, what can you say?' – David gave no vocal instructions. Initially bemused, groups of pupils soon began interacting with the exhibits and discussing their ideas. This unexpected start to the lesson – out of the normal routine – together with an invitation to look at everyday phenomena differently, provided the 'hook' needed to engage children's enthusiasm in a new scientific topic. It was a creative piece of teaching with no need for links to other curriculum areas. However, what this episode arguably lacked was a meaningful context. Why were children looking at marbles in a plastic cup, other than as a pedagogical device to introduce the notion of particle motion in gases? The main reason for linking science to other subjects is to contextualise children's learning and give it a purpose which makes sense to the children and helps them to make sense of scientific learning in relation to their everyday lives.

Setting learning experiences in a cross-curricular context can also support children's creativity in science; for example, the teaching of magnetism within the context of designing and making a magnetic board game can lead children to explore the possibilities of what can be done with magnets more widely than could, say, an investigation to find out which materials magnetism can pass through. This links with the notions of 'diversive exploration' (Moyles 1989) and 'possibility thinking' (Craft 2000), introduced in Chapter 3, suggesting that while it is possible to *teach creatively* without making cross-curricular links, in order to *teach for creativity* we need to set scientific activities within a broader context. *From Context to Concept* (New Zealand Ministry of Education 1999a) suggests starting activities from everyday contexts such as the orchestra, the garage, the playground, the classroom, the backyard, the kitchen and the supermarket. Such starting points, while not explicitly cross-curricular in themselves, offer opportunities for taking learning in many different directions. In a study of primary teachers' approaches to planning cross-curricular links between science and mathematics, Hurley (2001) identified five different categories of curriculum integration ranging from sequential planning and teaching to being taught together in 'intended equality'; she concluded that achievement in science tended to be higher with more integration. So it seems that the more we link science with other subject areas to provide meaningful contexts for children's learning, the greater the potential for both their creativity and their scientific conceptual development. However, we need to plan with the 'big scientific picture' in mind (Shepardson 1997) to ensure that the concepts don't get lost in the context, and we need to monitor children's creative outcomes to ensure that they include *scientific creativity*. To use the example above, a beautifully designed magnetic board game might demonstrate children's creativity in the choice and use of materials, colours and media, yet employ a relatively pedestrian use of magnets to move pieces around the board. Conversely, a game with less obvious aesthetic qualities and creativity in design might exemplify a more diverse exploration of the possibilities of magnets attracting and repelling each other, 'flipping' over or 'hovering'. However, this is not to say that science does not itself have aesthetic qualities which may be incorporated in children's creativity, as we shall explore in the next section.

AESTHETIC STARTING POINTS FOR CREATIVE SCIENCE

We are used to thinking about the arts as providing children with aesthetic experiences in the primary school. Art and design, music, dance and drama can all engage children emotionally and help them develop an appreciation of beauty. Aesthetics are seen as part of our inner, subjective world which only the arts can reach, whereas science is usually regarded as part of the external, objective world. Yet science too can be beautiful: think of the exquisite symmetries of snowflakes or the elegance of a simple formula like $E = mc^2$ to describe the profound link between matter and energy. Wickman (2006) argues that aesthetic experiences are an inescapable part of *doing* science. Indeed, the word *aesthetics* is derived from the Greek *aistheta*, meaning 'things perceived' – the 'science of perception'. Scientists choose phenomena to investigate because they find them intrinsically beautiful, interesting or exciting; these judgements are aesthetic because they involve an evaluation of taste regarding objects and because these evaluations describe qualities that are not in the first place physical, objective qualities. Darwin used aesthetic terms like beauty in describing his theory of natural selection, yet over the last 150 years scientific papers have increasingly shunned aesthetic phrases, leading to the popular notion of cold, logical scientists. This reluctance to engage emotionally runs the risk of turning children off science, particularly where science 'facts' conflict with pupil 'values', which may be of an aesthetic or spiritual nature. For this reason, aesthetic experiences are fundamental to learning science, since children's expressions of wonder and fascination (or disgust!) help them to link previous non-scientific experiences – such as noticing slugs or snails underneath plant pots – with the scientific ideas underlying a more systematic study of these phenomena (Wickman 2006). The role of the arts then may be to provide the more obviously aesthetic experience through which children come to appreciate the aesthetics of science, and hence to explore scientific ideas more creatively.

For example, McMahon (2006) recalls how as a teacher she shared some of Georgia O'Keeffe's paintings of flowers with a class of children. They described looking at them as like imagining that you are a bee and 'zooming in'. This idea of 'zooming in' and also of 'zooming out' – of looking at things on different scales – is important to biology as well as to art. We zoom in by using hand lenses and microscopes to look at the detail of living things – a common woodlouse is pretty impressive when magnified! By zooming out we think about living things in relation to other living things and the environment, moving to global ideas about sustaining life on our planet and beginning to think about life on different scales. Twerton Infant School in Bath visited 'the egg' children's theatre to see *Petrushka* as a puppet performance. Back at school, they worked together to create their own performance using puppets and musical instruments they had made. The scientific learning from the project included the production of sounds using different vibrating objects, altering the pitch by changing the length of vibration and exploring the mixing of different coloured lights. Victoria Smart at Pensford Primary School near Bristol created a dance with her class of 7–9-year-olds based on the functions of a sun dial. Some touring theatre groups such as Kinetic Theatre (www.kinetictheatre.co.uk/) and Quantum Theatre (www.quantumtheatre.co.uk/) perform plays with specifically scientific content, e.g. *Lady Cecily's Soundbox*, *Fillacavity Hotel*, *Octopushy!* or *The Starry Messenger*.

Initiatives such as *Creative Partnerships* (Sharp *et al.* 2006) and *5x5x5=creativity* (Bancroft *et al.* 2008) have used practising artists to work with children and teachers across the curriculum, including science. For example, Beckfoot School in Leeds worked with dancers from Northern Ballet Theatre to explore ideas about space, stars, forces and black holes, and children from Hillfields Primary School, Bristol, danced behind a screen with different coloured projectors to explore shadows and mixing of light. The Momentum project – a Creative Partnerships initiative involving 15 teachers and 15 artists in Bristol – aimed to develop activities and strategies that would enable teachers to explore a more creative curriculum with their class. Through discussion meetings the group planned a series of video 'Wow!' lesson starters that would promote talk and discussion with pupils (see www.suitedandbooted.org/wow-starters.html). These were trialled within the classrooms. Creative Partnerships worked with the teachers on delivering these stimulating starters. A follow-up meeting discussed the work within the schools and evaluated the activities that provided the most stimuli for the children. These activities were then planned in more depth and detail and a select group of children were chosen to be filmed. Follow-up meetings evaluated the effectiveness of the DVD and considered what support materials should be available to ensure a complete package could be offered to teachers. A case study featuring the 'Coat hanger sounds' starter from the Momentum project in Summerhill Junior School, Bristol, is featured in Chapter 6.

LITERARY STARTING POINTS

Clearly, the idea of aesthetic contexts for science is not limited to links with art, drama, music or dance. Stories and poems have great potential for engaging children emotionally, and can provide great starting points for creative scientific enquiry, as suggested in Chapter 3. Of course, science too is not without its stories. Millar and Osborne (1998) recommend the use of 'explanatory stories' for science to help children understand how powerful ideas such as particle theory underpin different aspects of what they are studying in science. They suggest that the use of narratives in presenting historical case studies will help children to understand the human context of science and how the processes of science have led to our present-day understanding. Together these could help children to build up a coherent set of interrelated ideas and concepts that would form a framework in which details would have more meaning. Scientific 'stories' are present in many different literary genres including films, television documentaries, science fiction novels and newspaper reports, all of which can be used as engaging starting points (Rennie 2007). Stories can provide both everyday and fantasy contexts, allowing children to express their scientific learning through many forms. For example, the story of *The Enormous Turnip*, in which first the farmer tries to pull up the turnip, then one by one a series of other people and animals come to help, could be used to initiate a discussion with young children about forces: 'Why was it so hard to pull up? How did they make the pull bigger? What else do we pull? Which are big pulls and which are small pulls?' This could lead into an investigation in which children explore the different strength of pull needed to move different objects. Imagine this activity presented in isolation – it might seem rather pointless! The story also lends itself to systematically adding 'more pull' – another feature that could be developed in an investigation. Steve Marshall (2006) recommends using the story *When the Sun was Afraid of Shadows* by Janice Cox as a starting point for role-play. He suggests that children in the role of reporters from the *Scientific Weekly* interview the other characters in the story, each of whom saw, said or thought something different about the apparent movement of the sun across the sky and its effect upon shadow length.

Chris Astall and Warren Bruce have published a series of *science postcards* (www.sciencepostcards.com) as literary starting points for scientific activities. They suggest that the postcards can be used in a range of different ways by teachers:

- to provide a **stimulus** for discussion, e.g. 'Hey, look at this postcard we have just received';
- to **challenge** scientific ideas and beliefs of the children;
- to help **support** a particular science skill, e.g. creating and using data tables, measuring, etc.;
- to be posted home to develop the activity as homework;
- to support or develop an idea within a current science unit of work;
- as an **extension** activity;
- to **explore** scientific ideas in everyday situations – a 'Science in the Real World' approach.

For example, the 'No to Noise' postcard on the above website, linked to the story *Ruby Sings the Blues* by Niki Daly, introduces the ideas that loud sounds can be damaging to our ears, and that ear muffs can be used to protect our ears or screen out unwanted noise, leading to an activity to investigate how good different materials are at reducing the sound of an alarm clock. Poetry also makes a good starting point for science. It is particularly good for setting science within an emotive context since it often emphasises the aesthetic dimension of the natural world, provoking a sense of awe and wonder at the structure of everyday things.

Stories can also be set in different cultural contexts, allowing access to scientific ideas for children who may be more familiar with the context described in the story than the dominant cultural context of the classroom. For example, Joanne Hobson used the story *Nanny Mihi's Garden* by Melanie Drewery to initiate a topic about the seasons. She started by asking questions to help the children make links with their own experiences – 'Who has a vegetable garden? Where is the vegetable garden in the school? Who knows what's growing?' – and to establish the connection between plant growth and seasonal change. She then moved on to a card sorting activity involving a number of pictures of 'everyday' things such as woolly hats and ice-creams, together with more 'scientific' links such as shadows, the sun and night-time. Children were asked 'Does the card have anything to do with the seasons?' and to sort their cards collaboratively into yes, no, and maybe piles. Next they walked round the room to look at other groups' choices and discussed their sorting decisions as a whole class. Finally, Joanne asked the children what they would like to find out about the seasons. Their questions revealed a real thirst for scientific knowledge which had been stimulated by both the story and card-sorting activity:

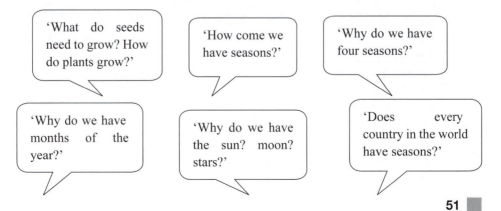

'What do seeds need to grow? How do plants grow?'

'How come we have seasons?'

'Why do we have four seasons?'

'Why do we have months of the year?'

'Why do we have the sun? moon? stars?'

'Does every country in the world have seasons?'

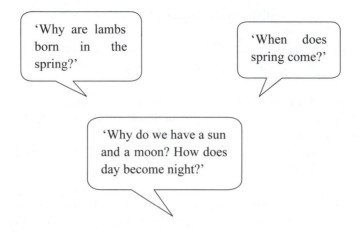

'Why are lambs born in the spring?'

'When does spring come?'

'Why do we have a sun and a moon? How does day become night?'

Joanne's creative approach to the beginning of this topic had generated enough questions to last the rest of the term!

MATHEMATICAL STARTING POINTS

It is perhaps easier to see the links between science and mathematics than those between science and literature. Gardner (1983) even regards them as part of the same 'logico-mathematical' intelligence. Mathematics, as a form of symbolic language representing precise relationships between variables, is often better suited to communicating scientific ideas than is verbal expression. Take the example of Newton's Second Law of Motion. It is much simpler – and more informative – to express it as $F = ma$ than to say something like 'the force needed to make a mass move with constant acceleration is directly proportional to the size of the mass'. Some scientists claim that mathematics is the language of nature itself, providing a 'mirror for the physical world' (Wolpert 1992). So why do pupils (and many teachers!) have such resistance to using numbers in science? Hawking (1988) claimed that the sales of a popular science book would be halved for every equation that appeared between its covers. The explanation lies in our deep-seated fear of mathematical abstraction, and the perception that it is unrelated to our everyday lives. Science teachers have a mission to perform in opening for children the 'secret garden' of a numerical universe and showing just how important a tool mathematics can be. Interpreting a set of real or 'dummy' numerical data from a piece of science in the news can show children how statistics can be manipulated to give misleading information. For example, the *Primary upd8* site (www.primaryupd8.org.uk) uses topical events in the media to present simplified scientific data and create engaging science lessons. The topical *Primary upd8* activity 'Spreading Swine Flu', aimed at 10–11-year-olds, invites children to predict the next points (extrapolate) in two-line graphs – one of 'total UK cases of swine flu' and the other of 'new cases' – and to consider why they have such different shapes. An earlier *Science Year* activity, 'A Discovery' (ASE 2002), describes the fictional observations of a scientist that eating spring onions appears to improve athletic performance. The pupils are asked to interpret the dummy results from an experimental and control group of high jumpers, and later to plan an investigation to test this theory. Through teaching them to take a critical approach to scientific data, children can conclude that, in this experiment:

- improvement overall was very slight in both groups;
- two jumpers in the experimental group declined in performance;
- one jumper in the experimental group made a significant improvement, weighting the figures.

Starting with data is a particularly useful approach, given the comparative underdevelopment of pupils' data interpretation and reasoning skills (Goldsworthy *et al.* 2000b).

Mathematical modelling, particularly when combined with a kinaesthetic activity to link the maths to children's experiences, can also be a stimulating starting point. For example, teachers of 10–11-year-old pupils in 20 Bristol schools that were part of the *Improving Science Together* project (Davies and McMahon 2004) initiated the theme of 'projectiles' in the playground with children exploring what happens when a ball or 'soft javelin' is thrown. They noticed that the angle of throw and the strength of the push affected the distance the object travelled, with gravity and air resistance thwarting their attempts to create a new school record! They used digital video to study the trajectory of the projectiles in slow motion. This led to investigable questions such as 'What is the best angle to throw a ball?', 'Why do some balls swerve more than others?', 'Does a shuttlecock always land nose down?' Pupils modelled the trajectory they had observed on the video using an angled board covered in graph paper, onto which they rolled ball-bearings covered in ink from different angles, leaving traces which could be measured. They tested their finding – that 45 degrees was the 'best' angle to make the projectile go furthest – by launching 'stomp-rockets' in the playground. A stomp-rocket fires a foam dart a considerable distance at a pre-set angle when its air sack is stamped on (or has a brick dropped on it from a measured height once the children realise that how hard you stomp is a difficult variable to control).

TECHNOLOGICAL STARTING POINTS

The relationship between science and technology in the primary curriculum has shifted backwards and forwards a number of times over the past 20 years in both England and New Zealand. An original intention to create a single subject in the National Curriculum (DES 1987) was resisted by those who wished to champion design and technology as a separate discipline and not merely an application of scientific knowledge (Davies 1997). In New Zealand, however, the relationship between the two areas was much closer during the 1990s, with pupils expected to: 'explore the relationships between science and technology by investigating the application of science to technology and the impact of technology on science' (New Zealand Ministry of Education 1993). There is within this statement a sense of equality and mutual support, reflected in the finding by Jane and Jobling (1995) that teaching integrated science and technology with equal emphasis in the primary classroom led to higher levels of pupil engagement and metacognition than treating them as separate subjects. More recently, the two countries appear to have swapped policies, with New Zealand establishing separate 'essential learning areas' for science and technology (New Zealand Ministry of Education 2007) whereas both of the recent reviews of the primary curriculum in England recommend a joint learning area/domain of 'scientific and technological understanding' (Alexander 2009; Rose 2009). What are primary teachers to make of this confused picture?

If our concern is to develop children's creativity, we need to acknowledge that most of the ways that children encounter scientific principles in their lives is through the technology that surrounds them and which they appear to master so much more easily than adults! Their creativity with ICT will be covered in Chapter 8, but even the use of simple technology such as a torch can open up a number of possibilities that a more conventional approach to the topic of electricity might neglect. Most young children will have seen, and may have played with, a torch – the ability to shine a light where you want it is fascinating and seems like magic. Manufacturers have cashed in on this sense of wonder with a range of different styles, some based on cartoon characters and featuring various battery configurations and switch mechanisms. A collection of torches, while offering rich evaluation potential for children's own designs, can also be used to focus their attention on the electrical concepts they embody, such as circuits, switches, conductors and insulators. The Nuffield Design and Technology free resource 'What light will work for you?' (download from www.primarydandt.org) can help structure a sequence of lessons on this theme. For example, Kate Angus at Northleaze Primary School, near Bristol, invited her class of 9- and 10-year-olds to design a torch for a certain kind of user, such as someone who explores caves, fishes at night, is 9 years old, attends accidents, etc. After taking apart a range of different kinds of torches to see how they worked, the children annotated their design drawings to show:

■ the jobs the person using it would want to do;
■ how the torch would be held or how it would work if not held;
■ where switches would go and how many would be needed;
■ the types of batteries to be used and how they would fit in the case.

They came up with lots of ideas for potential users, including 'a camper', 'a late-evening shopper', 'a child reading under the bed covers', or 'playing games such as hide and seek'. This last idea involved embedding the torch within a foam ball (Figure 4.1), a design which proved challenging to make because of the difficulties of incorporating a 'spring-loaded' switch in the circuit. As part of the preparation for building their designs, children undertook a range of science investigations, such as one to 'make different circuits to find out which batteries made the bulb the brightest'. This involved three girls in trying out a range of different sizes and numbers of batteries with their bulb to find the ideal combination to fit with their design. They recorded their investigation by taking digital photographs of each combination to compare brightness.

Another starting point using a familiar – if somewhat more sophisticated – form of technology is a supermarket scanner. This uses a laser to read barcodes on our shopping and calculate our bills. An activity recommended by the New Zealand Ministry of Education (1999a) is to approach a local supermarket to show children their checkout scanners and allow them to hold a blank sheet of paper in front of the laser

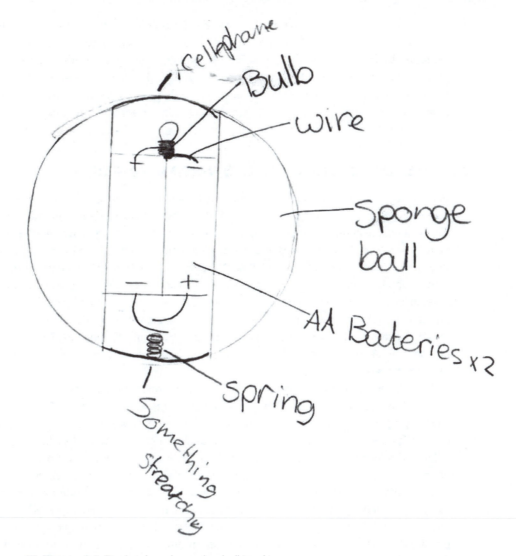

■ **Figure 4.1** Design for a bouncing ball torch

beam, taking care not to shine it at anyone's eyes. It then suggests the following activities:

> Move the paper or box upwards from the scanner and observe the lines of laser light on it. As you move the paper or box, what do you notice about the clarity of the light and the spaces between the lines? How can you explain what you observe? Hold the paper or box at a variety of angles. What do you notice about the light and the spaces between the beams now? (Laser beams do not spread out in all directions like normal light.)

> (1999a: 34)

Children could follow this up in the classroom using a 'laser pen', which are cheap and readily available, though again need to be used with care. For example, 9–11 year-old children in Neston Primary School, Wiltshire, designed a mirror maze which they would eventually build full-size in the playground. In order to determine the correct angles and positions of the mirrors in their model they tested it with a laser pen, which gives a clear, narrow beam of light whose path can be seen zig-zagging through the maze as it reflects.

HISTORICAL AND GEOGRAPHICAL STARTING POINTS

Part of adopting a 'socio-cultural' approach to science education (see Chapter 2 and above) is to set scientific ideas in a range of different historical and cultural contexts. This can enable children to see science as a human, social activity which has been relevant to people in different times and places, and which can still be relevant to their own lives now. Children at La Sagesse Primary School in Newcastle upon Tyne developed a Roman apothecary garden with help from the educators at nearby Segedunum Museum on Hadrian's Wall. They learned how to extract vegetable dyes and found out which plants were used by the Romans for their medicinal properties. They then compared these ancient remedies with modern drugs used to treat similar illnesses, learning about human health and the sorts of decisions people make between taking herbal or manufactured medicines.

Using a photograph as a starting point for scientific exploration can be very powerful, particularly if it is of an unfamiliar place or taken from an unfamiliar angle, encouraging children to 'see differently' (see Chapter 2). If we are using a geographical context for our science topic, photos can be useful in establishing a baseline of knowledge and understanding that children might already have about another place or other people's lives. They can provide a neutral starting point, a forum in which children can begin to share, discuss and question their ideas with confidence. Another advantage of using photographs is that children can connect science to everyday activities, such as cooking or looking after plants and animals. They will learn that science is universal. Children will be able to see that although life in other countries may differ in terms of facilities, climate and customs, it also bears many similarities with their own lives (Oxfam 2001). For example, the Oxfam *Photo Opportunities in Science* pack contains an image of bread-making near Lima, Peru, in a bakery set up by local women. Children can be asked what they notice about how the bread is being made and cooked, relating it to their own experiences of changing materials by using heat in classroom bread-making.

Danieka Rivers, a primary school teacher, used a set of images from the internet printed as A4 photographs for her 5–6-year-old children to examine as the starting point for a topic on 'Day and Night'. The photos included one of a city at night; the Earth seen from space; sunrise over the sea; the moon in the daytime; and the sun streaming through windows and casting shadows. These beautiful images immediately engaged the children's attention as they discussed them, first in pairs, then in groups of four (Figure 4.2, plate section). They stimulated some very thoughtful responses:

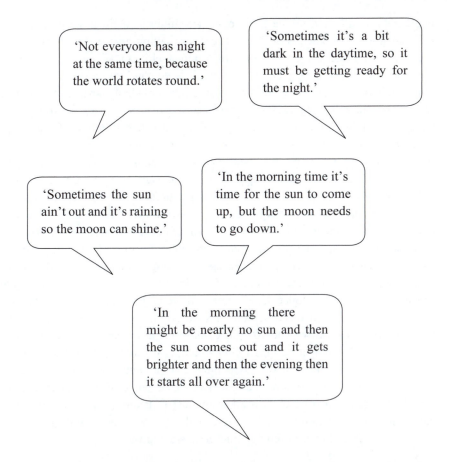

'Not everyone has night at the same time, because the world rotates round.'

'Sometimes it's a bit dark in the daytime, so it must be getting ready for the night.'

'Sometimes the sun ain't out and it's raining so the moon can shine.'

'In the morning time it's time for the sun to come up, but the moon needs to go down.'

'In the morning there might be nearly no sun and then the sun comes out and it gets brighter and then the evening then it starts all over again.'

These statements vary in their degree of scientific accuracy, but all demonstrate the careful reasoning of which young children are capable. In order to probe their ideas further, Danieka asked them to draw 'a picture of how we get day and night', and to explain their drawing to their partner. She followed this by seating the children in a large circle and inviting pairs to come and model the movement of the Earth and sun using a swivel chair and torch, with other children taking it in turns to direct the 'movement of the spheres' and relate this to day and night (Figure 4.3, plate section). Finally, children were asked individually to come up and explain how day and night happen in different places on Earth using a globe and an overhead projector (Figure 4.4, plate section). This teaching sequence was creative in that it used an initial 'Wow!' stimulus (Feasey 2005) but followed this up with in-depth exploration of children's ideas, using a range of different modes of expression – talk, drawing, writing, kinaesthetic modelling – to look at a scientific phenomenon from different angles and help children make connections between ideas they may not have previously linked together.

RESOURCES FOR CREATIVITY

Many of the cross-curricular starting points referred to above involve the use of resources which may not at first sight be obviously 'scientific', such as story books, photographs, balls and torches. Although we might sometimes need specialist equipment such as thermometers or data loggers for making precise observations and measurements in science, resources we use to stimulate children's ideas at the beginning of a topic or lesson will usually be more general, 'everyday' things such as the interesting objects children might bring in from home, or something 'special' or 'magical' the teacher provides. Feasey (2005) suggests a set of criteria for choosing resources to support creativity in science, including 'Will it motivate staff to try different approaches to teaching and learning in science?' and 'Will it provide a "Wow!" factor in the classroom?' She suggests the use of a 'surprise box' containing a mystery object each week – perhaps linked to the science topic for the term, such as a prism, a kaleidoscope or a hologram – about which the class has to ask questions to identify its contents.

Resources do not have to be expensive or difficult to come by in order to stimulate children's curiosity. For example, a team of teachers at Red Beach Primary School used plastic bottles, paper towels, water and umbrellas to start a whole-school topic on 'air'. The school has developed cross-age 'learning communities' and has adopted a philosophy of 'going deeper, doing less', which means that depth of understanding of fundamental scientific concepts is more important than curriculum coverage. Their learning model in science is based on three questions: 'What do we think?' (prediction, hypothesis), 'What do we notice?' (observation) and, perhaps most importantly 'What do we wonder?' (conjecture, possibility thinking, creativity). Sue, Cathy, Andrea and Fleur, the teachers of the school's 'Archimedes community' developed their topic on air around a series of 'immersion' challenges based on some of the fundamental concepts they wished to communicate: air is all around us, air takes up space, you can trap air, air can be squashed, air can be strong. These challenges were organised as a circus around four classrooms and undertaken by children in small groups:

■ Can you squash a plastic bottle (with the lid on or off)?
■ Can you run with an umbrella (different sizes, pulled behind them for safety)?
■ Will the paper towel get wet (stuffed into a glass, inverted into a tub of water)?
■ How quickly can you blow up the bag?

In response to the bottle-squashing activity, 'What do we think?' elicited the following responses:

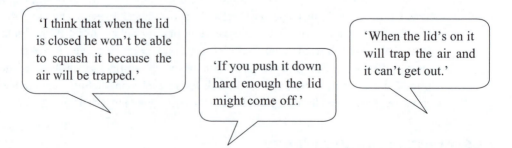

'I think that when the lid is closed he won't be able to squash it because the air will be trapped.'

'If you push it down hard enough the lid might come off.'

'When the lid's on it will trap the air and it can't get out.'

Once the children had tried squashing the bottle with and without its lid they responded to 'What do we notice?' with the following observations:

'When you had the lid on you could squeeze it a tiny bit except a lot of that air went out to the sides.'

'But with the lid off it's more squishy … the air blows out.'

'Hold your hand there, you can feel the air can't you.'

Asked to respond to 'What we wonder?', one child came up with the following:

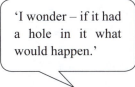

'I wonder – if it had a hole in it what would happen.'

The paper towel challenge produced the following predictions ('What do we think?'):

'The water will go up and the paper towel will get wet.'

'I don't think the paper towel will get wet because when you put a glass over water it just goes round it.'

'Tip it up the right way then it will get wet.'

Their observations ('What do we notice?') also contained a high component of explanation and hypothesis:

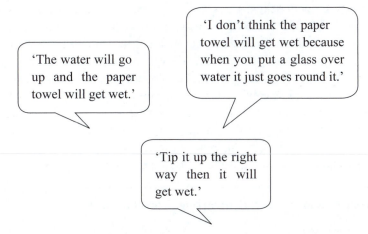

'I think the glass is trapping the air in, so there's an air pocket that's keeping the paper dry.'

'I also think the water is making a seal on the glass to stop the air getting out, so they're both like sealing it in and the water is pushing on the glass to seal it in there.'

'And when we tipped it to the side all the air came out with bubbles and that meant the pocket had opened.'

The activity itself had produced considerable wonder:

> 'We really, really wonder why the water is coming on the piece of paper but it still isn't getting wet!'

Sue, Cathy, Andrea and Fleur had used simple, everyday resources to produce challenges for children that invited them to think around the problem, conjecture and put forward alternative explanations for intriguing phenomena. This creative starting point was set within a whole-school ethos of enquiry in which children were expected to think deeply, and where scientific phenomena were providing the contexts through which their thinking skills were being developed.

SUMMARY OF CHAPTER 4

We have seen in this chapter how combining science with other curriculum areas can help to contextualise children's learning and make our classroom teaching less predictable and formulaic. I have argued that this process of combining ideas from different disciplines not only demonstrates teachers' creativity but also creates some of the conditions for children's creativity to flourish. However, the creative teacher needs to be more than a children's entertainer; constant novelty will soon wear thin if it is not followed up with in-depth learning experiences in which children investigate thoroughly the science behind the starting point. It is here that teachers' subject knowledge and confidence in handling scientific concepts becomes important. If we are familiar with the 'big picture' in a concept area then we can more easily scaffold children's understanding from their starting points towards a more scientific view. Perhaps the most powerful way in which we can help children follow their own paths to the big ideas is through scientific enquiry, which forms the focus of the next two chapters.

Practical resources for the creative starting points in this chapter

- ▨ Candle and sand tray
- ▨ Plastic cups and marbles
- ▨ Pair of rugby balls
- ▨ Materials to make a magnetic board game – card, magnets, scissors, felt pens
- ▨ Georgia O'Keeffe's flower paintings viewed at www.okeeffemuseum.org/
- ▨ Materials for making torches: bulbs, batteries, wire, switches, card tubes, acetate, foil
- ▨ Storybooks, e.g. Drewerey, M. (2002) *Nanny Mihi's Garden*, New Zealand: Raupo Publishing
- ▨ Science postcards, available from www.sciencepostcards.com
- ▨ Plastic bottles, paper towels, water, umbrellas
- ▨ Newspaper articles with science stories, science fiction novels
- ▨ Laser pen and plastic mirrors to design a mirror maze
- ▨ Overhead projectors and coloured acetates to provide coloured lighting for shadow dances
- ▨ Photographs of everyday activities in different countries
- ▨ Images of day and night, sunset and sunrise

CHAPTER 5

CREATIVE EXPLORATION

*Ian Milne**

INTRODUCTION

Creative exploration is an approach to science teaching and learning that mirrors many aspects of the ways in which scientists work. It requires both the teacher and children to make the science and scientific processes involved explicit. It is about 'children's science': children personalising their science activity leading to their development of creative explanations of natural phenomena. It requires children to be involved in exploration, enquiry, explanation and making connections and is often ignited by aesthetic experiences that promote affective and sometimes emotional responses. It is associated with dispositions such as fascination, anticipation, engagement, awe, wonder, interest and curiosity and can lead to the use of scientific enquiry to develop explanations of natural phenomena. This chapter will first introduce and justify this approach, and then provide examples of the approach in action.

Creative exploration is a sequential or cyclic model of exploring for understanding in children's science. It is based on the assumption that children naturally seek explanations for experiences that have some effect on their feelings, attitudes and the manner in which they think about or view natural phenomena. Children will often construct creative explanations when seeking to understand and explain the phenomena involved in their aesthetic experiences. The outcome of such creative explanations is a greater depth of understanding, especially if the learner involved has communicated and justified their ideas with others. In a teaching and learning situation children participating in rich

* Ian Milne has recently retired as Senior Lecturer in Primary Science and Mathematics in the Faculty of Education, University of Auckland. He has taught in a range of Auckland primary and intermediate schools and continues to work on a number of NZ Ministry of Education professional development contracts. He is Past President of the NZ Association of Science Educators (NZASE), National Director of NZASE Primary Science Conferences, and a member of the editorial board for the ASE journal *Primary Science*.

▨ **Table 5.1** Sequential elements of the creative exploration model for developing personal understanding in primary science

Creative exploration

Explore	A problem, situation, phenomenon, artefact, model, event, story	**Wonder**
Observe	What is happening? What changes happened? What materials are involved? What are the main parts? What are the key aspects? What do these parts/structures do?	**Wonder about**
Identify evidence	What is the cause and effect of changes? What is the function? What parts are interacting with other parts? What are the outcomes of these interactions? What trends and patterns keep occurring?	
Create explanations	Personal explanations supported by evidence are created and processes to test them are planned	**Wonder at**
Investigate	Find out, measure, compare, verify, test, clarify, identify	
Evaluation	A self-evaluation of these investigations may lead to new or modified explanations, doubts about existing ideas or tentative conclusions. These tentative explanations need to be communicated to others for peer evaluation and feedback	
Further investigation	Evaluated explanations can lead to: re-exploration, seeking further explanation, leading to further investigation	**Wonder whether**
Making connections	Explanations are used or applied to make sense of or clarify other contexts where similar phenomena are involved	

aesthetic experiences of natural phenomena can be guided by informed facilitation towards a greater depth of personal understanding. This authentic process of enquiry not only leads to the development of personal conceptual understanding but also to the development of procedural knowledge and skills and an appreciation of the tentative nature of science. Although the approach is presented here in a linear fashion (Table 5.1), it should be viewed as cyclic in nature. A child can follow the whole process or may only complete certain parts. The more elements of the process used, the deeper the depth of engagement and subsequent understanding.

CHILDREN'S SCIENCE

Creative exploration is a co-constructive enquiry learning approach to teaching primary science that requires both the teacher and learners to be involved in doing science. A fundamental cornerstone is that the nature of the science involved is made explicit. At any time the teacher and the children will be able to answer the question: 'What makes this activity I am involved in science?' This assumes that both the teacher and the learners have a personal understanding of what science is and that aspects of the nature of science are discussed, explored and applied in a natural enquiring manner. As discussed in previous chapters, children use their previous experiences and imagination to create explanations for experiences of natural phenomena that intrigue or interest them. For these ideas to be classified as science ideas the children need to be able to identify and share the evidence they have used to formulate their explanations. These explanations supported by evidence are what can be loosely termed 'children's science'. Children's creative explanations are the building blocks for further learning. They are used by children as evidence to support their thinking and view of the world. It is important that primary school children develop an appreciation that there may be other explanations for the same evidence. Therefore it is important that teachers and pupils need to have an explanation for what the term science means.

So what do children think about the nature of science? The following extracts were taken from across Remuera Primary School, during preparation for their science expo (see Chapters 7 and 10). After a school-wide emphasis on science, the children were sharing the outcomes from their science investigations with their families and other members of the local community. This is a selection of children's responses to what they thought science was about. Science is:

'something that helps you find out things and you do experiments.'

(child in Year 1)

'discovering stuff and you find out about the whole wide world.'

(child in Year 1)

'things that you do. It makes water rise. Professors are scientists. It's like magic.'

(child in Year 1)

'about learning, doing fun things and you find out stuff. You learn new things. You can record ideas and find out information.'

(child in Year 2)

'about lots of different things you haven't done before. You do stuff that is really different. It's about making things.'

(child in Year 2)

'investigating new things. Science is finding things out, information about things that is unknown.'

(child in Year 3)

'about food. It is solids, liquids and gas. You test things you don't know about and you change one variable at a time.'

(child in Year 3)

'everything – the world, biology, life, space, astronomy. You try to discover new things. You do experiments to find new things so the world can be better.'

(child in Year 4)

'something to find out things from objects and sometimes it helps people with problems. It can help people in space. You do research and investigate things.'

(child in Year 5)

'when you put a little bit of something and a little bit of something else and what ever happens you use that information to find out new information. Science is always truthful, it can't lie, it's the bare facts!'

(child in Year 6)

'something that you research and find things out. You can do experiments so you can test things out and learn stuff.'

(child in Year 6)

By Year 6 the children have moved from viewing science as a way of 'finding out stuff' to understanding that it is way of testing out ideas. In the process the children have developed an understanding that science is important and can help solve problems. The children's explanations include knowledge, skills and value elements. The expression of value elements by the children supports the contention that an emotional attachment or involvement with the experiences is important. A feature of creative exploration is the assumption that the expression of an aesthetic reaction of wonder to experiences of natural phenomena increases the engagement and subsequent science learning for the children involved.

AESTHETIC APPROACHES

It is claimed that a more phenomenological aesthetic approach to teaching and learning needs to be implemented in science education classrooms if students are to become engaged with and continue their studies in science (Dahlin 2001; Girod and Wong 2002; Wickman 2006). This is an approach to teaching and learning in science that Wickman suggests 'shows the intimate connections between learning science and interest in science' (2006: 145). Dewey's notions of educated experiences, or fulfilled experiences of phenomena over time, are described by Girod and Wong (2002) as being dramatic events. They contend that these events, which they refer to as aesthetic experiences, can have a significant influence on learning in primary school science. Similarly, Dahlin argues that there needs to be a greater 'emphasis on the aesthetic dimension of knowledge formation' (2001: 130). He defines aesthetic as 'a point of view which cultivates a careful and exact attention to all the qualities inherent in sense experience ... an approach to natural phenomena would not merely be to appreciate their beauty but also understand them' (2001: 130). It can be argued that there is a strong similarity between the notions of awe and wonder and the elements of fascination and anticipation that children engaged in aesthetic learning experiences may undergo. The awe and wonder factors, often referred to as the 'wow' factor (Feasey 2005), can become the focus or motivator for further thinking and enquiry.

Godlovitch suggests that an aesthetic experience could be defined 'as an elemental mode of awareness, one special way we make contact with experiential content, that which is the focus of attention of a special sort of appreciation' (1998: 3). He contends that fascination develops very early in life and suggests that because of the complexity of the sensory and affective dimensions of aesthetic experience, 'fascination stands proxy for a cluster of terms all of which accent a powerfully personal bond (analogous to affection) that develops in aesthetic experience between the subject and object of experience' (1998: 3). Wickman (2006) refers to Kant's definition of aesthetic experiences as the judgements which are related to experiences. For research purposes he defines aesthetic judgements as:

> utterances or expressions that either deal with feelings or emotions related to experiences of pleasure or displeasure, or deal with the qualities of things, events, or actions that cannot be defined as qualities of the objects themselves but rather are evaluations of taste – for example about what is beautiful or ugly.
>
> (2006: 9)

65 ■

Wickman examines aesthetic experiences from both a positive and a negative view as they appear as part of the practice and the life of pupils involved in science education activity. He focuses on the aesthetic judgements made as pupils react and communicate their feelings and emotions about their experiences of phenomena. This idea that aesthetic experiences may strongly influence how children approach their learning is supported by Egan (2005), who argues that 'whatever content is to be dealt with needs to be attached to students' emotions in some way'. Whatever teaching and learning approaches we use, there needs to be a period of exploratory activity that, with teacher direction and input, provides aesthetic experiences of natural phenomena that will assist the promotion of a sense of wonder, leading to a desire for understanding and explanation.

THE ROLE OF WONDER IN CREATIVE EXPLORATION

As indicated in Table 5.1, three specific aspects of wonder – 'wonder at, wonder about, and wonder whether' – are significant in creative exploration. These three elements of wonder were presented collectively for the first time by Goodwin (2001) and more recently by Naylor and Keogh (2009) when exploring factors that impact positively on children's engagement in school science. The importance of wondering is supported from historical and contemporary perspectives that include Socrates' 'wisdom begins in wonder', Aristotle's 'It was through the feeling of wonder that men now and at first began to philosophise', Gasset's 'to be surprised, to wonder is to begin to understand', Carson's (1956) need to develop a sense of wonder in all children, and Neil Armstrong's 'mystery creates wonder and wonder is the basis of Man's desire to understand'.

From an educational perspective the significance of developing a sense of wonder and its conjoint elements, awe and interest, are highlighted in the goals of science education from the *Beyond 2000* science education report (Millar and Osborne 1998). Experiencing and showing awe, wonder and interest are also identified as key aspects of learning of the New Zealand science assessment goals of 'developing interest' and relating scientific learning to the wider world (New Zealand Ministry of Education 1993). Egan (2005) identifies wonder as one of the tool kits of romantic understanding, the third of five stages of understanding that are featured in the work of the Imaginative Education Research Group. He suggests that the content of science education at the romantic stage should 'best be able to stimulate the student's sense of awe and wonder' (2005: 218), and in the process ensure ready engagement by the learners involved. The next section explores different notions of wonder and links these to questioning and enquiry.

The category of wonder in which children 'wonder about' pertains to questions relating to the processes of exploring in science: 'How does that work?', 'What will happen if we change this?', 'I wonder what made that happen?', 'How long will it take?', 'What will happen next?', When children 'wonder at' they may make exclamations like: 'Wonderful!', 'Wow!', 'How interesting!', 'How exciting!', 'How beautiful!', relating to the appreciation phase of an aesthetic experience of nature (Dahlin 2001). The third aspect, 'wondering whether', involves value-laden questions such as:

'Should I do this?', 'Would this be better than that?', 'Why is this significant or important?' These aspects of wonder represent the humanising of the science content that may be involved as science activity is presented in contexts that are engaging and contextually relevant. An aesthetic experience like patting a calf (Figure 5.1, plate section) could generate all three types of wonders and be the basis for further enquiry while also promoting further engagement. For example, children might ask: 'Why does the calf feel warm and soft?', 'I wonder how old she is', 'How much milk does she need every day?', 'I wonder how long she needs to stay with her mother.'

Creative exploration is a teaching and learning approach in science that is based around children seeking understanding of their experiences of natural phenomena. It requires the learners involved to create tentative explanations and in the process test the evidence they have used before sharing it with peers and other members of the community. The next section introduces examples of aspects of creative explanation in action.

EXAMPLES OF CREATIVE EXPLORATION

Ice hands

Recently I was invited to assist a group of primary class teachers to plan and teach a material world unit based around kitchen chemistry with the key idea of changes that occur when preparing food. There was a school focus on lifting the level of investigative skills in science. I was asked by a teacher to model the identification and testing of variables with 5-year-old children. The key science understanding involved was change in the state of water through melting.

The introductory stage of the lesson was spent revisiting the children's understanding of melting. There had been some prior exploratory activity and experiences of changes in material when heated. First the children were asked to share their understanding of melting in a general way. To support this process the children sat around a pan on an electric hot plate and were asked to predict what would happen when materials were placed first on the cold pan and then heated. In the process of testing the materials we established the idea that some form of heat energy was required for materials to melt. The children also noted that some things melted while others did not – they only got hotter. Several children were asked to touch the cold pan and hold their hands above the hot pan to establish that there was temperature change between the two.

The children were next introduced to an ice hand made out of frozen water and red dye (Figure 5.2, plate section) and asked to predict what would happen to it in the hot pan. The children enthusiastically responded, 'It will melt.' I then asked, 'I wonder what part would complete melting first?' The most common response was, 'The pinkie [the little finger] would melt first.' When asked why they thought this, one child suggested that the 'pinkie' would melt first 'because it is smaller than the other parts'. A short discussion with the children established the shared theory: 'the size of the piece of ice will affect how long it will take to melt'. As a class, we set out to test this theory. Working in pairs, the children were each given three different-sized pieces of ice and a dish to test the theory out. In the process we established the idea that the only thing that was different was the size of the ice cubes. In their pairs the children found places around the classroom to observe the melting process. I visited each group, discussed the progress of their investigation and asked the children to identify the relationships between the different-sized ice cubes and the different parts of the ice hand.

After the consultation with each group had taken place we returned to the hot plate and redid the investigation as a group. Sets of different-sized ice blocks were tested and the prediction that the smaller sizes would melt first was confirmed. The slowly melting hand was placed on the hot pan and the children observed the melting process. The children were spellbound and the engagement was intense. At the conclusion of the melting process the children revisited their theory and decided that their observations from the investigation had confirmed their explanation. To further aid their understanding the children were then asked to role-play what had happened to the ice blocks. Each child was asked to pretend to be a very cold ice block. The children then stood tall and erect and then acted out the melting process until they were spread out on the floor. Selected children were asked to model the process in front of the class; the observing class members then explained the process that was being modelled. There was an emphasis throughout on working with the children's ideas, prompting and challenging their thinking, and introducing them to the key idea that science is about developing explanations that can be supported by evidence. Throughout the process the classroom teacher was taking digital photographs which were later used in literacy time to develop a record and account of the activity and to revisit later as the experiences were relived as a power point presentation.

The Gingerbread Man

The second example of creative exploration in action also relates to the material world. I was invited to work with a group of junior class teachers at Botany Downs School, Auckland, who wanted to put a bit of excitement back into their science lessons. After discovering that they were due to be working on a literacy theme based on traditional stories, we decided to use these stories as a basis for doing some science. Stories selected were *The Little Red Hen*, *The Gingerbread Man* and *Goldilocks and the Three Bears*. *The Gingerbread Man* provides a natural context for developing creative exploration, starting with the question: 'Why on earth did the gingerbread man decide to climb on the fox's back to cross the river?' What did he already know and why did this knowledge influence his subsequent actions? The children responded that he would go mushy and soft quickly; this provided a context for exploring and investigating. The first time I did this with children we did not have gingerbread men so we immersed gingernuts and ginger cake into jars of water and watched closely. Slowly over time the gingernuts and cake sank to the bottom and the colouring and sugar started to diffuse through the water, turning it a dark yellow colour. After a time the gingernuts absorbed water and expanded slowly, then floated to the surface where they stayed until touched. The children quickly discovered that the hard, crisp gingernuts were now soggy and mushy.

We then asked, 'I wonder if there is any other reason why the gingerbread man climbed onto the fox's back. Could it be that he wanted to protect his special buttons?'

(These were made of M&M sweets.) Placing an M&M into a clear glass jar of water and watching it provided children with an aesthetic experience. The dissolving of first the colour and second the white sugary layer and their diffusion had a significant impact on their sense of 'wondering at' as the form and beauty evolved. We started to explain it by talking about everything being made up of little bits. A quick stir and then pouring off the liquid left a chocolate-only M&M. The whole process was modelled by the class members; first an M&M was constructed with three children bonded together a bit like a rugby scrum, each person representing a particle of chocolate. Two layers of colour were added, with the first layer of children being the white bits and the second layer the colour. At this point each child was given an M&M and bit it in half to identify the different layers and the different parts in the model. Now the remaining class members became water particles and as a class they modelled the changes that had taken place. First, the outside colours were tugged away from the M&M and diffused across the room, followed by the white parts of the model. Despite being bombarded with water particles, the chocolate particles stayed bound together as a lump.

I have led the M&M role-play with 5- to 14-year-olds and all ages of student teachers. It is important for the learners involved that a discussion is held about the importance of the use of models to demonstrate our ideas and understanding in science. It is also important to ensure that the science ideas being modelled are made explicit and reinforced at this point, including ensuring that appropriate language is used. Creating models in the form of role-play can be a very effective way to communicate our understanding of the phenomena involved; it also can be a creative way to provide formative feedback to the learners about their understanding of the concepts involved.

Testing our ideas about air pressure

The third example has been selected to demonstrate the use of children's drawings to help them develop their thinking, share their ideas and make connections with the examples of the phenomena in their real environment. After investigating and exploring properties of air, including the effect of temperature change and pressure, the children of Class 1C at Remuera Primary School settled on the following 'big question' to investigate: 'Can air lift or carry heavy things?' Their initial thinking was that air can't lift or carry heavy things such as a book or a person. I challenged them by asking: 'If you put a person on top of some balloons filled with air, what will happen? Will the balloons pop? Will the balloons be squashed? Can the air lift the person off the floor?' The children illustrated a set of instructions for what to do to answer these questions: 'First blow up some balloons.' 'Then put the balloons in a bag.' 'After that put the balloons on the floor.' 'Next put something flat on the balloons.' 'Lastly carefully get down and lie on the balloons.' The children expressed wonder and incredulity that the air could actually hold them up!

After trialling with children and teachers, they noticed the effect of changing variables by having heavier and lighter people on the balloons and measuring their height off the floor. After talking and thinking about the results the children were asked to draw a picture that explained what had happened (Figure 5.3). As a class and with the teacher's help, the children created the following three statements as a record of their

■ **Figure 5.3** Using symbols and diagrams to explain forces

current thinking: 'The air in the balloons could not escape out of the balloons. The people stayed up off the ground because the air in the balloons pushed the people up. There were a lot of balloons and so there was a lot of air pushing up.'

From a science education perspective, Figure 5.3 provides a rich context for exploring how scientists use symbols and diagrams when communicating their explanations. When asked if they had found an answer to their questions the class came up with the following response: 'Yes, air can lift heavy things. It can lift people and books. If air is trapped inside tyres, it can carry bikes, trucks, cars and buses. When air is trapped inside a bouncy castle, it can carry us.' The final stage of the investigation was making connections to their world and again drawings became the medium. The drawings were later photographed and turned into a Powerpoint presentation to show at the school science expo (see Chapters 7 and 10). This investigation clearly demonstrates that with assistance and support even very young children as a group can follow through the whole process of creative enquiry.

SUMMARY OF CHAPTER 5

In this chapter I have introduced the notion of 'creative exploration': an approach to teaching and learning that models many aspects of scientific enquiry in a way that engages children emotionally and builds upon their natural wonder at the world around them. It requires an exploratory phase that essentially provides children with rich learning experiences around everyday scientific phenomena. Out of these aesthetic experiences authentic questions can be generated that the children can investigate to test their own creative explanations. It requires enthusiastic teachers who personalise the science activity and not only provide support for but also challenge the children's thinking as they develop and share their explanations. We need to support children as they move their creative thinking from 'children's science' towards the creative world of 'real science'.

Practical resources to carry out the creative enquiries in this chapter

- Ice hand, made by filling a glove with coloured water and freezing
- Gingerbread men, gingernuts or ginger cake, M&Ms (or Smarties), water
- Balloons, very large plastic bag, large flat piece of hardboard

CHAPTER 6

COLLABORATIVE SCIENTIFIC ENQUIRY

INTRODUCTION – WHY COLLABORATIVE?

Children rarely do practical science on their own. It is perhaps worth pausing to consider why as teachers we tend to group children together to undertake scientific enquiries. One reason is practicality; we tend not to have enough equipment and resources for each child to undertake an individual investigation. Another rationale is peer tutoring: if children can help each other solve the practical problems they encounter they are less likely to come to us for help and we can direct our scarce adult support to groups or individuals who find the activity difficult. Linked to this is the development of children's speaking and listening skills as they 'talk science' to each other in groups. This aspect of language development is something we will consider further in Chapter 7. But I wonder whether the idea that doing science collaboratively enhances children's creativity enters our rationale. This links back to the notion of 'social creativity' (Harrington 1990) I introduced in Chapter 2, with 'middle c' creativity (Craft 2008) – which groups of people are able to create in the space between their minds – lying between the 'Big C' creativity of genius and the 'little c' creativity in which originality is unique to the individual. In other words, children are able to be more creative when they have the opportunity to 'bounce' their ideas off each other in collaborative work than they would be on their own.

However, experience tells us that not all groups are natural forums for creative thinking. In a study of children's creative group work, Mardell *et al.* (2008: 114) found that 'while some groups come together quickly, exude a sense of purpose and vitality, and provide a context for both individual and collective learning, others lack flow and do not promote creative learning'. Part of the reason for this lies in group composition: we may need to try out several combinations of children with different temperaments, friendships, ideas and capabilities to find the optimum combination for groups to 'gel'. Group size is also crucial: many scientific activities work well in pairs, whereas more complex activities with clearly defined roles may need group sizes of up to five. However, we may also need to teach children how to cooperate, particularly if they have little previous experience of working in collaborative groups. In Mardell's study the crucial factor was the opportunity for children to talk about their experience of working in a group and to come up with their own theories of how to make the group work well. Presenting children with stories about group learning helps foster metacognition – an awareness of their own learning processes in groups and an ability to discuss how well they have worked together. For example, Leanne, a teacher of 5–6-year-olds, wanted children to work together to explore a collection of puppets in order to investigate the properties of the materials they were made from. In order to raise children's awareness of the cooperative skills that the children would need to develop in order to progress in this kind of group enquiry she acted out two 'stories' of groups: one in which two children argued over resources and tore the puppet, then another, which involved speaking very loudly over each other. These scenarios allowed her to make some teaching points about the need to speak, listen and cooperate in appropriate ways. One of the criteria for children's evaluation of the subsequent investigation was 'how well we worked together'.

Working in groups can develop in children a wide range of personal attitudes and dispositions which are essential for success in science as well as contributing to their broader well-being. The traditional image of the lone scientist tinkering away in the laboratory is far from the truth. Scientists in the twenty-first century tend to collaborate in multi-disciplinary, often international teams, with frequent informal communication in addition to the papers and conferences on which the scientific community depends. Scientists, like most professionals, need what Gardner (1999) calls 'interpersonal intelligence' and what Goleman (1996) calls 'emotional intelligence': an ability to perceive what others are thinking and feeling and adapt our speech and actions accordingly. Fortunately, our primary curricula have recently recognised the importance of developing in children these wider aspects of learning to be able to relate to others and act effectively in the world.

A published primary science scheme which seeks to develop children's emotional intelligence and group working skills is *Smart Science* (Bianchi and Barnett 2006) – see Chapter 1 – which builds upon the *Personal Capabilities in Science Project* at Sheffield Hallam University (Bianchi 2002) and is linked to several UK government initiatives such as *The Children's Plan* (DCSF 2007), *Social and Emotional Aspects of Learning* (SEAL) (DCSF 2005) and the latest version of the Northern Ireland curriculum statement (DENI 2007). For example, in the *Smart Science* 'eco-consultants' task (free to download from www.personalcapabilities.co.uk/smartscience/) children are asked to share ideas to give advice to a conservation group in the Galapagos Islands, predicting the effects of changes of habitat on the populations of interdependent living things within the food web. The groups use a set of hoops with different numbers of children standing in each to model their ideas about what will happen to the numbers of various organisms such as whales, penguins, sardines, zooplankton and phytoplankton. At the end of the activity children review how well their group has collaborated to create and communicate an effective exploration using a 'thumbs up, thumbs sideways, thumbs down' self-assessment against a 'Smart grid' with the following criteria:

▧ We shared our ideas and what we already knew about...

▧ We made links between our ideas by...

▧ We agreed on an outcome by...

▧ We talked about how different organisms in the food web could affect each other, e.g....

▧ We explained how different factors affected the food web, e.g....

These prompts for discussion, while developing children's metacognition about how they collaborate in groups (Mardell *et al.* 2008), also require children to think about the process of generating new ideas and developing their understanding as a group, key to developing their social creativity.

TYPES OF SCIENTIFIC ENQUIRY

Much as we tend to think of the solo scientist beavering away on their own experiments, we also tend to assume that there is one 'scientific method' which all scientists must follow in order for their findings to be accepted by the wider scientific community. The traditional secondary school version of the 'scientific process' – apparatus, method, results, conclusion – has been adapted into the primary 'fair test', which tends to follow a similarly predictable path from 'observation' through 'questioning' to 'planning', 'predicting', 'testing', 'recording' and 'interpreting results'. This is a version of the 'inductive' method of scientific enquiry, developed by the Franciscan monk Roger Bacon in the thirteenth century from the work of the Ancient Greek philosopher Aristotle. The idea here is that to find out about the world we must observe it closely, inducing our theories from the evidence of our senses and testing these theories through experimentation. Over the centuries this process has become – at least in popular imagination – a rigid set of rules that scientists must follow systematically, leaving little room for creativity. However, in practice different branches of science have developed different versions of the experimental method (Polanyi 1964), and the most creative scientists have always interpreted the 'rules' flexibly according to their own judgement. Feyerabend (1994) has claimed that the most creative examples of scientific thought have come from 'chaotic' processes where scientists have dismissed reason and broken all the rules. Although we might not appreciate such anarchy in our science lessons, insights from the 'real' world might make us look at the procedural elements of scientific enquiry slightly differently. If science is a combination of systematic, careful data collection, together with the insight and inspiration of individuals and of scientific communities that lead to new explanations, then science in school should reflect this creative and sometimes 'fuzzy' process, rather than pretend that science is a linear path from question to answer.

The *ASE–King's College Science Investigations in Schools (AKSIS)* project (Goldsworthy *et al.* 2000b) found that scientific enquiry is associated in the minds of many primary teachers with the idea of a 'fair test': changing one factor and observing or measuring the effect, while keeping other factors the same. Interestingly, in the context of mathematics we tend to think of an investigation as a more open-ended problem-solving activity in which many solutions are possible (often starting with the phrase: 'How many ways can you find to…?'). So in this respect maths investigations appear to offer more scope for creativity than their scientific equivalent. In order to develop a more creative approach to scientific enquiry we need to move beyond the 'tyranny of the fair test'. *AKSIS* offers the following alternatives:

1   *Pattern seeking*: observing and recording to find patterns in data, or carrying out a survey. For example, a common activity of observing the changes in shadows caused by the sun involves children standing some kind of stick upright in the playground on a sunny day, and marking the position and length of the shadow every hour using either chalk directly onto the asphalt or marker pen on a large sheet of paper. Once children have identified the pattern observed and offered hypotheses to explain it, this activity can be followed up by simulating the sun's 'movement' using a torch in the classroom (Howe *et al.* 2009). Another pattern-seeking enquiry is to count the number of reflections of a small object between a pair of hinged mirrors placed at different angles to each other, which can be related to the beautiful reflected images we see in kaleidoscopes. This activity rapidly becomes a mathematical investigation as children begin to see a pattern in the numbers emerging (the number of reflections is 360 divided by the angle between the mirrors, minus one – so with the mirrors at 90 degrees we would see the object itself with three reflections). In the ubiquitous topic 'Ourselves', children can undertake the kinds of pattern-seeking enquiries which look at the relationship (correlation) between two variables, answering questions such as: 'Are people with the biggest arm span also the tallest? Can people with longer legs jump further?' This kind of investigation is best recorded on a scattergram, with one of the two variables on each axis. Any patterns can be looked for in the clusters of data points arising from measurements – another mathematical link (see Chapter 4).

2   *Classifying and identifying*: arranging a range of objects into manageable sets and allocating names. For example, sorting games based upon collections of objects can be used in a variety of ways to develop enquiry skills and understanding of properties of materials, helping children to become aware of the variety of materials that form the world around them. An excerpt from the *Making Sense of Science* series (Dickey 1995) shows a teacher working with a group of young children to sort a collection of objects by what they are 'made from', using different hoops for 'metal' and for 'plastic' objects. The teacher introduces a pair of scissors with plastic handles which initially puzzles the group, before one child decides to 'balance' them on the touching edges of the hoops, so that the metal part is in one and the plastic part in another. Next comes a more challenging example: a stapler with overlapping metal and plastic parts. She uses this to introduce the concept of overlapping sets, by moving the hoops across each other and asking: 'This space in the middle – which hoop is it in?', eliciting the response: 'It's inside both of the hoops' and leading the group towards the solution of placing scissors and stapler in the overlapping section. This kind of logical thinking is also stimulated in the process of designing an 'identification key' using a collection of found objects

such as autumn leaves. After using published keys to find out what their specimens are, children can use a programme such as *Flexitree* (available from
www.flexible.co.uk) to create their own key by coming up with binary questions (to which the answer is either 'yes' or 'no') to sort their collection into
progressively smaller groups.

3   *Exploring*: making careful observations using all senses. Often seen as prelimi-
nary to more systematic investigation using a fair test, exploration is usually
associated with the early years (see Chapter 3). However, older children need
to explore – and play too, for example with magnets or a 'scientific' toy such
as a gyroscope. Claxton (2002) questions the extent to which the current
emphasis on clearly focused learning objectives actually leads to 'better' learning. However, he also suggests that moving between focused and more diffuse
forms of thinking is important in developing children's creativity, so it is
important to allow children 'playing time' to try things out with the materials
and resources that you hadn't necessarily planned for (within the bounds of
health and safety). Instead of launching straight into an investigation of, say,
shadow size when moving an object backwards and forwards between a light
source and a screen, children can be asked to look carefully for all the shadows
they can find around the room, identify which light source is causing each
shadow and explore the effects of using more than one source (e.g. two torches)
at different distances from an object. If the torches are giving different coloured
light – by putting, say, a red filter over one and a green filter over another – the
shadows produced can be quite surprising and children will find out some
unexpected things about mixing colours: red and green light gives yellow
rather than the brown they are more familiar with in mixing paints. Children
can make careful observations using all their senses when exploring a habitat,
such as a tree, stream or space under a lifted stone, asking questions such as
'how much light is there?', 'how damp is it?', 'does the temperature vary
through the habitat?' and 'what sorts of living things are there here?' This
might lead on to another kind of enquiry: designing a habitat for a particular
kind of creature or community of living things.

4   *Investigating models*: trying out explanations to see if they make sense (also
called 'illustrative' activities). One of the biggest tensions in teaching science
practically is that between wanting children to carry out their own investigations
and yet needing them to develop certain specific scientific concepts, e.g. about
the relationship between layers of insulation, and how quickly an ice cube melts
(Driver 1983). Decisions about how much the focus of an enquiry should be
directed by the teacher and how much by the interests of the child are not easy.
There are times when teachers can see how an investigation might challenge or
extend the ideas of a whole class in a certain direction and they may frame the
enquiry more closely. On other occasions they may help an individual child or
small group to test their own hypotheses in order to help them see limitations in
their ideas. At other times, opportunities can be given for children to follow their
own lines of enquiry within a topic without a pre-defined direction. We tend to
imagine that the more an enquiry is child-driven, the more potential there is for

creativity. This is not necessarily the case. For example, when using analogies to explain particular phenomena, such as the flow of blood round the body carrying oxygen from the lungs via the heart to our tissues and organs, children can be asked to invent their own model to explain their understanding to others. Given a set of ready-made resources – say, a washing line with cardboard symbols that can be pegged on representing red blood cells, oxygen and carbon dioxide – children can experience for themselves the journey of oxygen around the body. There is also such a thing as a 'creative demonstration'. For example, when exploring the concept of 'upthrust' in liquids – related to Archimedes' principle of floating objects displacing their own weight – we can give children a ball or inflated balloon to press down into a tank of water, feeling the force of the water 'pushing back'. This can then be followed up by handing round lumps of plasticine with the challenge, 'Can you make it float?' Shaping the plasticine into a simple boat so that it displaces more water can then be incorporated into the teacher's explanation of Archimedes' principle.

5   *Making things or developing systems*: problem-solving activities to design, test or adapt artefacts. If asked which kinds of enquiry activities are most likely to require creative thinking, many primary teachers would answer 'those with problems to be solved'. This is because we tend to associate problem solving with the ability to think laterally ('outside the box') or to be able to generate novel and innovative solutions. This impression has been reinforced by government policy; for example, one of the 'creative thinking skills' identified in the 1999 version of the English National Curriculum is 'problem solving' (DfEE/QCA 1999). Problem solving is a thinking skill that has received much attention over the years, and might be thought of as 'hard-edged' creativity as distinct from the more 'fluffy' end of the creativity spectrum associated with imagination, whimsy and intuition. It is not that there is no place for emotion and aesthetics in science – quite the opposite, as I have argued in previous chapters. It is just that scientists face problems to be solved every day, so their creativity needs to be purposeful (NACCCE 1999), as does children's creativity when solving a problem. The purpose may change during the process, but a sense of purpose must remain. A goal is mostly likely to be achieved through a process of raising questions, imagining possibilities, playing with materials, resources or ideas and coming up with an original solution (at least original to the child). Creative problem solving can be approached in a systematic way and one technique that has found widespread application in the USA and Canada is known as the Osborn–Parnes process (Parnes 1967). The model consists of six stages – objective finding, fact finding, problem finding, idea finding, solution finding and acceptance finding – each of which involves both divergent and convergent thinking.

'Objective finding' involves defining what we want to achieve as closely as possible. This might be a brief from the teacher, e.g. 'I want to be able to turn the landing light on from the top or bottom of the stairs – can you design me a circuit that will do this?' But it might be better approached divergently, e.g. 'What sorts of things might we want to do with lights and switches in the home?', before converging on a particular challenge. Having identified a challenge and written it down, we now diverge by finding 'facts' and identifying other related challenges. Who might live in the house? How might they want to use the lights? What sorts of switches are available? Having converged on answers to these questions children might then start work building their circuits, listing 'problems' as they arise – 'This bulb's too dim', 'This switch won't work if the other one is on'. One of these problems might be the crucial one upon which the others depend, so we converge on that one. 'Idea finding' is a divergent process that might draw upon prior experience – 'Do you remember when we made a parallel circuit?' – or insights from other areas of science ('Magnets can push things at a distance'). Note that idea finding is the fourth stage in the Osborn–Parnes process, not the first. Often 'brainstorming' sessions begin at this idea-finding stage before the real problem has been identified. Furthermore, they often end here too with a list of ideas but no further action. 'Solution finding' might involve trying out one or more of the ideas in the circuit, while 'acceptance finding' will involve discussion between group members – 'Do we all agree that this is the best way to do it?' – and the 'client', often the teacher, in the role of gatekeeper (Csikszentmihalyi 1990) deciding upon which solutions meet the criteria and which need further thought.

Problem-solving activities in which children make things tend to be associated with the link between science and technology, explored in Chapter 4. To maintain the distinction between the scientific and technological aspects of a designing activity it is worth thinking about purpose; if the purpose is to improve something or meet a need, the activity is probably more technology-oriented. If, however, it is to help children understand a scientific principle in greater depth or in a practical context it is probably closer to science. For example, Suzie Chard, a trainee primary teacher, asked her class to design seed pods that would demonstrate different modes of dispersal. One child used a Smarties tube to model an 'exploding' seed pod, scattering 'seeds' over a wide area. Another used pipe cleaners to attach hooks to his seed enabling it to be caught in a mammal's fur. Some children designed different versions of floating pods which they went on to test in water. Clearly, the children involved in this activity had undertaken some divergent thinking – 'What kind of seed could I make?', 'What resources could I use?' – but also some convergence ('I'll use these pipe cleaners to make hooks'). Kaufman and Baer (1998) argue that divergent-thinking exercises need to take place in a wide variety of contexts (not just the 'what use could you put this to?' activities used in many American primary schools) in order to allow children to exercise their divergent-thinking 'muscles' in different domains. Also, as has been demonstrated, there's more to creativity than divergent thinking.

SCIENTIFIC ENQUIRY SKILLS

If problem solving can be thought of as a creative thinking skill, other skills which children need whatever the type of scientific enquiry they are engaged in can also be regarded as thinking skills, e.g. hypothesising, interpreting and evaluating, while others might be classified as physical or motor skills such as using measuring or magnifying equipment.

However, this distinction can become somewhat 'fuzzy' in practice, since some scientific skills involve manual dexterity – holding, pouring, cutting – but also have a conceptual component. For example, to use a hand lens, a thermometer or a Newton meter requires a combination of physical manipulative skills and an understanding of what the tool does. One characteristic that thinking skills share is that they are 'procedural'; they are about carrying through a course of action, which led Harlen (2000) to refer to them as 'process skills' in the context of children's scientific learning. Learning experiences which are relatively open-ended, involve trying things out, testing ideas and communicating what has been discovered, generally make use of and develop these skills in a holistic way, and are consistent with a view of science as a blend of skills, concepts and attitudes that should remain intertwined during teaching. However, the *AKSIS* project (see above) has promoted the explicit teaching of individual enquiry skills, noting that teachers felt they had to cover the entire investigative process each time they taught science, which they found time-consuming and off-putting (Goldsworthy *et al.* 2000b). Children find some of the 'higher-order' skills – such as recording and interpreting data in graphs and charts – very difficult, so exercises involving the presentation of 'dummy' results for analysis have become increasingly popular in schools. Science subject leaders have planned whole-school schemes of work with a built-in progression of process skills, including units of work and lessons with particular skills emphasis, such as those developed in the *Improving Science Together* project (McMahon and Davies 2003) and featured on the AstraZeneca Science Trust website (www.azteachscience.co.uk).

This process of breaking down the scientific enquiry process into its component parts – what we might term an 'atomistic' approach – has its dangers. Treating the skills as distinct may lead children to a simplistic view of science as a set of standard procedures that have to be gone through, rather than as a complex relationship between creative thinking, and production of evidence. However, to understand the holistic nature of scientific enquiry, it is often helpful to think about the different aspects that make it up, just as to understand creative activity we might find it useful to break down the process into phases (Dust 1999). Furthermore, it is then possible to appreciate the similarities between scientific enquiry and creativity (at least in the 'Western' sense of the process) and how the use of children's process skills might contribute towards their own creative processes, as suggested in Table 6.1.

■ **Table 6.1** Correspondence between scientific and creative processes

Scientific process skills	'Western' view of creative process (see Chapter 1)
Observation, questioning, planning	Preparation – investigating the problem and gathering data
Collecting data, gathering and considering evidence	Incubation – usually an unconscious/subconscious phase
Interpretation, explanation, hypothesis	Illumination/revelation – the insight, the moment of creation
Recording, presentation, evaluation	Verification/reframing – the 'testing' of the idea, usually through communicating the outcome to peers or 'gatekeepers' or 'field' of the domain

So when children are observing and exploring an interesting phenomenon – colours in bubbles, patterns of seeds in a sunflower – asking questions about it and planning how they might investigate it further they are engaging in a process analogous to 'preparation' for creativity. There is not really a direct parallel within school versions of science to the 'incubation' phase in creativity, but when children are finding out more – perhaps by testing, measuring or further observation – and particularly when they are thinking about what they have found, they could be considered to be incubating their ideas. For this reason it is helpful to build in a break between the 'doing' part of a scientific enquiry activity and the subsequent 'thinking' part when children discuss their findings and develop new understandings, because of this need for incubation of ideas. The moment of 'illumination' is often the restructuring of previous understandings in the light of new evidence: for example, the realisation that the flow of electricity is the same all the way round a circuit rather than getting 'used up' in the bulb. However, these new insights need 'verifying' through the presentation of experimental evidence and children's evaluation of their own enquiry methods – do our findings really show this, or might we have got different results if we'd changed our approach? In this way, children's scientific enquiry skills can combine into a process that at least mimics the creative process. However, the individual skills themselves can be used with different degrees of creativity, as we will consider in the following sections.

OBSERVING CREATIVELY

Part of the 'myth of objectivity' in science is that scientists see what is really there. In practice, all scientific observations are mediated by our expectations of what we will find – for example, seventeenth-century scientists imagined they could see a 'homunculus' (tiny human being) in the head of a sperm – our eyesight, our cultural background, what we consider to be important and our aesthetics. According to Wickman (2006), aesthetics are linked to 'the right way to act' in science. In observations of science classrooms, he noticed that pupils' negative aesthetic experiences tended to be excluded from their observations, while those that were positive were more likely to be included. We like looking at things we consider to be beautiful or interesting, and tend to disregard what seems to be boring or ugly. This presents a challenge to teachers helping children recognise the beauty and fascination in the everyday, perhaps by using close-up photos or those taken from unusual angles. We can also encourage children to go further with their observations, to look more closely or to use more of their senses. A common approach is to use the acronym 'WILF' ('what I am looking for'), as in the phrase 'I am looking for children who notice something about the plant (which nobody else had observed).' This may be spoken, written or preferably discussed with the children. This helps to make success criteria clear to children: what counts as creative observation? We can also introduce a range of tools to aid our observation. Hand lenses or mini-microscopes are invaluable for studying 'minibeasts' closely, finding the intricate and beautiful structures in insect wings and centipede legs that children may have previously disregarded or that may have prompted negative aesthetic experiences – 'uggh!' For things that stay still – grains of sand, salt or sugar, leaves and petals, hairs – a digital microscope can enhance children's observational experiences, enabling images to be projected onto the whiteboard, captured in time-lapse photography or recoloured psych-edelically. When studying our own bodies, a mirror can be used to study the shapes of our ears or teeth to relate them to their functions. McMahon (2006) suggests that children can make use of art materials to make detailed observational drawings of living and non-living things, engaging their aesthetics and strengthening cross-curricular links (see Chapter 4). For example, the artist Georgia O'Keeffe has produced some striking paintings based on animal skulls that the children could look at and respond to when making their own drawings of a collection of (clean) animal bones that have been brought into the classroom. The very act of drawing can itself be a process of scientific discovery as children notice the shapes of the ends of the bones: how they might join onto each other, and their hollow or honeycomb structure giving them strength. That their drawing might also have some aesthetic qualities is a bonus.

QUESTIONING AND PLANNING CREATIVELY

Scientific enquiry often (but not always) starts with a question. Some questions arise spontaneously during observations. In the above example of our bodies, children can be encouraged to note down questions that occur to them on Post-it notes, e.g.: 'Do people with bigger ears hear better?', 'Which smells do different people like and dislike?', 'Can we identify different surfaces better with our hands or our feet?', 'How far away can we hear a pin drop?', 'How do we feel after running on the spot?', 'Why do bones have holes in?', 'Are my legs longer than my arms?'

   Not all of these questions are investigable in a scientific sense, so further discussion will be needed to choose one to look at more closely. However, having plenty to choose from is a good start. But what happens if children can't think of any questions? How can we stimulate children to ask more creative, or more scientific, questions? One approach is to start every enquiry lesson with a handling collection – say a collection of candles, or leaves, or balls, or moving toys – and to set each group a challenge of how many questions about the collection they can generate in 10 minutes. Another suggestion is a 'wonder wall' next to a display of photographs or a nature table, to which children can attach Post-it notes with statements beginning 'I wonder…' Post-it notes again come into play with the 'planning board' approach (Goldsworthy and Feasey 1997) which seeks to scaffold the formulation of an investigable question by starting with a 'variable scan' (Harlen 2000). Starting with the 'independent variable' (what we can change) children are invited to brainstorm 'all the things we could change about … a parachute, an ice cube, a bubble-blower, etc.' Deciding together which factor they will change, all the others recorded on the separate Post-it notes are moved to the section 'keep the same' (control variables). Once they have undergone the same process with 'all the things we could observe or measure' (the dependent variable), the planning board helps to model the construction of a scientific question by providing the formulation: 'How does changing the (independent variable) affect the (dependent variable)?' This approach only works for 'fair test' investigations and is potentially quite limiting to the types of questions children can ask.

   A more flexible approach is to classify a set of questions – either generated by the children or provided by the teacher – in terms of the type of enquiry that might be needed to answer them. For example, in considering the properties of a collection of materials, questions like 'What colour is it? What texture is it?' could be answered by observation; questions such as 'Which object will float or sink? Which material allows light through?' could be answered by exploration. 'Which material is hardest? Which is most flexible?' could be answered by comparison and fair-testing, while 'How is it made? Where does it come from?' are best answered from research using secondary sources such as books or the internet. Of course, some of the questions may be unanswerable – children are fond of asking questions that are not easily answered, and perhaps this may be regarded as an example of 'creative questioning'. It may be worth pointing out that science does not have an answer to some questions, or that there may be an answer but teacher doesn't know! Rather than seeing this as a problem, it could be an opportunity to value children's contributions by emphasising that genuine questions are worth asking even if they cannot be answered. Goldsworthy and Ponchaud (2007) have devised a game to make this classification process more enjoyable, engage them in discussion and kinaesthetic learning, and begin to think about the decisions that need to be made in planning a scientific enquiry. Called 'Planning posers' it presents children in groups with a set of definitions of different types of enquiry (which are also presented as labels round the walls of the classroom) together with a range of ways they could present the evidence from the enquiry – tables, bar charts, line graphs, scattergrams. Next the teacher reads out a scientific question, e.g. 'Which is the best material for making a tea cosy?' Through discussion, the groups need to decide which is the most appropriate type of enquiry and recording format, then send a member to run to the appropriate 'enquiry label' and act out their chosen presentation style, for example getting down on all fours for a 'table'. It is great fun, if a little chaotic, and can lead to valuable discussions about the different choices the groups have made. Some questions suggest an appropriate enquiry type very strongly, whereas others can be approached in a range of different ways, i.e. creatively.

As teachers, we have a role in modelling some of the more 'wacky' questions that children might investigate, maybe based on traditional folklore or everyday observations, for example: 'Does bread always fall butter side down?', 'Do we get taller during the day?', 'Does eating carrots really help us see in the dark?', 'Which kind of biscuit is best for dunking?' This last question was actually investigated by the Physics Department at the University of Bristol, which came up with a mathematical formula governing the optimum 'dunking time'. Children can have a go at designing experiments to answer these bizarre questions simply as a creative thinking exercise, without actually having to carry them out. However, it is only when actually trying to do some practical science that children realise just how many decisions there are to be made. For example, a common investigation under the heading of 'the Earth and beyond' is to simulate meteor impacts upon the moon by dropping a marble into a tray of sand. This will make a crater, and a little exploration will reveal that the higher the drop, the bigger the crater. Once children have decided on an aspect of this phenomenon to investigate, they will soon come up against some of the practical issues involved in testing their hypotheses. For example, how can they change the mass of the marble without changing its size? How will they measure the diameter or depth of crater accurately, since its edge is rather indistinct? Will they need to make repeat measurements? Similarly, when investigating the factors that might affect how tall a plant will grow, actually planting the seeds outside will raise a whole range of new questions to consider: 'Shall we put netting over the flowerbed to keep the birds off?', 'Shall we bury them all in the same depth of soil?' They may have planned to take photos, or to measure the plants every day, but decide that twice a week is going to be enough as the plants are growing more slowly than they predicted. In this way children will realise that planning isn't just something you do at the beginning of an enquiry; plans need to be adapted throughout and they will need to use their creative problem-solving skills to think of ways round all the obstacles they encounter.

PREDICTING AND HYPOTHESISING CREATIVELY

Children sometimes get confused between a prediction and a hypothesis. One straight-forward way of distinguishing between them is to say that a prediction is what we think will happen, and a hypothesis is why we think it will happen. A prediction without an underlying hypothesis is a guess, not a creative prediction! Children tend to find it easy to make predictions but less easy to explain the thinking behind them. Engaging them in creative exploration with innovative ways of recording their ideas can help to make their thinking more visible; it is often in the hypothesis that children's creativity lies. For example, as part of the Momentum project (see Chapter 4), Christine Bradnock at Summerhill Junior School, Bristol, used the 'Wow starter' video *Coat Hanger Sounds* to start her new science topic on sound with her class of 9–10-year-olds. She started by asking 'How do you think you hear sounds?', immediately inviting the children to start hypothesising. She then showed the short video showing children tying string to a wire coat hanger, and letting it hang loose and hit the edge of a table while pressing the ends of the string into their ears. Before letting them try the activity out for themselves she asked, 'What might happen?' One child answered, 'You might hear things through it, 'cos you can hear the sea in a sea shell.' Christine praised this answer as 'fantastic science thinking', since the child was making links between this activity and another phenomenon she had experienced. Another used more overtly scientific language: 'It might send vibrations up to the string.' She then asked the children to try out the activity themselves in pairs, and to discuss their ideas about what was happening. While they were doing this, Christine handed out Post-it notes, inviting them to write 'one thing you felt or noticed about it' and to stick them on a flip-chart stand. At this point, stopping the class, Christine read out a selection of the observations on the board, several of which took the form of hypotheses:

> The sound goes up the coat hanger and goes all the way up and you can hear it in your finger.

> It made a vibration against your ear and it had a bell ring.

> It was like the waves.

> I think that if you let it dangle that metal it is louder.

> It banged but if you hold the string the sound minimises.

For the next phase of the activity, Christine played the next section of the video, which opened up other possibilities for exploration, modelling questions such as 'Do different metal objects make different sounds?', 'What's the difference between a tin can and a finger in your ear?' She showed the children a range of objects they could choose from in order to extend the activity – large tin cans, different types of string, other metal utensils – and invited the pairs to talk to each other about what they could try next. This was a relatively open-ended exploration, with children invited to try something nobody else had thought of, but before she allowed them to go ahead she referred to a model of the 'investigation cycle' on the wall, reminding them of the need to formulate a question to answer and to make a prediction. The children went off in their pairs to use the resources provided, for example to answer the question 'Is there a difference between the sounds I hear with different sized tin cans?' (Figure 6.1), while Christine distributed another set of Post-its asking them to record: 'your prediction and what happened, something you've observed, something you've learned'.

■ **Figure 6.1** Investigating 'tin can sounds'

Again, the children's findings and thoughts were shared by sticking their Post-its on a board, several noticing unexpected findings:

'I think it will be the same as the coat hanger. When you put the tin by your ear and tap it with a knife it is quiet and when you put your finger and a tin it is quiet but when you just have a finger it is the loudest.'

'It wasn't what I expected, it was quieter than I imagined with the big tin.... Maybe because the can can't get into your ear, and the end of the string is at the end of the can.'

'When you use a can it doesn't work as well because there were too many holes in the bottom so it travelled through.'

Christine was able to explore these ideas further by asking children to think about the materials through which the sound had to travel in order to reach their ears – gas, solid or liquid – and which might conduct the sound most effectively. Overall there was a freedom to think in this lesson which was facilitated by the relatively open structure of the activity and the strategies Christine used to invite children's creative hypotheses.

RECORDING DATA CREATIVELY

One of the biggest complaints children have about science – particularly in the later primary years – is 'too much writing!' (Murphy and Beggs 2005). Children say they love investigating in science, but hate having to write it up, particularly in the formulaic ways we often impose on them in order to gain what we perceive as important assessment evidence (Collins *et al.* 2008). This is a great shame, considering the many creative ways in which children can record science: making video or audio recordings, taking and annotating photos, making multimedia Powerpoint presentations, designing posters, using the interactive whiteboard, presenting a news report, acting out procedures or explanations in drama, using puppets … the list is endless. For example, in the *Eco-monitoring at Key Stage 2* project (see Chapter 8), groups of children participated in a science conference, presenting their environmental data collected around the schools as Powerpoint slides using tables, charts and maps, incorporating photographs and video clips and occasionally employing role-play and drama, as in a spoof television programme 'Britain's got science'. Yet underlying these exciting and spectacular ways of communicating scientific enquiry lies the rather more mundane process of deciding how to represent the numerical data children may have collected in a table. The **AKSIS** project (Goldsworthy *et al.* 2000a) identified specific difficulties children experienced with the following aspects of data recording:

▨ transferring information from tables to graphs;
▨ choosing whether to use a bar or a line graph;
▨ understanding scale;
▨ describing relationships in data;
▨ explaining results;
▨ understanding why measurements need to be repeated.

To provide support for teachers in this area, *AKSIS* mapped out a progression in data recording and graphical understanding, also introducing some creative ideas to make graphs 'fun'. For example, in the case of bar charts, young children can construct them physically – e.g. by putting a block in the stack next to a picture of their favourite food – or visually – e.g. by cutting a strip of paper to match the length of their foot and comparing it with those of others in the group. For older children there is the 'human bar chart': one child stands up straight as a 'Y axis' while another lies on the floor at their feet to represent an 'X axis'. Looking at the data in the table they want to represent, the class now chooses a sensible scale for the Y axis and the teacher or another child writes the division markers on Post-it notes (e.g. 10, 20, 30, etc.) before sticking these on the child representing the Y axis at equal intervals. Similarly, appropriate labels are chosen for the X axis; for example, if the investigation was to measure the height bounced by different types of ball, the X axis labels might be 'golf', 'tennis', 'squash', etc. Finally, children are selected to be the 'bars' in the chart. Each one wears a label indicating the data reading for that bar (e.g. if the golf ball bounced 39 cm the child representing the bar would have a Post-it with '39' on his or her forehead) and stands behind the corresponding label on the X axis. The rest of the class decide on how much each bar must stoop or stretch – 'up a bit, down a bit' – so that the top of the child's head is roughly level with the appropriate marker on the Y axis. So the child representing the bar for the golf ball bounce would have to crouch just below the '40' marker on the Y axis. This proves to be a collaborative and hilarious process which involves kinaesthetic learning for the participants and makes the process transparent for the rest of the class looking on.

INTERPRETING AND EXPLAINING CREATIVELY

Perhaps the highest-level process skill of all is the ability to make sense of the patterns in the data children have collected, recorded and presented, linking these back to the original question the investigation was supposed to answer and comparing them with children's previous predictions and hypotheses. To scaffold children's data interpretation we can ask them questions: 'When the … increases, what happens to the…?', 'Some people say that children's hearts beat faster than adults'. Is this what our survey shows?', 'We predicted that … Is that what this shows?', 'How big are the differences between … and…? Do you think they matter?', 'Could there be anything else that would explain our results?'

One of Goldsworthy and Ponchaud's (2007) science enquiry games is 'table talk': groups of children are given blank tables of results to complete, together with 'conclusion' statements expressing a possible relationship within the data. The game is set within the context of a visit to an alien planet, where the different creatures ('squags', 'thrubs', 'drobbles', etc.) are assigned numbers of legs, antennae, eyes and wings at random by the throw of a die. The game is played rather like Bingo, with the teacher calling out numbers to insert in the table while children keep an eye on their conclusion statement until they have sufficient data to call out 'results support the conclusion' (or not). ICT resources such as data loggers can also help with data interpretation, since they produce 'real-time' graphs of changes in physical conditions. Children can see the line representing temperature drop as the sensor is held in a cup of hot water, and can even compare two line graphs being generated on the same axes by sensors in cups with different insulating materials. In the *Eco-monitoring at Key Stage 2* project (see above and Chapter 8) children had the added benefit of a *Google Earth* image of where they had been with the data logger. For example, after conducting a sound walk around the school grounds, one 9-year-old girl gave the following commentary on the graph which had been superimposed on an aerial map of the local area:

> 'We started round about there [pointing] when we came into the conservation area and it was quite quiet, then when we went past the diggers in that corner it was quite high, because the diggers are quite loud. Then along this stretch here [pointing] it was probably just the birds making the sound, then there was an air vent about there [pointing].'

This ability to make the links between what they had done and the data generated, while linking individual changes in readings to the physical changes she observed, is the first stage in explaining her findings. A child in New Zealand took this a stage further by comparing her findings with her hypothesis. She had heard about the ability of cola to eat away at hard surfaces. She had learned that kowhai seeds have very hard coats and that gardeners have to scarify them with hot water or a knife to get them to germinate, and she wondered if she could use cola to achieve the same end:

> In my hypothesis I thought that the seed I soaked for 5 days would grow the best, but I found that the seed I soaked for 3 days grew the best. It is possible that when I soaked the seed in cola for 5 days it was too long and the cola started to kill the seed and that 3 days was the longest amount of time I could soak the seed before it started to die.

Meyer and Woodruff (1997) suggest that to support children in developing scientific explanations we should make it a collaborative process. In their study of 11–12-year-olds learning about light, the children conducted enquiry activities, then discussed their ideas and explanations in small groups, aiming to reach a consensus before sharing them more widely. Then these groups shared and justified these explanations with other groups, undergoing several cycles until there was a single explanation across the whole class. This 'consensually driven' explanation was usually greater than the sum of its parts, since it incorporated a wide range of ideas from across the class.

SUMMARY OF CHAPTER 6

In this chapter we have outlined a rationale for children undertaking scientific enquiry in groups, in terms of the added scope for creativity that collaboration provides. We have considered how teachers might take a more creative approach to investigation by choosing from a wider range of enquiry types – pattern-seeking, classifying, exploring, modelling explanations, making things – and how the process of creative problem solving (which may be required during any kind of enquiry) can be explicitly taught. We have looked at the parallels between scientific and creative processes, and how the 'process skills' of science can be combined in a creative sequence. Finally, we have broken down scientific enquiry into its component thinking skills, examining how each of these can be developed more creatively through the instructions we as teachers give and the resources we provide. There should be no excuse for the regulation 'fair test', repeated endlessly and recorded laboriously through children's primary science experience. This does not represent the creative and collaborative processes of 'real science' and threatens to turn children off. Fortunately, many teachers have recognised this and have begun to let children decide – with guidance – some different ways to go about answering their scientific questions. Of course, language plays a central role in both questioning and group collaboration, so this will be the focus of the next chapter.

Practical resources for teaching the collaborative enquiry activities in this chapter

▪ Shadow stick for playground, torch and squared paper
▪ Hinged pairs of mirrors, coins, kaleidoscopes
▪ Range of objects with metal and plastic parts, sorting hoops
▪ Gyroscope
▪ Torches, object, metre rule and screen
▪ Outdoor habitats: tree, stream, large stone
▪ Ice cubes, insulating materials (foam, card, foil, etc.)
▪ Materials to model circulatory system: washing line, pegs, card, scissors, felt pens
▪ Newton meters
▪ Bubble mixture and range of differently sized and shaped frames to blow bubbles
▪ Plasticine or modelling clay to design boats, water tray
▪ Materials to design seed pods (e.g. Smarties tube, pipe cleaners)
▪ Coat hangers, string, range of metal utensils and cans
▪ Drawing materials, cartridge paper
▪ Post-it notes
▪ Sand tray with range of different-sized marbles and ball bearings, metre rule
▪ Digital video and stills cameras, *Powerpoint, Moviemaker* and *Photostory* software (available from www.microsoft.com), interactive whiteboard

---

Figure 4.2 Discussing a photograph of the Earth in space (p. 56)

Figure 4.3 Modelling day and night using a torch and swivel chair (p. 57)

Figure 4.4 Explaining day and night using a globe and overhead projector (p. 57)

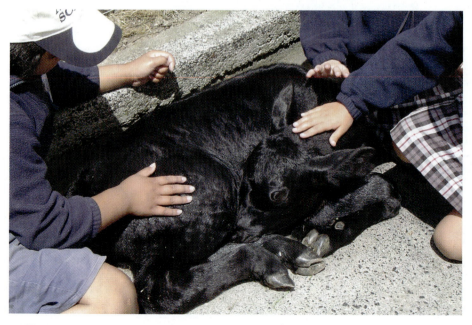

Figure 5.1 Experiencing wonder through patting a calf (p. 67)

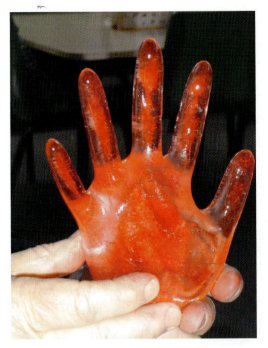

Figure 5.2 Creative exploration of an ice hand (p. 67)

Figure 7.2 Writing about science using a display board (p. 100)

Figure 7.3 Recording scientific learning using a board game (p. 100)

Figure 8.1 Using position-linked data logging in the school playground (p. 104)

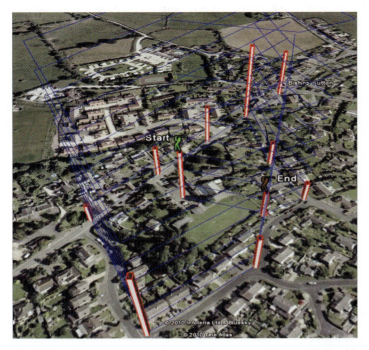

Figure 8.2 *Google Earth* visualisation of sound level readings taken by children at Bishop Sutton Primary School (p. 104)

Figure 8.4 Using stop-frame animation to explain forces (p. 107)

Figure 8.5 The Neston 'moonbase' (p. 109)

Figure 9.1 Building prototype 'pop-up' shelters (p. 118)

Figure 9.3 The willow tunnel and sensory garden at Neston Primary School (p. 120)

Figure 9.5 Building a den from found materials in the playground (p. 123)

Figure 9.6 Ascension Day walk up Kelston Round Hill (p. 125)

Figure 10.1 Creative demonstration (p. 133)

USING LANGUAGE CREATIVELY IN SCIENCE

INTRODUCTION – 'DIALOGIC' TEACHING

One of the reasons why we ask children to work together in groups during science lessons – as discussed in the previous chapter – is so that they can talk to each other. Children's talk, we are increasingly discovering, is fundamental to their scientific learning. Through talking to each other they can rehearse their own scientific explanations, debate different ideas about a phenomenon and construct shared understandings. Our education system tends to socialise children out of talking in class. Yet, far from being a distraction from learning, allowing children to talk about their science actually increases the percentage of the time they spend 'on task' (Alexander 2004). Our understanding of the social nature of learning and the role that language plays in thinking derives from the work of Vygotsky (1986), but this has been taken a stage further by the introduction of the 'socio-cultural' perspective on learning (see Chapters 1 and 2), which seeks to explain the relationship between human action and the cultural, institutional and historical contexts in which this action occurs (Wertsch 1998). From a socio-cultural view, every classroom embodies a set of cultural norms that children need to adjust to, and a set of cultural tools (such as specific vocabulary and ways of expressing themselves in speech and writing) that children need to appropriate in order to participate in joint meaning making. These classroom cultures reflect the wider culture of society; for example, in a comparison between primary class-room culture in different countries, Alexander (2001) observed that there was more robust debate in Russian and French classrooms than in England, where concerns for children's self-esteem and well-being led to avoiding controversy or labelling ideas as 'wrong'. Science too has its own culture and its own specialist vocabulary, which children need to make their own in order to participate in the social learning of the classroom. In other words, learning science is learning to talk science (Lemke 1990).

One of the central ideas in socio-cultural theory is 'dialogue'. For Bakhtin (1986), all speech is dialogue, either with another or internally with ourselves. When children are talking together they are establishing a 'dialogic space' (Mercer and Littleton 2007) where ideas can be shared and meanings negotiated. This is important for 'possibility thinking' (Craft 2000), an important component of creativity in which children envisage what might be. Through dialogue, children can open up a 'dialogic space of possibility' (Maine 2009) in which meanings are not yet fixed and new ideas can emerge. Wegerif and Dawes (2004), studying children's dialogic interaction during group work, reported 'highly significant learning gains' and improvements in the quality of shared thinking. Of course, dialogue in the classroom is not limited to interactions between children; it is teachers who largely create the culture of learning and engage in discussion with groups, individuals and the whole class. This has led to the idea of 'dialogic teaching', which Alexander (2004) defines as communication between teacher and pupils in which ideas are developed cumulatively over sustained sequences of interactions. In the field of science education, Mortimore and Scott (2003) have distinguished teaching which is 'interactive' – in which a range of children contribute to discussion – from that which is 'dialogic', in which children's ideas are given status. They have developed a framework for analysing the 'communicative approach' of teachers in two dimensions, contrasting dialogic with 'authoritative' and interactive with 'non-interactive'. They define the four resulting types of communicative approach as follows:

- Interactive/dialogic: the teacher and students explore ideas, generating new meanings, posing genuine questions and offering, listening to and working on different points of view.
- Non-interactive/dialogic: the teacher considers various points of view, setting out, exploring and working on the different perspectives.
- Interactive/authoritative: the teacher leads students through a sequence of questions and answers with the aim of reaching one specific point of view.
- Non-interactive/authoritative: the teacher presents one specific point of view.

Becoming aware of the communicative approach we are using with children is part of becoming a creative teacher, since it requires us to move beyond the standard 'initiation–response–feedback' (IRF) model of classroom discourse, where the teacher asks a question, a pupil responds and the teacher provides feedback on their response (Sinclair and Coulthard 1975). Diversifying our 'communicative repertoire' – particularly making more use of 'interactive/dialogic' teaching – is more likely to offer space for children's creativity. Rojas-Drummond and Mercer (2004) found that Mexican primary teachers employing more 'dialogic-interactive' approaches were more effective in developing pupils' learning. Dialogic approaches in primary science lessons can help to link children's everyday language with the language of scientific procedures and draw attention to salient features of their experiences of a phenomenon while also valuing the children's observations. They also provide a supportive forum in which children can apply their scientific ideas to new situations (McMahon 2009). Consider these two excerpts from Zoë Lowe's lesson on 'gravity, weight and mass' with 10- and 11-year-old children at Wribbenhall Middle School, Worcestershire (available online at www. teachers.tv/video/1451). In the first, using a giant inflatable globe and a teddy bear in a space suit ('astrobear'), Zoë is teaching the concept that gravity pulls us towards the centre of the Earth.

Zoë: Astrobear is at the North Pole. If he jumps, where's he going to land? Shaun?

Shaun: At the South Pole?

Zoë: So he's going to do that (moves Astrobear around the globe to the South Pole). If you were stood up there Shaun, and you jumped, where would you land?

Shaun: In the same place.

Zoë: In the same place, that's right, exactly. In the same place. (Moves Astrobear to the side of the globe.) In China, Astrobear jumps, where's he going to land? John?

John: Same place.

Zoë: Same place, correct (moves Astrobear to other side of globe). South America, where's he going to land if he jumps? Chrissie?

Chrissie: Same place.

Zoë: Same place (puts down globe). What is it that's making Astrobear not fall off the world? Gina?

Gina: Gravity.

Zoë: Gravity. Now, gravity is a force that pulls us where? Kirsty, what do you think?

Kirsty: The centre of the Earth so it's then like all around us.

Zoë: Something all around us. So where does the gravity pull us to, is it just the Earth or is there more?

Kirsty: To the Earth's core.

Zoë: To the centre, doesn't it. So gravity is a force, a force that pulls us downwards.

This teaching sequence is clearly interactive in that Zoë is involving several members of the class in answering questions as she moves the 'scientific story' forwards. However, the idea that has status in this discussion is the accepted scientific explanation for gravity, not the children's ideas. Zoë uses positive reinforcement (repeating children's answers in a tone which implies that they are 'correct') to move towards this 'authoritative' truth and there is little room for children's alternative ideas or for following a different chain of enquiry. Therefore, we could classify this short extract as an example of 'interactive/authoritative' teaching. Compare it with the next episode, which follows on almost immediately. Zoë uses a smaller ball to represent the moon, and asks what would happen if Astrobear jumped on the moon:

Zoë: Tom, what do you think, would it still pull him?

Tom: On the moon, when he jumps he goes higher and stays there for longer.

Zoë: OK.

Girl 1: So the mass is like pulling us to the ground so when we jump it's like an elastic band tied to our feet, 'cos when we jump we always come down.

Girl 2: On Earth, the gravity is pulling you down (*Zoë*: uhuh) but on the moon there's hardly any gravity, so you're more likely to float.

Boy 1: When, when you're on the moon the gravity changes so you're just, when you jump you're just high and you stay there for like a couple of minutes or something.

Zoë: Megan?

Megan: Is it like magnets because when you put a South Pole and a North Pole together with magnets they both connect, and, um, when you put weight and gravity together they work together to pull you down.

Zoë: The thing that keeps cropping up and I know this links back to your work last year is this idea about magnets and forces and all that thing, and you're absolutely right with magnets and forces; magnetism, North and South Poles, all those sort of things.

In this episode, Zoë allows the discussion to flow, inviting children to contribute and offering encouraging noises to indicate that their thinking aloud is valued. She does not evaluate the contributions until the end, when she affirms the link between the forces of magnetism and gravity (even though Megan's explanation was not strictly in line with the accepted scientific version). The teaching was 'dialogic' in that it valued children's ideas and allowed them to build upon each other cumulatively. Zoë spoke less, the children's utterances were longer and they began to engage in possibility thinking (imagining what it would be like to jump on the moon) and to make connections between ideas from different areas of science: both characteristics of creativity.

TEACHERS' QUESTIONS, CHILDREN'S QUESTIONS

Asking questions is fundamental to science, probably more important than finding answers. As teachers, we ask children questions for a wide range of reasons (see Chapter 5), many of which are unrelated to learning (Wragg and Brown 2002). Even our questions to probe children's understanding often end up being 'closed' or 'subject-centred' questions (Harlen 2000) that 'test' whether children know the 'right' answer, as in the first episode from Zoë's lesson above. Harlen (2000) suggests asking 'person-centred' questions of the 'What do you think…?' variety, which will be interpreted by children as an invitation to express their own ideas. Having a list of 'question stems' in our heads or on paper as teachers can help us probe children's thinking rather than test their knowledge. The following list was compiled by OFSTED (2004: 8) from observations of 'effective' science teaching:

- 'Why do you think that…?'
- 'How do you know that…?'
- 'What does that tell us about…?'
- 'Can you be sure about that…?'
- 'How can you explain that…?'

Hoath (2009) suggests that we allow children individual thinking time and the chance to discuss their answers with a talk partner after we ask a question. She argues that teachers tend to become uncomfortable after around four seconds of silence following the asking of a question, but that this may not be an indication that children 'don't know the answer'. It may simply be that they need more processing time and the opportunity to try out different versions of their response with each other, rejecting unworkable ideas before offering their thoughts to the teacher. By resisting the opportunity to rephrase the question or fill the gap with our own answer, we are opening up a 'dialogic space' which children can populate with their own emerging ideas. Our questions don't even have to be 'open' ones; even closed questions can be thought provoking if they are asked in a 'What if…?' format. Naylor and Keogh (2009) use the example: 'What would happen if you tied a knot in a doctor's stethoscope?' At one level this question has only three responses: either the doctor could still hear the patient's heart just as well, or she could hear nothing, or the sound would be muffled. However, discussing this 'thought experiment' with each other could explore all sorts of aspects of children's ideas about how sound travels. Steve Marshall (2006) suggests the use of 'red herrings' as discussion starters – scenarios which invite lateral thinking. For example, 'Out for a drive, he stopped for gas, but when he filled up, the fuel indicator never budged. Why not?' Again, this is a closed question (the answer is that the 'gas' he used was air to pump up the tyres) but the learning derives from the discussion children have to solve the puzzle. Sometimes a more creative approach to classroom dialogue is to try and avoid asking too many questions. Children can become immune to a constant torrent of questions from a teacher, which may tend to lead the discourse down a predictable IRF pattern (see p. 90) and avoid challenging them to think through ideas. An alternative approach is to restate a pupil's answer, thus inviting them to enlarge upon it, as in the following example cited in McMahon and Davies (2001):

Teacher: What is it that makes it living? If you had to explain to someone else what it is about the plant that makes it alive, what would you say?

Matt: It's a plant.

Teacher: It's a plant.

Matt: It has either a seed or a bulb to make it grow and it needs water and light.

Teacher: So it needs water and light, it might have a bulb to make it grow. Lots of ideas there. Anyone else? Toby?

Toby: It moves.

Teacher: It moves, in what way might it move?

Toby: Side to side, to get the sun … when it…

Teacher: So it might follow the sun.

Max: If it's living, it has to eat or drink to live. Say like a table, is non-living because it doesn't eat, it doesn't drink!

Although the teacher does ask questions here, she intersperses these by echoing Matt's and Toby's rather limited responses, leading to amplification and explanation by the children. She also rephrases Toby's attempts to explain phototropism, which invites a third child (Max) to contribute without being asked a specific question. This could lead to a longer chain of dialogue in which the teacher plays a less prominent role.

What is missing from the above sequence is the opportunity for children to ask questions. Although we claim to value children's questions, we do not always invite them in class discussion. In Chapter 5, Ian Milne suggests that children's questions tend to arise from an aesthetic response to a phenomenon they observe or explore, and that the types of questions that arise can be linked to Goodwin's three categories of wonder: 'Wonder about', 'Wonder at' and 'Wonder whether' (Goodwin 2001). Sometimes the most creative questions children ask are those without answers (see Chapter 6), which might be more philosophical than scientific. It is important for children to realise that science has its limitations, and that there are many perfectly valid questions that we cannot currently – or may never be able to – answer. Other questions may be answerable, but are rather tangential to the current topic or relate to aspects which may be covered later. In order to give value to such questions and avoid channelling children into only asking 'testable', 'relevant' questions, Hoath (2009) suggests a *scruffy question wall*. Pupils write a question on a Post-it note and, throughout the teaching of that section of work, regular checks are made to see if the questions have been answered and what still needs to be addressed before moving on. Variations on this include a 'wonder wall' on which all questions begin 'I wonder...' or a 'Q and A wall', which encourages children to post a range of possible answers to each other's questions. A class 'wiki' (from the Hawaiian word implying something that's not hanging about) could also be set up within the school website, inviting children to contribute to the pool of knowledge about a science topic by posting their questions and answers.

If we see the classroom as a community of enquiry, we should sometimes be asking questions to which we don't ourselves know the answer. This can help challenge children's perception of the teacher as the 'fount of all knowledge' and can prompt a wider range of creative responses. For example, during a lesson on 'animal adaptation' with 7–8-year-olds, science coordinator Sandy Jackson showed a photograph of her Siamese cat and posed the question: 'Why do Siamese cats have points?' (dark patches of fur at the ends of their ears, feet and tail). The first response was: 'It's camouflage.' However, thinking this idea through, another child responded: 'It's not camouflage – unless it was a polar bear.' This prompted a third child to hypothesise: 'If they were first found in Canada or something where it's snowy it would be good because if it's a bit rocky...' Here Sandy followed the chain of thought and finished the sentence: 'the points would look like rocks.' However, rather than leaving the discussion at this neat solution, she introduced an additional piece of information: 'Originally the breed came from Thailand' (where it doesn't snow). At this point the conversation moved away from camouflage, as one child observed: 'They're the sticky out bits, that will get colder easier', prompting Sandy to introduce another piece of information: 'When she pulls her fur out it grows back darker.' The class now picked up on this idea of temperature regulation with the following observations:

> 'The sun is attracted to black so when the sun shines down on something black it gets really hot but light colours like white don't attract the sun.'

> 'When she pulls her hair out the cold goes onto it so when the hairs grow they turn a darker colour and the dark hair keeps her warm because they're fat.'

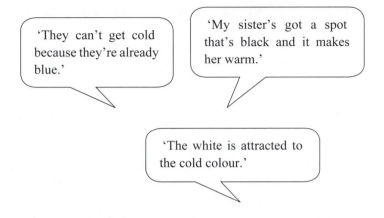

It appears unlikely that living in a hot country like Thailand a Siamese cat would suffer from cold feet, yet by being prepared to 'run with' this hypothesis, Sandy invited children to think more broadly about the question, making links between their observations in different contexts to build up a creative theory.

CHILDREN TALKING IN GROUPS

So far in this chapter we have tended to focus upon the teacher's interaction with children, either in whole-class discussion or when communicating with smaller groups. This is the focus of 'dialogic teaching' and might be regarded as an aspect of 'creative teaching', whereas the ways in which we set up the sorts of discussions that take place when the teacher is not present are perhaps closer to 'teaching for creativity'. According to Mercer *et al.* (2009), dialogic teaching involves a mixture of whole-class discussion and group work, for which the teacher needs to establish 'talk rules' and provide 'talking points' to enable children to use talk more effectively for learning. The *Discussion in Primary Science* (DIPS) project (Braund *et al.* 2007) established the notions of 'talking science frequency' (TSF) – how often a particular child contributes to a group scientific discussion – and 'talking science efficacy' (TSE) – how effective children's talk contributions were for their scientific learning. They found a strong association between TSF and TSE, indicating that the more children contributed, the more they learnt, yet group dynamics often limited the contributions of particular individuals. The project developed a number of strategies for getting everyone involved in group discussion, including talk cards in sets of four, with pairs of numbers, letters, colours and animals on them to facilitate dialogue between children in twos, fours and eights in the classroom. For example, in a 'DIPS lesson' on micro-organisms with 10–11-year-olds at Maybury Primary School in Hull, class teacher Kate Holloway started by assigning children to groups of four using the talk cards. She then gave them some ITT (independent think time) to consider the question: 'What do you know about micro-organisms?' before asking child A in each pair to tell child B anything they thought they knew. Child B then had a turn to share their previous knowledge with child A before they pooled their understandings with the other two children in their group. Kate next sent the pairs on an 'information hunt' around different 'stations' she had set up in the classrooms. These included:

- finding out about Tudor illnesses by using the index of an information book to research relevant information;
- looking at yeast under a microscope;
- watching a set of video clips about bird flu with questions for discussion;
- planning an investigation to test whether skin keeps fruit protected from bacteria;
- a photograph of somebody sneezing with the accompanying question: 'What could have happened to prevent this?'

One of the 'rules' of the information hunt was that both members of each pair had to find and agree on their answer. This idea of shared responsibility is central to DIPS, in order to avoid children becoming 'passengers' in groups, contributing little to talk and getting 'left behind'. Sometimes when working in groups of four, Kate chooses one child at random using the talk cards to answer a question that the group has found out about. If that child is unable to answer, it is the whole group's responsibility. DIPS is a highly structured approach which may at first glance appear to inhibit children's creativity, but by increasing 'talking science frequency' (TSF) for all children it can allow them to verbalise scientific ideas that might otherwise remain undeveloped.

Another, looser approach to group talk is exemplified by Sarah Earle, a specialist science teacher at Elmlea Junior School in Bristol, who places emphasis on group auton-omy in planning scientific enquiry collaboratively. In the following example from a lesson on forces with 10–11-year-olds (cited in Davies and Howe 2007), a group comprising three boys and two girls were working outside the classroom. One of the girls (Jasmine) assumed a leadership role, leading discussion while completing the group planning sheet Sarah had provided to structure the discussion. The other girl took a supporting role, with the three boys coming in and out of the discussion as their attention engaged and wandered.

Jasmine: We have to do a test don't we. We can see how fast it goes, we can do differ-ent types of car. We can see how far it goes.

Clark: We could test which car goes fastest.

Jasmine: Yeah good idea, we could test which type of car goes fastest.

Clark: Yeah, is it the heaviest or the lightest?

Jasmine: We're going to change the type of car.

Lydia: What are we going to measure?

Ben: The car.

Jasmine: (reading what she has just written) We will measure or observe how fast the car goes.

Michael: How are we going to do that?

Clark: We could do how far it goes if we drop it and how far it slides along.

Lydia: Yeah, so how far it goes.

Jasmine: OK and (reading) we will keep these things the same … We will keep the height of the ramp.

Others: Yeah.

Jasmine: The height of the ramp the same and, anything else?

Lydia: Oh, yeah the same strength you push it with.

Jasmine: Do you mean the same person?

Lydia: Yeah, the same person pushing the car.

Clark: The same surface.

Ben: Don't you think you should let it go because if you push you can't get it exactly…

Jasmine: Yeah so it's a hard thing to control.

Lydia: Stopwatch.

Jasmine: Oh yeah, stopwatch, same person on the stopwatch.

Ben: Same two people on the stopwatch 'cos then you're just doing the average. Otherwise you might stop it a second too fast.

Jasmine: (writing) So our question is when we change the type of car what will happen to the distance it travels? Our prediction, what do we think?

Clark: No we don't need the stopwatch because if it's just the…

Lydia: We need a metre stick.

Jasmine: We can use a metre stick to see how far it's going, the distance.

Lydia: We could use blutack or something to stick in it.

Michael: No because we're doing distance not weight.

Lydia: The heavier the car, more speed less friction.

Clark: So like all the cars we have we're going to see how far the different cars travel.

Jasmine: The heavier it is the farther it goes because it's got more weight to pull it down the ramp.

Michael: No, I think the lighter car will go quickly.

Jasmine: The heavier the car, the faster it goes because gravity…

Clark: Just write that … just say it's got more weight so it might go faster.

Lydia: Cos it's got more weight to pull it to the ground.

Clark: Pull it down the ramp.

Ben: It might slow down a bit quicker because the carpet…

Clark: When it gets to the ground it might pull it instead of pushing it along.

Ben: When it's going fast down the ramp then it's got quite a lot of speed to just push it when it gets to the ground.

Lydia: It relies on its speed.

Michael: When it gets to the bottom of the ramp there's a step and it might flip.

The children in this example were engaging in a high-level discussion about factors they could realistically change about their investigation and the likely effects of such changes. They demonstrated creativity as a group in considering a range of alternatives, engaging in possibility thinking and in designing an investigation which – while it would almost certainly require adjustments when they tried it out – combined equipment in unexpected ways. The comparative openness of the brief and the autonomy given to the group in negotiating their plan were elements of the 'creative ecosystem' (see Chapter 2) that Sarah puts in place within her classroom.

Argumentation

We cannot leave this section on children talking in groups without a brief consideration of scientific argumentation. This is the logical, cumulative process by which scientists arrive at a new theory or new interpretation of evidence by providing 'grounds' (evidence) for their statements and building upon – or arguing against – previous statements. According to Kuhn (1970), science moves forward more through controversy and disagreement than through harmony and consensus, because new ideas always challenge existing theories. Naylor *et al.* (2007) suggest that this process has not found favour in English classrooms, perhaps because 'argumentation' suggests conflict. Using the statements in concept cartoons to stimulate argumentation in 7–9-year-olds, they have developed a seven-point scale to classify pupils' argumentation skills:

Level 1: Pupils are unable or unwilling to enter into discussion.
Level 2: Pupils make a claim to knowledge.
Level 3: Pupils begin to offer grounds to support their claims.
Level 4: Pupils offer further evidence to support their claims.
Level 5: Pupils respond to ideas from others in the group.
Level 6: Pupils are able to sustain an argument in a variety of ways.
Level 7: Pupils evaluate the evidence and make judgements

(Naylor *et al.* 2007: 23)

Naylor *et al.*'s research suggests that children can talk collaboratively and co-construct arguments, even when they have not received any training in argumentation and the teacher is not present to direct their conversations. Such arguments tend to have a common goal of reaching a shared understanding, rather than being argument for argument's sake. The provision of resources such as concept cartoons with a ready-made disagreement presented in the different ideas of the characters can allow children to side with one of the ideas they find convincing, providing 'grounds' for it within their own experience. One example, cited in Naylor *et al.* (2007: 31) is a group's response to the statement 'the black card will make the darkest shadow':

Child 1: Say like you wear dark clothes and have fair hair. Your shadow is like normally like all the same colour. It is like all black. Think. I haven't seen a purple shadow.

Child 2: I think it will make some difference but not much. Black is stronger. If you wear white on a black floor you wouldn't see the white, only the black.

Like the children in Sandy Jackson's class (see p. 27), this pair are using evidence from their own experience to theorise creatively about a situation. The difference here is that the concept cartoon is fulfilling the teacher's role in prompting the argument and suggesting lines of enquiry. This particular argument might only be resolved by empirical enquiry, yet a creative teacher listening in might want to offer the challenge: 'Can you make a purple shadow?'

WRITING ABOUT SCIENCE

There is nothing so deadening to a creative, hands-on experience of scientific enquiry or a lively debate than the requirement to write about it afterwards. This is not to say that writing cannot be a creative activity, it is just that the ways in which we approach the genre of the scientific report in schools tend to be formulaic and concerned with providing evidence for assessment rather than being a meaningful communication of children's findings and explanations. Science writing, we assume, must be written in the past tense; it may be chronological, but does not have a narrative voice; it is often structured into sections such as 'Method' or 'What we found out'; and tends to be heavily scaffolded with sentence openers and connectives, e.g. 'I predict that...', 'We think ... because...', '...however our evidence shows that...'. Creative use of written language in science needs surely to move beyond this convention. For example, Christine Bradnock at Summerhill Primary School, Bristol (see Chapter 6), uses Post-it notes for children to record 'something you noticed', 'something that excited you', 'something that was unexpected' (Figure 7.1).

Children at Remuera Primary School produce display boards in groups for a school 'science expo' to which parents are invited. Every group stands beside their display to explain their project, just like a poster presentation at a scientific conference. They have to communicate in writing and speech – using 'props' if necessary – what

■ **Figure 7.1** Using Post-it notes to record scientific enquiry

they have found out and how it will be useful, exploring the science behind the topic they have chosen to investigate. This can be anything the group is passionate about; for example, the children who produced the poster in Figure 7.2 (plate section) were interested in mountaineering and wanted to explore the types of fabrics that would be good to protect climbers from mountain weather.

Another school, which teaches science from a fundamentalist Christian perspective, used board games to communicate children's understanding of the Earth and space (Figure 7.3, plate section). To develop these games, children needed to formulate questions to test the knowledge of the 'astronaut' players, together with a set of instructions for the game. This form of 'instructional text' represents a very different genre from the standard scientific report.

Children can also use traditionally 'creative' forms of writing such as fictional prose and poetry to communicate their sense of wonder at natural phenomena. For example, the Bristol Chem@rt initiative (www.chemlabs.bris.ac.uk/outreach/primary/WhatIsChemart.html) is an online gallery of images produced during scientific research in the School of Chemistry at Bristol University, designed to be used as a stimulus for creative writing. One electron microscope image of a 'nano brush' inspired a 10-year-old pupil to write the following poem:

A hazard of pencils dance in under water caverns,
Prickly pears point at passing pomegranates,
Razor sharp teeth bite the breaking waves,
Mushy mushrooms move magnificently,
Scales of a trout swish
Chalky cues go for the eight ball,
Transfixed crowds gather for the Moon landing
Penguins huddle facing icy winter
Spiked triangles weep the beating vibe,
Rockets depart the Earth's warming embrace.

(cited in Rivett *et al.* 2009: 11)

The dry forms of written communication in scientific papers and children's investigation reports entirely fail to capture the aesthetic response to our universe which is the hallmark of creative science. Whereas Darwin was unafraid of using words such as 'beauty' in his scientific writings, as argued in Chapter 4, scientists have increasingly shied away from revealing any kind of emotional engagement in communicating their work. This need not be the case for children: play scripts, novels, science fiction stories, blogs, diaries and poetry are all relevant genres for expressing their scientific creativity.

SUMMARY OF CHAPTER 7

This chapter has argued that the ways in which we communicate with children in the classroom can expand or limit their opportunities for creative thinking in science. Adopting a 'dialogic' approach to classroom discussion can open up more space for children's ideas to be given status on the 'social plane' of the classroom, and for children to engage in speculation or voice ideas that are only half-formed. While 'dialogic' teaching may be regarded as part of the repertoire of the 'creative teacher', there are also ways of promoting discussion and argumentation among groups of children working on their own that are more characteristic of 'teaching for creativity'. Ways of structuring talk such as the DIPS project 'talk cards' or stimulating debate using resources such as concept cartoons can help children contribute to group discussion that is purposeful and playful. Creativity with words in science is, however, not limited to spoken language; in the latter part of the chapter we looked briefly at a number of examples of scientific writing that transcend the restrictive forms imposed on us by our limited conception of the nature of science.

Practical resources used in the case studies featured in this chapter

■ Talk cards, available from www.azteachscience.co.uk/ext/cpd/dips/index.htm
■ Chem@rt images, available from www.chemlabs.bris.ac.uk/outreach/primary/WhatIs Chemart. html

USING NEW TECHNOLOGIES CREATIVELY IN SCIENCE

INTRODUCTION

Scientists have been, on the whole, early to adopt information and communication technologies (ICT). This is because science requires accurate measurement – sometimes in dangerous or far-away places – storage and manipulation of large amounts of data and rapid communication with other scientists around the world. The email, internet and database software we all use in the twenty-first century were developed initially for scientific purposes several decades ago. Scientists use technology to develop both scientific content knowledge (e.g. generating patterns about complex ecological systems) and scientific reasoning skills (e.g. analysing DNA data, making hypotheses). By contrast, ICT in primary science got off to a slow start, but is now gaining momentum as primary teachers make increasing use of ICT tools to support children's scientific learning. Common examples include using an interactive whiteboard to present scientific concepts visually or to allow children to move objects and labels around the board to explain or categorise. Children often use websites to research or revise aspects of science, or present their findings from scientific enquiry using text, photos, charts and video in a multimedia package such as Powerpoint. Slightly less common is the use of data logging equipment to measure and monitor physical quantities such as light, sound or temperature during scientific enquiry, or carrying out 'virtual experiments' which would be difficult to undertake in the classroom using simulation software. It is easy to assume that merely by using ICT we are making the experience of learning science more creative for children, since they appear to be highly motivated by it, and it is often presented in attractive, slick packages. But is this really the case? Is a child answering a multiple-choice quiz in a web-based revision package really exhibiting creativity? Is there even the danger that by 'sanitising' science and removing some of the practical difficulties of real scientific enquiry, ICT might be limiting children's creative opportunities?

We might argue that by using a wide range of resources in our teaching – including those such as ICT applications which present science in a colourful, attractive and interactive way – we are teaching creatively. However, to teach *for creativity* (see Chapter 2), we need to examine the 'affordances' of the technology (Gaver 1991) more critically to see where children are being offered choices to solve problems in different ways, or where they are being prompted to engage in possibility thinking. Loveless and Wegerif (2004) argue that there are distinctive features of ICT that can support children's creativity, which they identify as follows:

- provisionality (the ability to make changes easily);
- interactivity (the feedback given to the user);
- capacity (ability to hold vast amounts of information);
- range (ability to source information from great distances);
- speed (processing large amounts of information in a very short time);
- accuracy (particularly in measurement);
- quality (for example of visual images);
- automation (ability to bypass mundane tasks);
- multi-modality (communication in text, charts, images, sound, video);
- neutrality (presenting data without comment for the user to interpret);
- 'social credibility' ('coolness', facility to produce 'professional' outcomes).

They particularly point to provisionality and multi-modality to enable children to experiment with different juxtapositions of text, image and sound, but stress that the mere presence of these features will not guarantee that children will use them creatively. As with any resource, the creative potential is only released by a combination of skilful pedagogy and children's ICT capability. As teachers we need to ensure that children have exploration ('playing') time with any new piece of hardware or software to enable them to develop sufficient confidence with it to be able to experiment and use its features creatively. As 'digital natives' (Prensky 2001), most children will rapidly familiarise themselves with a new piece of technology, learning more from each other in half an hour than the teacher has managed in a whole evening. However, it is sometimes useful to teach them some problem diagnosis and solving strategies for when the software malfunctions or they find themselves somewhere they don't recognise; the solution of pushing all the buttons until something happens may be counter-productive! The case studies in this chapter examine how teachers have carefully selected an ICT application to enhance children's learning in science and, beyond that, have trained the children in the use of what might at first seem highly technical equipment beyond their levels of understanding, and have encouraged them to exploit the affordances of the ICT to generate outcomes that are original and of value (NACCCE 1999).

USING NEW TECHNOLOGIES TO OBSERVE CREATIVELY

Using a digital camera or digital microscope to record observations can help children to look more carefully, and can help them to see familiar objects in an unfamiliar way. For example, when studying plants children can use the 'macro' setting on the camera to get in really close to a leaf or flower, revealing detail that might not otherwise be apparent, and 'framing' the image to focus their attention on specific aspects of the specimen. They can try lighting the plant in different ways (from above, from behind) to bring out different patterns, and can even take the photo through a hand-lens to add further magnification. The resulting images can be projected on the interactive whiteboard to create a slide show of beautiful and strange shapes and patterns, or could be labelled to teach the parts of a flower in a rather more imaginative way than the usual two-dimensional drawing. To get in even closer, samples of leaves, stems and petals can be examined under the digital microscope, revealing the fine structure, if not the individual cells. These images can be re-coloured or sequenced to produce a time-lapse study of a flower opening or a leaf decaying. In a study of light and shadows as part of the *5x5x5=creativity* project, five- and six-year-olds at Moorlands Infant School, Bath, worked with staff from the Holburne Museum on a digital photography project. Alongside the children's inventive use of the camera was an evident pleasure in their individual creative relationships with the world around them – presenting their unique eye view. They loved shadows and patterns and had a natural sense of composition. Children can also use their creativity in manipulating the captured digital images, either on the camera or by uploading them into a computer. For example, one 11-year-old from Saltford Primary School, near Bristol, produced a series of images on the theme of 'movement'. One of these shows the process of descending a staircase, while the other captures the movement of a model aeroplane as it swings on a string suspended from the ceiling. While such images clearly have an aesthetic and artistic quality, they are also important scientific explorations of changes in position over time.

USING NEW TECHNOLOGIES TO MEASURE AND MONITOR CREATIVELY

The 'Eco-monitoring at Key Stage 2' project, funded by the AstraZeneca Science Teaching Trust (AZSTT), worked with 9- and 10-year-old children and their teachers in 10 schools to enhance data reasoning skills within scientific enquiry through the use of position-linked data logging. The project aimed to improve participant teachers' confidence in the use of data logging and the teaching of data interpretation skills by introducing the software package *JData3D*. It integrates data from Global Positioning Satellites (GPS) with sensor data collected outdoors to produce *Google Earth* visualisations of environmental quality in particular locations. Children walked around their schools and local areas with data loggers and GPS receivers, taking readings of either sound, light, temperature, carbon dioxide or carbon monoxide levels – see Figure 8.1 (plate section).

They then uploaded the data from both sources to classroom computers using the *JData3D* software, produced by local firm ScienceScope (www.sciencescope.co.uk) and interpreted their readings by presenting them as bar charts or line graphs superimposed on the track of their walk drawn on *Google Earth* – see Figure 8.2 (plate section). One girl's description of the *Google Earth* visualisation of the sound walk she had undertaken around the school grounds is given in Chapter 6. There was also the option of taking digital photographs at the places where they were collecting data; these photos could be synchronised with the sensor readings and would appear as camera icons in *Google Earth* which could be clicked on to remind children of the link between the physical conditions and the data they were collecting. Some chose to annotate these photographs and their associated data points to provide a written record of their interpretations.

Once they had become familiar with the equipment and confident in trouble-shooting the technical issues associated with synchronising the various data sources, groups of children and their teachers planned projects to monitor particular local environmental indicators. Several of the schools selected projects that they could present as part of their submissions to gain 'eco-school' status (www.eco-schools.org.uk). For example, children at Bishop Sutton Primary School near Bristol – which registered on the eco-schools programme at the beginning of the eco-monitoring project – decided to mount a 'Powerdown' campaign with their class teacher, Katie Green. They monitored light and temperature levels around the school before and after a whole-school initiative to switch off unnecessary lights and electrical equipment. The project started with children producing a range of promotional posters and leading an assembly to raise awareness among other pupils in the school. They used data logging equipment to compare light and temperature levels around the school before and after the campaign, monitoring the school's electricity bills and calculating the savings made. The eco-monitoring project provided a data-sharing website www.participateschools.co.uk which included poster templates for children to use in presenting their findings to each other. Some children at Bishop Sutton chose to present their data in this way – see an example in Figure 8.3. Along with representatives from all 10 schools they also presented their findings to a wider audience at a children's scientific conference held in the Science Learning Centre South West at the end of the project. Children made creative use of multimedia to communicate their findings at the conference, including video, drama, sequenced photographs, poetry, music and a game-show format. Bishop Sutton's use of data logging to monitor and implement changes in their energy use gained them an eco-school bronze award by the end of the project.

The eco-monitoring project made use of the speed, accuracy and multi-modality of ICT to enhance children's creativity by enabling them to collect real data relevant to a pressing environmental issue, visualise and interpret the data in a variety of ways and choose how they would present their findings to audiences well beyond their classroom. Even without sophisticated equipment such as that used in this project, teachers can take a creative approach to environmental monitoring by downloading current or past weather data from the Meteorological Office (www.metoffice.gov.uk) to compare with today's conditions. For example, sending children out into the playground with a temperature sensor or thermometer, together with a rainfall gauge on a day which lies on the transition between two seasons – say 1 December – with the question 'Is it autumn or winter?' can challenge them to use a range of different indicators to answer the question. Comparing their temperature and rainfall data with that from the same day in previous years can give an indication of seasonal variation, or even climate change, though children need to be aware that daily weather is only the 'noise in the climate signal' and that scientists need to look at trends over much longer periods. A few snowy days in January do not disprove the theory of human-induced global warming, whatever

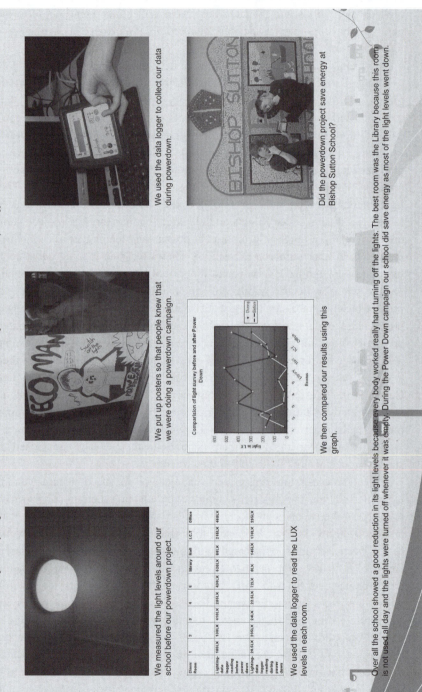

Power Down at Bishop Sutton primary school

Bishop Sutton Primary, Teacher Group; 13/05/2009

Schools through out the country are using too much energy which comes from the burning of fossil fuels. We decided to collect data from our school and then we Powered Down, for two weeks, turning off every thing that we did not need. We decided to monitor the light levels. Did we save any energy?

We measured the light levels around our school before our powerdown project.

We used the data logger to read the LUX levels in each room.

Class Room	1	2	3	4	5	6	library	Hall	I.C.T	Office
Lighting-data logger reading before power down	146LX	52lLX	416LX	299LX	439LX	626LX	89LX	246LX	466LX
Lighting-data logger reading during power down	29.5LX	295LX	24LX	22.5LX	73LX	8LX	146LX	176LX	395LX

We put up posters so that people knew that we were doing a powerdown campaign.

Comparision of light survey before and after Power Down

We then compared our results using this graph.

We used the data logger to collect our data during powerdown.

Did the powerdown project save energy at Bishop Sutton School?

Over all the school showed a good reduction in its light levels because every body worked really hard turning off the lights. The best room was the Library because this room is not used all day and the lights were turned off whenever it was empty. During the Power Down campaign our school did save energy as most of the light levels went down.

▪ **Figure 8.3** Children's online poster produced during the eco-monitoring project the media might say. This is an example of where children need to develop the scientific literacy to weigh up the evidence and arguments for themselves, and could form the topic of a lively classroom discussion or debate.

USING DIGITAL ANIMATION TO EXPLAIN CREATIVELY

Liz Ireland, science coordinator at Redfield Edge Primary School, South Gloucester-shire, wanted to find a way of helping her after-school science club – 21 pupils aged 8 to 11 – to understand forces in real-life situations. She decided to involve the children in using stop-frame animation, using a digital camera and plasticine models (like the Wallace and Gromit films). Her aim was to learn to use the digital camera and anima-tion software alongside the children as part of an action research project for her Master's degree dissertation. The children, working in groups of two or three, were asked to tell a story with their short animations that would involve everyday examples of forces in use. For example, one group of three girls shot a simple story of two boys having a fight – 'pushing each other over' – and a dog jumping on top of them (see Figure 8.4, plate section for the animation in progress). One child described the process: 'Each picture you move it a bit but you have to keep your hand out of the way.' Next they loaded all of the frames on to *Animation Shop* software and selected the period of time that each would be displayed. They then annotated the resulting short movie on the computer with 'push', 'pull', 'gravity' or 'air resistance'. One child commented: 'It's good being able to make it, and to put it all together, and to see what you've done.' Another added: 'You can be more creative when you do animation, because you can design what you're going to do, and you get to think things through, like what forces you're going to use and how the forces work.'

Not only had this experience helped reinforce children's understanding of the tricky and abstract conceptual area of forces, it had also enabled them to exercise choice, make links with other curriculum areas and engage in critical reflection as they viewed their results. Critical reflection has been identified as a creative behaviour (QCA 2003), which can be greatly enhanced by the provisional of ICT and children's ability to con-tinuously edit their work without having to start again. Liz concluded that the project was an example of teaching for creativity in science because,

> You're wanting them to think outwardly. A lot of the time science uses left brain thinking – quantitative, sequential enquiry methods. The other side is about making things link, making leaps of understanding. Often we stifle this kind of learning in science, but the story element helps get both sides going and provides a kinaesthetic experience.

For the next cycle in the research, she decided to focus more on children's explanation of ideas about forces – specifically gravity, air resistance and friction – while helping them to annotate their cartoons with arrows showing the size and direction of the forces. Since by now children had gained familiarity and confidence with the animation process, many of these second-generation films were more ambitious, for example involving people falling from aeroplanes, with and without parachutes!

USING COMPUTER SIMULATIONS CREATIVELY

One of the most powerful applications of ICT, widely used by scientists, is to model complex phenomena so as to understand them better. Of course, it takes considerable expertise to build the sophisticated mathematical models needed to simulate weather systems or the flow of blood around the body, but once the model is built scientists can try out different scenarios by altering various parameters (e.g. wind speed, blood viscosity) to see what happens. Creativity is required both in the development of the model in the first place and in the possibility thinking to ask the question 'What if...', change the relevant factor(s) and interpret the outputs. All this might seem beyond the reach of primary-age children, but fortunately several ready-made simulation applications are available that can enable them to exercise creativity in the design and testing of different kinds of models. One of these is *Bamzooki* (www.bbc.co.uk/cbbc/bamzooki), which is linked to a children's television programme and enables them to 'design' creatures to see how well they adapt to various environments. Children can change the animals' body plan and shape, its number of legs, how the legs move in relation to each other and many other factors affecting its survival within an ecosystem. They can then 'test' their designed animal in competition with others, making amendments to some of its characteristics to better adapt it to its virtual habitat. Although some scientists and teachers might object to this process in that it appears to reinforce the idea of 'intelligent design', children can learn some of the biological principles of adaptation and make use of the provisionality of ICT to make progressive refinements to an idea in the light of testing. Another example in the physical sciences is *Sodaplay* (www.sodaplay.com) where children can design and test a range of 3D shapes and machines – built by connecting masses with springs – in different conditions. The physical variables that children can alter in this virtual environment include the stiffness of springs connecting the masses together, the force of gravity (they can even make gravity 'negative' so that the models fly upwards!), and the amount of friction between their model and the 'ground'. This ability to experiment with the forces of nature can enable children to try out their possibility thinking – e.g. 'What if the force of gravity was only half as strong?' – in a virtual environment. Somewhat more realistic, though potentially more conceptually demanding, are the simulations on sites such as www.fearofphysics.com which enable children to change the height they drop a virtual object from or change the mass of a pendulum. While virtual experiments such as this do not offer children the opportunity to alter the laws of nature, they do allow some possibility thinking and arguably lead to a more scientific understanding of how and why objects move through the influence of various forces.

USING CONTROL TECHNOLOGY CREATIVELY

Using control technology to create, test, improve and refine sequences of instructions to make things happen exemplifies what Loveless (2003) refers to as the 'conjectural paradigm' for learning experiences. Loveless regards this as more open-ended and of a higher order than many of the other uses of ICT by children, since: 'the rules and relationships in the model are set up by the learner in order to investigate how they develop'

(Loveless 2003: 39). Children undertaking a control activity have to solve problems and continually ask the question 'What would happen if…?', requiring a methodical yet creative approach and a relatively high degree of autonomy. Since children often work in pairs or small groups in designing control programmes, the activity also highlights the role of collaborative learning (Yelland 2003). However, achieving the 'holy grail' of independent, collaborative problem solving through the use of control technology is difficult to achieve and places high demands on the teacher, requiring new roles as 'consultant, technician, project manager, assessor and evaluator' (Loveless 2003: 45). The ability to take on these new roles depends upon the teacher's expertise, their beliefs about teaching and learning, and their understanding of the role of ICT in teaching and learning (Cox and Web 2004).

Linda Davies, headteacher, and Steve Heal, senior teacher at Neston School, Wiltshire, responded to this challenge by developing a 'moonbase' in the school grounds: a geodesic dome containing technological applications which could be controlled remotely from the ICT suite in the school building (Figure 8.5, plate section). The project was driven by perceived weaknesses in the use of control technology and specific gaps in pupil understanding of the science topic 'Earth and Beyond'. The project started in 2002 with an application to NASA to link up with the International Space Station (ISS) through the Amateur Radio in Space Station Programme (ARISS). This successful link-up stimulated children's enthusiasm to design their moonbase, which was built in stages, just like the international space station. The finished dome contains a computer-controlled robotic arm complete with miniature camera, allowing remote imaging of arm operation. Batteries with solar panel charging are available to run equipment. The computers in the dome are wirelessly networked to the school network. Remote cameras in the dome and school computer suite enable pupils to set parameters and zones around the dome with warning signals. They can also send instructions directly to 'astronauts' working within the dome and can monitor their movements. Sensing software has been installed, with a portable PC enabling teachers and pupils to conduct a wide variety of science experiments including impact testing, pH testing, temperature logging, sound analysis and light monitoring. *Flowol* software enables pupils to learn control technology programming. For example, they have sequenced instructions for a full-sized traffic light controlled via a *FlowGo* control interface. They have also practised programming instructions for a *Robosapien* micro-robot. An electronic message display board, controllable from the classroom, has been installed in the dome to give instructions to 'astronauts'. By placing a 'mission control' group in control of the moonbase team, children have practised giving instructions to carry out scientific investigations, for example: 'Get some rocks out then test them please to see if they're limestone.'

The 'astronauts' demonstrated effective listening skills and trust in following the instructions, which were monitored from 'mission control' by a video link. Testing 'moon rocks' for their solubility offered the children an intriguing opportunity for conjecture: what would be the implications of finding limestone on the moon? Using *Flowgo* to control the temperature in the moonbase involved them in thinking about the lunar environment and what the likely effect of sunlight on the glass dome might be – how could they monitor the temperature and alert astronauts to potential danger? Even solving the various technical problems associated with the wide range of equipment developed their troubleshooting and problem-solving skills. Several children demonstrated a methodical yet creative approach, with relatively high degrees of autonomy in working in a location remote from the classroom. Through the moonbase project, children were able to experience control technology in an exciting, practical and innovative context. While the experience of most primary school children is of small-scale simulations of control technology in the real world, this project has involved researching and developing the possibilities of control technology in a futuristic setting.

USING HAND-HELD TECHNOLOGIES TO ASSESS CREATIVITY IN SCIENTIFIC ENQUIRY

The use of small, hand-held computers (sometimes called 'personal digital assistants' or PDAs) has grown in science education since they offer children the opportunity to record their thoughts, observations and collected data in a range of different formats – text, speech, photographs, video. They are small enough to be carried around, for example when exploring eco-systems in the school grounds. Hand-held devices can also be used to record practical investigative work since they take up much less working space than a class set of laptops and so can more easily be used alongside other equipment and resources. If the data children record on hand-held devices during scientific enquiry can be collected together in one place it can offer great potential for assessment, since as teachers we can potentially capture children's thoughts and ideas as they emerge, recorded in the ways children choose to express them. For example, a child who has good scientific understanding and creative ideas for how to make an investigation work well, but finds it difficult to express themselves in writing, can record their thoughts in a voice memo or as a commentary to a piece of video they take of the experiment the group is carrying out. Such valuable assessment information might be lost for ever if the child is asked to write about their investigation retrospectively, whereas if we listen to the sound file recorded at the time we can gain an insight into the child's creative thinking and scientific capability. This assessment principle is embedded in the 'e-scape' (e-solutions for creative assessment in portfolio environments) project, first developed by the Technology Education Research Unit (TERU) at Goldsmiths' University of London, to support design and technology coursework portfolio assessment at secondary school level. The project has since been extended to secondary science and geography, and more recently to primary scientific and technological understanding. The e-scape system consists of a web-based authoring tool in which teachers can develop assessment tasks, which are then run on a laptop server, communicating with a class set of hand-held devices via a wireless link (Figure 8.6). Each assessment activity consists of a series of 'boxes', each of which is presented as a separate screen on children's devices, controlled by the teacher on the laptop. Each box represents a stage of the investigation, giving instructions and inviting children's responses in text, drawing, sound file, photo or video via hyperlinks on the children's screens. As children enter their responses, these are sent back to the teacher's laptop via the wireless link and compiled in e-portfolios for each child, which can be subsequently uploaded to an online assessment forum for comparison across schools.

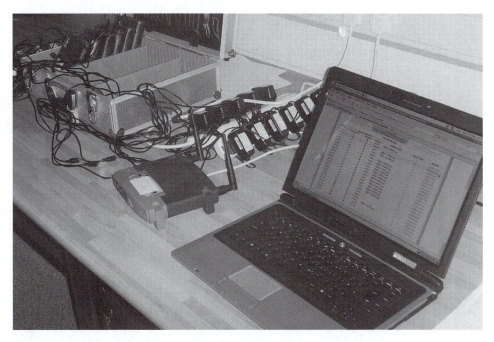

■ **Figure 8.6** The e-scape system ready to run a science assessment task

As part of the primary e-scape project, Pauline Hannigan, science coordinator at Nancledra Primary School in Cornwall, developed an assessment activity on bungee jumping for her class of 9- and 10-year-olds, using Ameo hand-held devices to record their ideas and data. Before handing out the devices she showed the children a video of someone bungee jumping, and invited the children to think 'just for a minute in your heads about the forces that might be happening on him'. She then distributed the Ameos for children to work on in pairs and started the activity. Box 1 invited the children to draw a picture of a bungee jumper and use arrows to show some of the forces acting on him or her.

Box 2 drew the children's attention to the jumper's bouncing on the bungee, with each bounce getting progressively smaller. It asked them to explain why this happens, using a 30-second sound recording. Children rehearsed their explanations to each other before recording and listening to them. This made effective use of the provision within the technology to prompt critical reflection; some pairs chose to rerecord their explanation several times before they were happy with it.

Before moving the activity to Box 3, which focused upon identifying potential variables to change about the bungee jump, Pauline drew children's attention back to the video, and what kinds of things the people in charge of the jump would need to take into account to keep the jumper safe. Box 3 then challenged children to list as many things as they could think of that might affect a bungee jump. The next box invited children to choose one of the factors they had listed that could be investigated in the classroom using a model of the real situation. Pauline showed the children a range of resources they could use – stopwatches, rulers, pieces of elastic, weights, bags – and modelled the sort of question that children might choose to investigate:

I wonder if a bigger, heavier person goes down further than a smaller, lighter person, then we could measure to see how high we came up, or we could see if it makes a difference how long the bungee rope is.

Box 5 required each pair to make a voice recording giving a detailed plan of how they were going to carry out their investigation, making sure 'you know what it is that you are changing, what you are measuring and what you are keeping the same to make it fair'. Although this was a standard 'fair test' type of scientific enquiry, the unusual context and degree of choice given to children in what to investigate and how to go about it increased its creative potential. For the next box Pauline invited the children to write their predictions on Post-it notes before speaking them into the device, another strategy to provide thinking time and encourage rehearsal before recording their thoughts. One pair had opposing predictions for their investigation: either a lighter jumper would bounce more than a heavier one, or vice versa. Pauline encouraged them to record both and praised the children's use of the word 'because' to back up their predictions with reasoning. During Boxes 7 and 8 children carried out their investigations, making video recordings of them to help with measurement of distance of drop or bounce against a scale, and recording their results on a spreadsheet. Once children had selected an appropriate chart to display their results, Box 9 asked them to make another voice recording, answering the question: 'What do your results show? You need to refer back to your question which you should now be able to answer. Try and explain your results in terms of forces.'

The next part of the activity went beyond science to assess children's technological understanding and imagination by asking them to design 'the ultimate bungee jump', drawing upon what they had learnt from their investigation. They could draw on the screen or on paper and photograph their drawing if preferred. Box 11 asked them to make a quick, simple model of their idea and video it in action, before reflecting upon its strengths and shortcomings in the final box. Once completed, each pair's work was automatically uploaded to Pauline's laptop via the wireless link so that she could click and view any part of the activity, for example the video of the investigation. After the activity the children were asked what they liked about using the hand-held devices for scientific enquiry; they mentioned the facility for recording their ideas in drawing using different colours; the transcribing tool for turning their handwriting into printed text; the potential for using multimedia such as video; and the fact that the devices were small, portable and 'fun'. The downside of this diminutive size was that they felt that the drawings were too small and the keyboard too 'fiddly'. This and other similar feedback have prompted us to use slightly larger 'e-book' sized devices for the next phase of the project.

Another creative use of hand-held technology to assess children's scientific understanding – as distinct from their enquiry skills as focused upon by the e-scape project – is the recent popularity of electronic voting devices in the classroom. For example, Michelle Grimshaw, science coordinator at Marsden School, Lancashire, used a set of Promethean *ActivExpression* pods to assess scientific ideas across a range of concept areas (Grimshaw 2009). These pods allow children to input numbers, letters and complete sentences, which Michelle used creatively by giving an answer to a mystery question and asking the children to text what they thought the question was. Michelle was able to identify children's misconceptions, by asking them to respond to the ideas expressed in a concept cartoon, with the software enabling her to review the results in a graphical form (the numbers of children opting for each idea) and record each child's progress through a topic by keeping track of their responses over time. She also found that the use of the pods could stimulate class discussion, for example by the facility for children to text questions to the interactive whiteboard. Such systems facilitate the use of a range of types of assessment question, for example statements with true/false or Likert attitude scale responses (five options from 'strongly agree' to 'strongly disagree'). Since the software allows for anonymous use where only the teacher knows what each child has answered, it can counteract peer pressure to an extent. Michelle found that she could also measure the speed of each child's response if she wanted to find out who was sure of their ideas or acting on intuition, by comparison with those requiring more thinking time. Overall, if used flexibly, such systems can promote more creative approaches to assessment as long as they are not used merely to find out who knows the 'right answer' in a sterile, quiz-type environment, which is always a danger of ICT-based assessment.

SUMMARY OF CHAPTER 8

This chapter has briefly reviewed examples of some of the features afforded by digital technology for enhancing the potential for both teaching science creatively and teaching for children's creativity. Such features have been summarised by Loveless and Wegerif (2004) and include, crucially, the ability for children to make changes to their work through critical reflection upon it – 'provisionality' – and the possibilities to record their ideas and present their findings using a range of different forms such as images, text, drawings and video, what we might call the 'multi-modal' potential of ICT. We have reviewed a number of case studies in which teachers have thought carefully about how new technologies can enhance children's experience of the world, for example by recording their observations in digital photographs and manipulating these images creatively to show movement and time passing, or by using stop-frame animation to create their own explanations of scientific concepts. The 'Eco-monitoring at Key Stage 2' project has shown how children can make use of cutting-edge satellite technology to record and visualise environmental data, making it more meaningful to them to facilitate interpretation and creative presentation. Children can also make creative use of scientific data available on the internet, such as that provided by the Meteorological Office, to compare with their own observations and measurements. They can exercise possibility thinking in the design and testing of physical or biological models using web-based simulations, and in the use of control technology to affect events at a distance. Finally, we have reviewed some of the potential of hand-held technologies to record valuable assessment information in 'real time' as children undertake a practical scientific enquiry activity or respond to a concept cartoon using an electronic voting device. If ICT is allowed to replace hands-on science or relegate its assessment to knowing the 'right' answer for a quiz, it can inhibit creativity in science. However, in the hands of a creative teacher who understands the conditions needed for children's creativity to flourish, it can greatly enhance it.

Practical resources used in the case studies featured in this chapter

■ Digital camera, digital microscope, digital video camera, interactive whiteboard
■ Data logger, GPS receiver, *JData3D* software (available from www.sciencescope.co.uk), *Google Earth* (available from http://earth.google.co.uk/)
■ Weather data available from UK Meteorological Office (www.metoffice.gov.uk)
■ Equipment for stop-frame animation: digital camera, plasticine, *Animation Shop* software (available from www.Corel.com/UK)
■ Web-based simulations and modelling software, e.g. *Bamzooki* (www.bbc.co.uk/cbbc/bamzooki), *Sodaplay* (www.sodaplay.com), *Fear of Physics* (www.fearofphysics.com)
■ Control software, e.g. *Flowol* (www.flowol.com), and control interface, e.g. *FlowGo* (available from www.dataharvest.co.uk), *Robosapien* robot (available from www.amazon.com)
■ Hand- held mini-laptop devices (personal digital assistants – PDAs), e.g. *Ameo* or *Fizzbook Spin* (available from www.argos.co.uk)
■ E-portfolio management and authoring software, e.g. *MAPS* (available from www.taglearning.com)
■ Resources for modelling bungee jumping, e.g. elastic of different thicknesses, brass weights, metre rule
■ Electronic voting devices, e.g. Promethean *ActivExpression* (available from www.prometheanworld.com)

USING THE OUTDOORS CREATIVELY IN SCIENCE

INTRODUCTION

Many children in Western industrialised countries spend a large proportion of their time indoors. The combined effects of increasing fear of paedophilia, rising traffic levels (partly caused by wider educational choice and the associated middle-class 'school run'), and the attractions of electronic games have led to a generation of children with little experience of outdoor play. This has worried many educators, some of whom also point to a decline in field studies undertaken as part of school curriculum time in science and other subject areas (Peacock 2006). The perceived bureaucracy associated with undertaking risk assessments – combined with the associated fear of litigation should an accident occur – is sometimes cited as a reason for teachers being unwilling to take children outside the school grounds. However, a study of teachers' attitudes to 'education outside the classroom' (EOtC) (O'Donnell *et al.* 2006) found a general perception that the extent of provision had either increased over the previous five years or remained broadly the same. The activities where a decline in activity was most frequently reported were off-site residential experiences in the UK and abroad, whereas school-site activities or off-site day visits were relatively common. However, most of these visits were to urban or built environments such as museums in which much of the learning was indoors, rather than to rural or 'natural' spaces. It is interesting to speculate why this might be the case. Are teachers more nervous about taking groups of children to natural, outdoor environments because there is less 'structure' and therefore more potential for losing control of the group? Are outdoor environments perceived as more risky, with the potential for falling into rivers or suffering allergic reactions to wasp stings? Or are teachers unconvinced of the value of outdoor learning and therefore less sure of what to do with an outdoor space?

There is plenty of evidence that outdoor learning is good for children, both cognitively and emotionally. For example, one review of research from around the world (Malone 2008) suggests that children involved in EOtC attain higher levels of knowledge and skills, have greater levels of physical fitness and motor skill development, increased confidence and self-esteem, show leadership qualities, are socially competent and more environmentally responsible. Opportunities for children to engage in explorative play and experiential learning activities in school grounds, wilderness camps, art galleries, parks or community settings can help them achieve aspects of all five of the UK government's *Every Child Matters* key outcomes connected with well-being (DCSF 2007). As a more holistic approach to teaching and learning, EOtC allows children to:

- become risk aware but not risk averse in managing their own safety;
- undertake meaningful exercise as a means of staying healthy and learning more about themselves and their environment;
- have fun and enjoyment and achieve negotiated goals;
- have the opportunity to work with others and to contribute as 'active citizens' in a vast array of activities, many in their local community;
- develop skills and self-confidence that can be applied later in their life.

(Real World Learning Partnership 2006: 3)

There are benefits for teachers as well: a review of 150 pieces of research published in English between 1993 and 2003 (Dillon *et al.* 2006) indicated that teachers often improved their subject knowledge and acquired new skills that could be applied in their own classrooms, while they also appreciated interacting with their pupils in relatively relaxed, informal environments. In the early years, outdoor activities were frequently used to enhance science-related topics, such as seasons, animals, mini-beasts and growth, while primary-age children learnt about biological topics such as plants, habitats, materials and forces. However, this review also suggested that opportunities for learning were not always fully exploited; preparatory activities in school tended to focus on practicalities and not on issues of curriculum, pedagogy and evaluation. Competing curriculum pressures limited the opportunities for extended follow-up work, so that children did not always see outdoor visits as connecting with their ongoing learning. In a study of the longer-term impact of out-of-classroom learning experiences connected with the National Trust Guardianship scheme, Peacock (2006) noted a failure to apply local issues to global matters. For example, while children could talk at length about the pros and cons of wind power in their area, they did not seem to relate this to global climate change. What seems to be needed is an approach which starts with the most local and familiar outdoor environments that children encounter every day, moving gradually outwards into the locality and beyond while emphasising the links between the different scales and the scientific learning going on in the classroom. To make this a creative learning experience, there also need to be opportunities for children to transform their surroundings in sustainable ways using natural materials. This chapter will examine a number of ways in which children have experienced scientific phenomena and exercised their creativity outdoors, starting with the school grounds.

USING THE SCHOOL GROUNDS FOR CREATIVE SCIENCE

Many science enquiry activities are more easily or safely carried out in the playground than in the classroom. Kinaesthetic modelling in which children are pretending to be the particles in a gas or the planets in the solar system need plenty of space, and some investigations into the properties of sound also require reasonable distances to produce noticeable effects. When children were investigating air resistance at Red Beach Primary School (see Chapter 4) their teacher took them out onto the school field to experience the differences between running when holding a small or a large umbrella behind them. This produced some enthusiastic and thoughtful responses:

'When you're using no umbrella you can run fast, then when you're using the small umbrella you can run quite fast. But the big umbrella will make you slow.'

'But I think it will be windier with the umbrella.'

'When you run sometimes you can feel loads of air on you, so loads of that air is going to get trapped in the umbrella.'

'I think the small umbrella will go quicker than the big umbrella because the big umbrella will take up more air and make it harder to run.'

'It'll act like a parachute and the bigger the parachute the more drag it makes.'

> 'I think when you have a small umbrella it makes you really faster because um somebody swallows the air.'

> 'The umbrella tried to whoosh away, and I couldn't hold onto it because it was trying to go away.'

While we might point to the use of umbrellas to teach air resistance outdoors as an example of creative teaching, one way of engaging children's creativity is to involve them in designing the outdoor environment of their school. The UK-based charity Learning Through Landscapes has been making grants to schools to develop their grounds over a number of years; projects to enhance the science curriculum have involved creating a wildlife area or digging a pond. In a survey of 351 schools receiving funding for this purpose, 65 per cent believed that improvements to school grounds had improved overall attitudes to learning and over half saw improved academic achievement. Such projects also appear to have made an impact upon the affective domain: respondents reported improvements in behaviour (73 per cent), social interaction (84 per cent) and self-esteem (64 per cent) (Learning Through Landscapes 2003). One school which took a novel approach to developing its grounds is Neston Primary School in Wiltshire, with its 'moonbase' project (see Chapter 8). Funded by the National Endowment for Science, Technology and the Arts (NESTA), the moonbase project involved children from the outset. Steve Heal's Year 5 and 6 classes (9–11-year-olds) designed temporary 'pop-up' shelters (see Figure 9.1, plate section) which they reasoned might be required as the first stage of establishing a new settlement on the moon. With the initial stimulus of a pop-up play tent, they researched geodesic domes and other flat-packed structures on the internet, rated criteria for a design specification collaboratively and constructed 3D shapes using triangles in preparation for designing the structure. The scientific learning from this process included considering the forces at different points on the frame and selecting lightweight, flexible materials for cladding. Steve commented:

> Over the weeks it was clear the children were getting very excited about making the prototype of the moonbase. The language they were using improved each week and their knowledge of which materials would be best for certain weathers and of making strong hinges was of a high standard.

He also noticed that the creative process during the design development went through a series of divergent and convergent phases, somewhat akin to the Osborn–Parnes Creative Problem Solving Process introduced in Chapter 6 (Parnes 1967).

However, in this case one child or a small group would light upon a particular solution to a structural problem – for example using string to lace the panels together – which all the others would adopt, such that the designs tended to converge towards each other. However, in subsequent development the prototypes would again diverge as groups made their own innovations.

Steve took advantage of a snowfall to link the design of the dome to the construction of an igloo in the school playground (Figure 9.2). For this, children had to compact the snow and cut it into blocks, comparing the very different properties of this building material with the wooden spars and plastic cladding they had been using for their pop-up shelters. The exploitation of chance events such as a fall of snow provides multiple opportunities for scientific learning for creative teachers, since water in its crystalline form exhibits such different properties from those of its more familiar liquid state. Children can take magnifying glasses out to examine individual snowflakes and see whether they can spot their hexagonal symmetry. They can explore the muffling effect of snow upon everyday sounds and the extraordinary creaking sound it makes when we walk through it. Comparing the 'stickiness' of snow with the 'slipperiness' of ice is also fascinating; why should these two frozen forms of water exhibit such different frictional properties?

Once the geodesic dome of the main moonbase had been built, it was gradually extended using more natural materials; for example, the children planted a willow tunnel to link the dome with the first of the modular zones in their original design: a 'rocket' greenhouse for science growth investigations. An attached weather station measures wind speed and direction and rainfall, and has three temperature/pressure/humidity sensors in different locations to enable comparisons. Remote cameras in the school pond and a nearby bird box provide opportunities to study living things. Another zone linked to the moonbase which children decided would be fun to play in was a full-size mirror maze constructed from large sheets of mirrored plastic mounted on metal frames. The design of this maze involved considerable cross-curricular learning:

'In maths we were finding out how many mirrors we need and how much each would cost.... We got the tallest person in the school to measure to get the size of the mirrors.'

(10-year-old pupil)

■ **Figure 9.2** Igloo designed and built by children in the school grounds

While constructing a prototype, children used a laser pen to look at the paths light took through the maze with different configurations of the mirrors. The design and prototyping of an outdoor mirror maze involved them in learning some advanced scientific concepts about light and reflection, as evidenced in the following quotes:

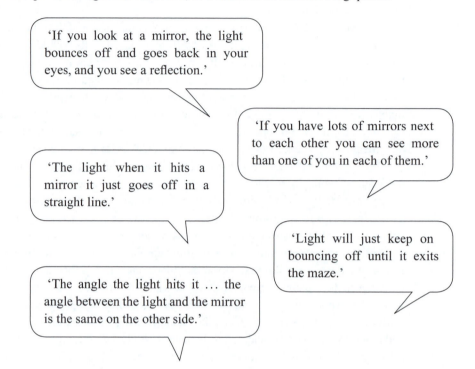

'If you look at a mirror, the light bounces off and goes back in your eyes, and you see a reflection.'

'If you have lots of mirrors next to each other you can see more than one of you in each of them.'

'The light when it hits a mirror it just goes off in a straight line.'

'Light will just keep on bouncing off until it exits the maze.'

'The angle the light hits it … the angle between the light and the mirror is the same on the other side.'

The final phase of the moonbase project was to design and plant a garden, since the children reasoned that astronauts would need to grow their own plants on the moon in order to survive. They decided to make the version for their school grounds into a 'sensory' garden to enable visually impaired children to enjoy it. They designed it in a star shape to reflect the overall 'space' theme of their project (Figure 9.3, plate section), including benches for a quiet place to sit during break times.

GARDENING

Every primary school should have a garden; not necessarily a 'designer' version like the Neston sensory garden, but somewhere that children can grow vegetables and other plants. The benefits to children's health from eating the vegetables they have grown are self-evident, and there are clearly scientific and affective learning outcomes from sowing, tending and harvesting their own produce; gardening may also develop aspects of creativity. Roach (2010) argues that teaching science through gardening in the early years increases young children's creativity by giving them the confidence and imagination to try out different ways to investigate things. She cites the example of Caerau Nursery School, Cardiff, where part of the curriculum is structured around learning through garden maintenance. Children observe seasonal change because every day they are out raking up leaves or grass cuttings. They learn classification skills by identifying which are weeds and which are sown plants as they tidy the beds. The staff set aside space for children to practise digging and putting soil into buckets, developing intuitive understanding of forces and levers as they do so. Briten (2006) suggests that gardening can develop problem-solving skills, for example through lawn seed trials, in which children can sow types of seed appropriate for differing situations – shade, full sun, drought-resistant – and monitor their growth. She also suggests extending the usual 'conditions for growth' experiments by using differing quantities of fertiliser, observing the effects and comparing them with plants not receiving the benefits.

Not all schools will be comfortable with such an experimental, intensive approach to gardening (Briten suggests calling the school garden a 'research station', which implies a certain view of plant science associated with government laboratories). Headteacher William Fuller noticed that two classes planting potatoes on the same day came up with very different ideas for how they should be planted and tended. He asked the children from both classes about the approaches they had taken and challenged them to monitor the growth of each crop, developing explanations for any differences. Other schools have used their gardens for producing crops other than food. For example, Firth Primary, Orkney, runner-up in the Rolls-Royce Science Prize in 2005–2006, established a 'Sally Garden': an area in the school grounds for growing and harvesting willow for shelter-belt fencing as so few trees grow on Orkney and winds tend to be strong.

THE SCHOOL WILDLIFE AREA

Few schools in urban settings are lucky enough to be able to set aside part of the playground for a wildlife area, but Learning Through Landscapes (www.ltl.org.uk) provides plenty of suggestions for planting up an underused corner to benefit wildlife – for example, growing a buddleia bush to attract butterflies. Once the wildlife area has been established, children will need to maintain it by cutting back some plants to prevent them from taking over (buddleia can become huge) or clearing the fallen leaves from a pond. Teachers also need to be creative in the ways in which they use the area with children to derive the maximum learning potential from it. For example, Colin Walton, science coordinator at St Stephen and All Martyrs Primary School, Bolton, wanted to make better use of an area of overgrown waste ground behind the school. Together with colleagues from the school and scientists from Bolton University, he developed the project 'Following in the footsteps of Darwin', which involved children in going on their own expeditions, mapping the fauna and flora in this 'uncharted area', inspired by Darwin's voyage on the *Beagle*. The project won the Rolls-Royce Science Prize in 2007 and can be found at http://science.rolls-royce.com/previous_entries/. The children started by plotting Darwin's voyage on the *Beagle* around South America to the Galapagos and across the Pacific, viewing all the locations he visited on *Google Earth*. They then planned their own expedition with the aid of a countryside ranger, deciding on their own objectives such as surveying, classifying and sampling fauna, soils or rocks, observing wildlife habits and relating these to the suitability of the habitat. Colin Walton and the countryside ranger planned a series of science lessons around the children's ideas, enabling them to carry out their objectives for the expedition. These included measuring the length and girth of saplings, and taking cores from a fallen tree. Children even had the opportunity to camp out overnight in the wildlife area, after being taught 'survival skills' in case of being attacked by pupil-eating tigers!

After overcoming such difficulties, the children drew detailed maps of areas of interest, using the resources of Bolton Museum to identify and classify wildlife and flora and developing their understanding of the ecology of the site. Some children visited Bolton University to analyse soil samples using the techniques usually reserved for undergraduates, including a light box to drive invertebrates downwards out of the soil samples to identify and count. They then compared their findings with the recorded work and botanical specimens taken 100 years ago by local scientist Thomas Greenlees, which are archived at Bolton Museum. The children devised signposted routes through the wildlife area with accompanying leaflets drawing other children's attention to particular features. During the school Science Week, they advertised and provided guided tours of the site for parents and local people. Although this was an extensive and intensive topic, involving several months of detailed research, aspects of it could be adapted for much smaller-scale activities in any school wildlife area. For example, inviting children to create their own mini-nature trails using lolly-stick markers joined together with string can help focus their attention on the smaller details of the natural environment, while allowing them creativity in the choice of what to highlight and how to guide other observers.

A pond is a key feature of many school wildlife areas, enabling children to participate in the enjoyable and fascinating activity of pond dipping. Carefully emptying their nets into plastic trays filled previously with pond water, examining and identifying the extraordinary variety of creatures they find – water boatmen, snails, larvae, newts – before dipping the tray back in the pond to allow their finds to swim away, can be one of the peak experiences of childhood. However, ponds are expensive to dig and time-consuming to maintain, so many schools prefer to visit a local environmental centre, many of which are run by regional Wildlife Trusts (www.wildlifetrusts.org). For example, Santa Formoso and her class of Year 5 children at Cherry Garden Primary School near Bristol decided to link their school eco-monitoring project (see Chapter 8) to work in a local environmental education centre – Willsbridge Mill, run by Avon

■ **Figure 9.4** Collecting data on pond temperature

Wildlife Trust. At the request of staff at Willsbridge, they monitored the temperature at different depths in several local ponds – looking at the effect of position, vegetation and depth of water on wildlife diversity (Figure 9.4). Their visits also included monitoring a number of other environmental indicators around the site. The children presented their data in character as aquatic creatures, talking about the warmth of the water near the surface on a sunny day and the temperature inversion in cold weather, when the surface of the pond might freeze but the animals could still survive in the depths.

DEN BUILDING

Den building is large-scale construction with found materials, offering plenty of scope for imagination and links to science. For older children it can be linked to the design of shelters (see the Neston moonbase project above), perhaps for temporary accommodation for people affected by a natural disaster like the 2010 Haiti earthquake. Dens can be indoors or outside, in the playground or in the woods. One purpose of indoor den building might be to give children an experience of darkness, perhaps linked to a story such as *Can't You Sleep Little Bear?* by Martin Waddell, exploring the science of light and dark. However, the best dens are constructed out of doors, using natural materials such as branches, bracken and moss. For example, children at Combe Down Primary School, Bath (part of the *5x5x5=creativity* project – see above), spend a number of creative sessions in a local wood with Sue Harper from the WILDthings partnership (www.wildthingsbap.org.uk/). Den building developed as a natural response to the woodland environment. Logs were moved to build fires and fireworks were made by wrapping brightly coloured wools around sticks. Some children made maps to show how to get to the den. At Freshford Primary School (see above) children drew up plans for dens they could make in the school playground (Figure 9.5, plate section). They expressed a desire to make 'the biggest den ever' incorporating all their plans. They began building using poles, pallets, sheets and netting. Inside the big den, tunnels connected a series of 'rooms', like a 'souk or market-place'. Developing a greater understanding of building and construction, the children made connections between the practical and the creative processes: as one child sculpted and moulded a brick for the wall of one of the dens, she stood back and reflected: 'A wall is a sculpture.' Working at this scale can give children a kinaesthetic sense of the mass and density of objects such as branches, the forces they exert on each other through their 'springiness' and the parts of a structure that are in tension and compression.

USING OUTDOOR PLAY EQUIPMENT CREATIVELY

Children don't have to build a den to experience forces in a kinaesthetic 'whole-body' way. Many schools have on-site play equipment, or are likely to be located near a play park with access to a slide, swings, a roundabout, seesaw and climbing frame. Teachers can use these opportunities creatively by engaging children in a pre-visit discussion to help them think in terms of pushes, pulls, starting, stopping, speeding up, slowing down and changing direction when they are on the equipment. The scientific learning from such an experience can be maximised by asking one group to play while another group of children watches and describes what is happening, e.g.: 'Karla is pushing the rounda-bout', 'Drew is sliding down', 'Nathan will fall down when he lets go'. Taking digital photographs or movies of the children, projecting these on the class interactive white-board and annotating them with the class afterwards can further enhance their under-standing. Asking questions such as 'Can we see anyone pushing?', 'Why did the seesaw go up and down?', 'What did it feel like on the swing?', can draw children's attention to the key concepts in the topic of forces. Their creativity can be engaged by going on to invite them to design and make play equipment as models or 'lifesize' examples, using large-scale construction kits (e.g. 'Quadro').

Although they are not strictly speaking outdoor play equipment, bicycles are ideal props to stimulate thinking about forces in an outdoor environment. With due care and appropriate permission from parents, a creative teacher might ask some of the class to bring in bicycles and ride around the playground to generate a discussion about how a rider starts, stops and stays at a steady speed. This could be extended to other wheeled vehicles, perhaps by observing the reception class at play or a teacher's car as it starts and stops. This topic may be developed alongside a road safety theme, asking 'Why do we wear seatbelts?', 'Why do we wear cycle helmets?', 'Why might a car skid in the rain?' Cycling is seen as a 'green' way to get around. This assertion could form the basis of an investigation into the environmental effects of travel – carbon 'footprints', CO_2 emissions and atmospheric pollution. Children might be motivated to develop a campaign to encourage more pupils (and teachers) to cycle to school. They could also investigate the reasons why many people prefer to stay in their cars. Walking to school presents another green option, but many parents are concerned about their children's safety as pedestrians and prefer to drive them to school, ironically increasing the risks for other children who choose to walk. One solution widely adopted by some primary schools is the 'walking bus', whereby a group of parents or other trained volunteers walk several predetermined routes to school, children joining them as they pass through their neighbourhoods. The gradual accumulation of children results in a lengthy 'croco-dile' by the time they reach the school gates, with an adult at either end to maintain road safety. Such communal walks to school could be the opportunity for monitoring sea-sonal changes together or discussing other scientific phenomena such as the 'Doppler effect' from an ambulance siren speeding past.

GOING FOR WALKS

One of the pleasures of many middle-class childhoods – though perhaps more fondly remembered in retrospect than enthused about at the time – is the family walk, either through the countryside or in a local park. However, there will be significant numbers of children in any primary classroom for whom this is not part of their cultural background, or who may be living largely indoor lives. This makes the provision of short 'welly walks' invaluable as a way of looking carefully at the local environment and experienc-ing seasonal changes. These need not be long-distance expeditions: for example, Fradley (2006) advises taking regular walks in the school grounds. She cites the example of a walk 'to find out which part of the playground is the windiest' with her Year 1 class of 5–6-year-olds at Upton Noble Primary School in Somerset. Each child took a paper windmill, and once outside observed that when they stood facing certain directions the windmills went round. They suggested the areas they thought were the windiest from their experiences at playtime, but when testing their predictions they noticed that wind is not constant and sometimes their windmills slowed down, stopped or went really fast. They discussed with each other which direction the wind was blowing in and found the most sheltered part of the playground, which they thought would be very useful on a cold day. Back in the classroom, Carol downloaded the photographs she had taken in the various parts of the playground and projected them on the smart-board, discussing with the children whether the windiest place was actually where they had thought it would be.

As part of their *5x5x5=creativity* project (see Chapters 3 and 4), young children at Freshford Primary School near Bath went somewhat further afield on a wet winter walk, collecting a number of natural objects including 'a stick what looks like antlers' and 'a piece of the moon' (conker shell). Back in the classroom they used the found objects as stimuli for sharing thoughts and memories, including walks with their families and things they had found in the past. The objects represented other things, real and imaginary; for example the collected sticks became 'a deer's hat', 'a pretend fishing rod', 'rockets' or 'a rainbow'. The children designed and made new objects with the sticks – a dreamcatcher, a picture frame, magic wands, swords and boats. This focus on found objects resulted in children and adults bringing in their 'special things' from home. The rest of the class tried to guess what some of them were: 'an olden day thing', 'a bit of a fallen off wooden church'. They listened carefully to each other's stories. 'We found it on holiday. First my daddy made it for my mummy ... she wore the necklace all the time on holiday.' The children enjoyed each other's memories, which prompted further recollections and prompted a decision to share the story and their memories with others. They could 'turn all the classroom and playground into a museum', but they decided to 'make the museum in the wall on the terrace'. They 'made a hole in the wall and dug it out and put the things inside' over the next three weeks, creating a 'museum of found objects', including photographs of their 'special things' and objects they made from the sticks and other things they had collected. While there was little explicit scientific content in this project, the children's hands-on experience of the properties of natural materials was enhanced by their emotional engagement with them and their possibility thinking about what the objects could become.

By the time they reach 9 or 10 years of age children are capable of walking much greater distances, enabling the creative teacher to make use of a wider range of local habitats for scientific exploration. Neil Baker, science coordinator at Saltford Primary School near Bristol, decided to structure his school eco-monitoring project (see above and Chapter 8) around a series of extended whole-class walks around the village of Saltford and beyond, monitoring sound, temperature and carbon monoxide levels along the busy A4 and Great Western railway line which run through the settlement. On Ascension Day they walked up Kelston Round Hill – a full day's expedition (Figure 9.6, plate section) – measuring temperature levels throughout the walk using a data logger linked to a GPS receiver.

This position linking of their temperature data enabled children to see their whole walk on *Google Earth* with the temperature levels at each point superimposed as a three-dimensional graph (see Chapter 8). Back in the school ICT suite, children interpreted this graph, making observations such as the following:

'I noticed that the temperature at point 2 was two degrees higher than at point 1.'

'I noticed that the temperature at points 7 and 8 were the same.'

Overall, they concluded that the temperature had increased towards the middle of the day, but had decreased slightly as they climbed the hill. The class then split into smaller groups to monitor variables of their choice around the school grounds, and tried to measure water flow in the river Avon to compare with data from another school further upstream. However, because readings were taken near the edge of the river during a dry spell, the flow was too small to be measurable!

FARM VISITS

Perhaps a neglected aspect of outdoor education, farm visits nevertheless play an important part in children's understanding of food production. However, in a recent survey of 822 children aged 7–10 years, Childwise (2008) found that 84 per cent claimed to have visited a farm in the previous three years. Farming was considered the primary purpose of the countryside, followed by food production and recreation. Increasing numbers of children assume that farmers are responsible for looking after the British countryside, prompting Ciaran Kinney (ASE Science Teacher Award winner) and children at St Anne's Primary School, near Ballymena in Northern Ireland, to develop a water filtration system for a local farm. Their project, 'Investigating water', in which children explored the water cycle and analysed the quality and treatment of water in their local community, was named winner of the 2008 Rolls-Royce Science Prize. As part of the project, pupils visited a local water treatment plant and, under the guidance of experts, used a variety of scientific tests to measure the quality of local water sources from three main rivers. They tested for a variety of parameters such as pH, turbidity, nitrate, phosphate, temperature and faecal matter, comparing these readings to those from farms' surface run-off. This suggested that the use of fertilisers and pesticides by local farmers was affecting the purity of the water, so the class invited the farmer parent of one of the children into school to discuss the problem. Once the farmer had explained the pressures on modern food production and the difficulties he experienced with preventing surface run-off, the children worked with a civil engineer to develop a water filtration system using sand and gravel and iodine to treat water at the farm before its release into the environment.

Designing a scientific solution to an environmental problem for a farm was also the focus of the 2009 winner of the Rolls-Royce Science Prize. Teachers at Kells Lane

Primary School, Gateshead, worked with an engineer to build a small-scale wind tunnel for children to safely test and evaluate different blade configurations for a wind turbine to be built at a local farm. The children quickly developed models from 150 mm diameter aluminium discs, altering the number of blades and their pitch. They then tested the efficiency of their models by recording electrical output at different wind speeds. The involvement of Ken Leung, lecturer in engineering at Northumbria University, in working with the children helped to scaffold their creative thinking and problem-solving skills in finding efficient turbine designs and relate their work to Ken's development of the Gazelle Wind turbine. The children then started to consider design ideas for the local farmer's turbine. The small-scale wind tunnel models were remade using corriflute sheeting so they could be tested outdoors. Groups tried different design ideas on squared paper before choosing one to make. There were lots of different ideas about how wide blades should be, or if they should be wider at the tip or bottom. Was it important whether blades were symmetrical or had square tips? It was really good to see ideas from earlier work involving air resistance and wind tunnel testing being applied to the challenge of creating a wind turbine of their own. A full-scale version of the most efficient blade was eventually installed on the actual farm turbine.

Of course, children don't have to become involved in solving farmers' technical challenges to learn science creatively on a farm. They don't even have to go very far because many city farms offer opportunities to get close to baby animals and help with feeding. In Switzerland, some farms are designated as 'school farms', operating a curriculum-based service to schools from local towns and cities, often with a specially trained farmer or on-site educationalist and a classroom. The UK-based charity Farms for City Children (www.farms4citychildren.co.uk/), run by children's author Michael Morpurgo, takes groups of up to 40 children and their teachers for a week at a time to work on one of three farms. Children are woken early to milk the cows, collect eggs or shovel dung in a sheep shed. Although soon filthy and exhausted, many love the experience and learn a great deal about themselves and the process of agricultural food production. There is even room for creativity in the many different ways they choose to record the experience.

SUMMARY OF CHAPTER 9

In this chapter we have explored some of the many opportunities afforded by the outdoor environment for creative teaching and learning of science. These start with the most local environments – the school playground and wildlife area; extend out into walks to the local park, through a wood or up a hill; and take in the very different environment of a working farm. Through experiencing the outdoors at first hand – getting messy, working with natural materials, observing plants and animals in their habitats – children's learning of scientific concepts will be deeper and more emotionally engaged; we might say more *aesthetic* (Wickman 2006). Often the most creative learning experiences out of doors are when children begin to affect their environment by making changes: planting a garden, building a den, designing a piece of play equipment, filtering farm run-off. However, teachers are rightly wary of some of the risks involved in taking groups of children beyond the school gates. Real World Learning Partnership

(2006: 20) makes a number of suggestions to help such visits run smoothly and safely, for example:

- set clearly defined objectives for the visit;
- prioritise these objectives so the visit is appropriate to the needs and competence of the group;
- make the amount of planning and preparation proportional to the duration and type of visit;
- check out the school's policy on educational visits;
- talk to the school's Educational Visits Coordinator (EVC);
- do a planning pre-visit, preferably with colleagues, to find out more about the site and its facilities;
- prepare a written risk assessment and safety management plan;
- involve pupils in planning the visit;
- take advantage of the wide range of training opportunities for staff involved in visits;
- find time to reflect on the experience.

Dillon (2006) adds that as teachers we should take more account of the context of the experience for children by, for example, being aware of their fears and phobias, and finding out whether they have been anywhere similar. This can be particularly important in activities with living creatures, such as pond dipping or feeding animals on a farm. Properly planned, however, outdoor learning can be one of the most memorable experiences children will have during their time at school.

THE WIDER ROLE OF THE CREATIVE PRIMARY SCIENCE TEACHER

INTRODUCTION

This book has focused upon what primary teachers can do to make science more engaging and stimulating for children, by recognising and unlocking our own creativity as educators and having the confidence to try something a little different. It has included examples of practice with a creative spark which has either provoked wonder in children, engaged them aesthetically in the broadest sense of the word or provided elements of a 'creative ecosystem' (Harrington 1990) to foster children's own creativity. Yet even the most creative teacher can become tired, so we need continual professional refreshment to support our creativity through involvement with wider networks and new initiatives. This chapter will introduce some of the agencies, professional development opportunities and links that can help to sustain and extend creativity in primary science education. There is also a role for creative teachers' support for colleagues' creativity in science, whether this is informally or through the appointment of a school science coordinator or subject leader. It is therefore necessary to consider the science subject leader's role in relation to promoting creativity across the school, through staff development, whole-school projects and science fairs. Finally, there is the vexed issue of public engagement with science. Should we, as informed lay people, have a say in the direction of science policy and practice in our democracy? As professional communicators do we have a wider role in society to promote and demystify science? These are questions we will consider as the book draws towards its conclusion.

SUPPORT AGENCIES AND NETWORKS

The following list is not exhaustive and tends to be rather UK-based, though similar opportunities and organisations exist in other countries. Some of them have been mentioned in previous chapters, but this is an opportunity to bring them together into a support directory for creative science educators.

The Association for Science Education (ASE)

The ASE (www.ase.org) is the professional association for teachers of science in the UK. It was officially constituted in 1963, but can trace its origins back to 1900. It is the largest subject association in the UK with around 15,000 members and can exert a powerful influence on science education policy and practice. For primary teachers, the ASE publishes the journal *Primary Science*, which is free to members and contains short, accessible articles based on classroom practice, much of which is innovative and promotes creativity. As well as its large annual meeting, held for three days in early January each year, the association runs a series of regional conferences and local training events. Many workshops at such events are aimed at primary teachers and tend to be highly practical, often with many creative ideas and free resources. The best way to become involved in the network of primary and secondary teacher members is to join a local section, many of which have an active programme of innovative projects and support events. The ASE also commissions and undertakes large-scale research projects, including one currently examining the role of practical enquiry in science learning. Regular updates and ways to become involved in research projects are posted on the website and through regular mailings. The ASE, in conjunction with the Centre for Science Education at Sheffield Hallam University, supports the *Primary Upd8* site (www.primaryupd8.org.uk, see Chapter 4). This subscription service takes topical news items and turns them into curriculum-linked classroom science activities, often set within an unusual or inspiring context. Regular email notification of new topics and activities can help to ensure that science lessons remain fresh and relevant, while the growing archive of activities can easily be incorporated into school schemes of work.

Science Learning Centres and the Rolls-Royce Science Prize

Funded by the Wellcome Trust, the network of Science Learning Centres (www.sciencelearningcentres.org) was established in England in 2004 to coordinate professional development in science for primary and secondary teachers. There are nine regional centres and a national centre based in York, which also runs residential courses for teachers in Wales, Scotland and Northern Ireland. Since 2008, continuing professional development (CPD) courses run by Science Learning Centres have been linked to the Rolls-Royce Science Prize (http://science.rolls-royce.com) through Project ENTHUSE, a partnership between industry, government and the Wellcome Trust, which provides teachers with funding to cover the cost of attending courses at the National Science Learning Centre. The Rolls-Royce Science Prize, established in 2005, is an annual awards programme that helps teachers implement creative science teaching projects with grants of up to £5,000. Several of the innovative case studies featured in this book have been developed as a result of funding from this scheme (see Chapters 4 and 9).

AstraZeneca Science Teaching Trust

The AstraZeneca Science Teaching Trust (www.azteachscience.co.uk) was established in 1997 and provides financial assistance to help improve the learning and teaching of primary science in the UK. Each year the trust funds several 'innovative projects', most of which are run by universities or local authorities in collaboration with groups of primary schools. The projects tend to combine research with CPD and are all reported on the website. Several of the case studies in this book have emerged from the eco-monitoring project (see Chapters 6, 8 and 9), funded from this source. The trust also funds clusters of schools who wish to implement one of the innovative projects collaboratively in their group. For example, the eco-monitoring project has been taken up by a cluster of schools in the London Borough of Hillingdon. CPD units, consisting of presentations and video clips based on a selection of innovative projects, are available on the trust website for use by school science coordinators in supporting the dissemination of innovative practices within primary education.

British Science Association: after-school clubs

The British Science Association (www.britishscienceassociation.org), formerly the British Association for the Advancement of Science formed in 1860, is a charity that exists to advance the public understanding, accessibility and accountability of the sciences and engineering in the UK. It runs the British Science Festival for five days in September in a different location in the UK each year. The festival, which is aimed at the general public as well as the world of education, includes scientific debates, talks by eminent scientists, films, field trips and hands-on workshops. The association also coordinates the National Science and Engineering Week in March each year. It includes local activities aimed at children, and many primary schools choose to link their own science weeks to the national one, registering events on the website to enter a prize draw for resources and free hands-on science shows. The British Association supports the development of after-school science clubs in primary schools through partnership in the STEM clubs network (www.stemclubs.net/). Primary schools can register a science club – or a more cross-curricular science, technology, education and mathematics (STEM) club – with the network to provide access to a range of support resources and activities. After-school clubs can enable enthusiastic teachers to try out a wider range of creative activities and strategies than might otherwise be possible under normal classroom conditions. For example, Liz Ireland's digital animation project at Redfield Edge Primary School (see Chapter 8) was carried out with the school's science club. Club members can also apply to become Creativity in Science and Technology (CREST) Star Investigators through the association website. CREST Star Investigators has three awards: Star, SuperStar and MegaStar. In addition, interested children are also offered the opportunity to become Young Science Ambassadors (YSAs), who are expected to communicate enthusiasm for science; encourage others to think about, and engage in, scientific activity; and promote interest in science at home, school or in the community.

SUBJECT LEADERSHIP FOR CREATIVE TEACHING

This is not a book about being a science coordinator, but it is inevitable that many primary teachers who demonstrate flair and innovation in teaching will be offered this role at some point in their career. For some reason, the job title 'subject leader' (Bell and Ritchie 1999) has never really caught on in English primary schools. Perhaps this is because coordination implies a supportive role, whereas the notion of leadership implies a position of power or authority over others (Howe *et al.* 2009), out of keeping with the collegial culture of most primary staffrooms. However, the role of the coordinator has changed over recent years to one of providing strategic direction to the development of a curriculum area, so perhaps the term 'leader' is becoming more appropriate, particularly if leadership is seen as distributed across the whole staff rather than located within a small senior management team. Providing strategic direction to the development of science means looking ahead to potential future curriculum changes, for example possibly the incorporation of science within the learning area of 'scientific and technological understanding'. It is also important to maintain ongoing discussion and debate across the school community about the 'flavour' of the science we wish to promote. Staff meetings, informal discussions, school council and governors' meetings can all contribute to this sense of what we value about science and scientific learning as a school. The value we place on creativity in science education can be enshrined in a policy document, but such statements tend to become stale and lack meaning in relation to the day-to-day practice in the school. Better perhaps to embody our values in the exciting science happening in the classroom or through initiatives such as science fairs, with 'pupil voice' statements on the school website capturing children's responses to such activities and their ideas about science (see Chapter 5).

Science fairs

The ASE and British Science Association (see above) provide support for primary science subject leaders wishing to raise the profile of science among children, parents and staff by running a science fair or week. For example, the *ASE Primary Science Year CD-ROM* (ASE 2002) offers the following advice:

- A science fair can be for the whole school, a single class or even a specific group of children. This will depend on the reason for holding the science fair, resources, staffing and space within school. It is often easier to run an event for whole classes as these would not then need to be split or another teacher found for the rest of the class.

- Depending on the size of the school, the numbers of children involved and the available space, the event can be scheduled over a week, two days, a single day, a morning or an afternoon. Holding the science fair over a morning or an afternoon means that there will be less impact on other events in school. However, it will mean that only a single year group or class would be able to participate. Extending the science fair over more than one day means that more children can be involved and the activities will not be rushed, but whether this is possible will depend on individual circumstances. It may mean that the activities have to be cleared away and set up again if the space is used for different purposes.

- There are different ways of involving the children in a science fair, depending on the aims for the event. One way is for the children just to be involved in the activities and recording their results on the day. Another option for involving the children is for them to research a scientific topic and produce a display for the science fair, or as the follow-up from it. This would probably help them to think more about what they have learnt, but it involves more organisation.

■ Science fairs can be given a theme so as to establish some continuity for the event or to fit in with a theme that is being followed at school. On the other hand, a theme may be too limiting for children to experience a wider range of activities.

■ Select from and budget for the wide range of possible visiting speakers, theatre companies, hands-on workshops and planetariums available to support science fairs. This may require booking several months in advance. Some visitors, such as parents or scientists from local universities, will not charge, but for others sponsorship is sometimes available from local businesses with a product that is relevant to the science fair topic or theme.

■ Class teachers and learning/classroom support assistants taking part in the science fair will be able to see new ideas for practical activities and the way that investigative science can motivate children. If it is possible for the science coordinator to be released during the fair they can be available to answer questions and give advice and support to colleagues and children.

■ A science fair can also be a good way of creating publicity for the school. Contacting the local newspaper (or local radio and television stations) before the event could be very fruitful, as they may be interested in taking photographs and interviewing children.

■ Inviting parents to come to the science fair can raise the profile of science in school, encouraging parents to talk about science with their children. It will also give parents the opportunity to see how science is taught. Visitors could take part in the activities, or just observe what the children are doing. On the day it may be important to enlist some help in setting up the activities before the children arrive.

■ At the end of the science fair it is a good idea to bring the children together to look at some of the recording they have done and to review what they have learnt.

Science fairs can provide opportunities for 'creative demonstration'. We tend to assume that teachers who stand at the front of the class and demonstrate a scientific experiment belong to the 'old school' of transmission pedagogy, in which children are not allowed to participate through hands-on investigation. The demonstration tends to be associated with a traditional form of secondary science teaching, but used interactively it can provide the 'Wow!' factor necessary for a memorable science fair experience. For example, David Young at Shoscombe Primary near Bath used a demonstration activity with his class to find out how much air was contained in different samples of soil (Figure 10.1, plate section). As well as showing the importance of careful measurement and pouring for children's subsequent investigations, he maintained a flow of challenging questions during the investigation and invited children's predictions and hypotheses. During a science fair, visiting scientists or specialists from local secondary schools may wish to use demonstrations as part of their input, in the format of the traditional Royal Institution Christmas Lectures. Within the constraints of health and safety requirements, this approach can be encouraged, if only because it may be an unfamiliar teaching strategy for children and so potentially disturb the predictability of their day (Oliver 2006).

An example of a variation on the science fair theme is provided by Remuera Primary School which every year holds a science 'expo', providing a showcase for children's scientific enquiry studies carried out over previous months (see Chapter 7). According to science leader Bernadette Hamlin, the staff found a weakness in children's scientific knowledge and were concerned about science disappearing from the curriculum, so decided to place a strong emphasis on science and enquiry learning, sharing this with the local community through a yearly 'expo'. The school curriculum is structured around 'habits of mind', which include 'wonderment and awe', 'getting excited' and 'wondering what happens'. Whole-school, whole-term topics are shared between science and other curriculum areas. The stimuli for these topics are A3 cards with 'big questions' on them, differentiated for the different age ranges in the school. Years 1 and 2 (children aged 5–7) explore their question as a whole class; Years 3 and 4 (children aged 7–9) select sub-questions to investigate as groups; while children in Years 5 and 6 each frame an individual question to guide an in-depth enquiry over 10 weeks. To prepare the older children for undertaking what is a demanding piece of work, teachers first engage them in a 'Wow!' circus of different activities over the first three weeks of the topic, modelling the enquiry process including a reminder of fair testing and variables. Children are presented with a list of possible science topics to inspire and enthuse them and they take home a planning booklet to discuss with parents or carers. After showing examples of finished posters and display boards from previous years' topics, teachers discuss children's ongoing planning on a regular basis, exploring the science behind their chosen topic and consulting on each stage of the investigative process from weeks 4 to 10. Each child is required to produce a display board reporting the findings from their enquiry, like poster presentations at a scientific conference (Figure 7.2, plate section). At the expo they each stand beside their board to explain it to visitors, using props if required. Although time-consuming, the expo has made a significant impact upon the status of science in the school and among parents, and has fired many children's imaginations to take their scientific enquiry forward both within and beyond school.

Supporting colleagues' creativity

One of the responsibilities of subject leadership is leading and managing change. Change demands flexibility and can require the establishment of a culture of creativity within the staffroom. I argued in Chapter 2 that creativity is not just the property of individuals; it can reside in the space between people when they collaborate together and spark ideas off each other, what Craft (2008) calls 'middle c creativity'. But how can a primary science coordinator engender this social creativity and bring it to bear on the difficult process of educational change? Howe *et al.* (2009) argue for a 'dialogic' approach to managing change, analogous to the process of 'dialogic teaching' (see Chapter 7), in which everyone contributes to the development of ideas over sustained periods of discussion. This is of necessity time-consuming, but is consistent with Michael Fullan's research on educational change which, he argues, is inherently problematic, dependent both upon school culture and the extent to which leaders are able to listen to the concerns of all stakeholders (Fullan 2007). Individual teachers' ideas matter because the way people understand things is central to what they actually do in practice. In the long run, it is not actually helpful to 'go along with' innovations that are not fully understood or actively opposed, and differences between ideas can be constructive and creative. It helps to foster a culture of creative collaboration if all members of staff are aware of the wider roles and relationships of colleagues and to support dialogues that are open and honest, but also caring and professional (Howe *et al.* 2009). A subject leader might use any of the following tools for communication and professional support, but they need to be exercised dialogically:

- ▨ introducing ideas or inviting discussion at staff meetings;
- ▨ leading or arranging INSET (in-service training) days;
- ▨ observing other teachers and feeding back;
- ▨ having other teachers observe the subject leader's teaching;
- ▨ co-teaching alongside colleagues;
- ▨ setting up working groups to focus on an issue;
- ▨ coaching or mentoring;
- ▨ informal discussions.

(Howe *et al.* 2009: 223)

Working with the Special Educational Needs Coordinator (SENCO)

Creative, open-ended approaches can benefit children with special educational needs (SEN). For example, during the Momentum project (see Chapter 4) a child who was usually difficult to engage both at home and in school was interested in an activity stimulated by the 'Wow' lesson starters on paper aeroplanes, but struggled with some of the practicalities. On returning to school the next day he told his teacher, 'I can make a paper aeroplane now – my dad taught me last night.' He had obviously enjoyed the lesson and was animated enough to talk about this at home. His excitement and enthusiasm were shared with his father who then helped him with the task. Back at school he was so excited by his discovery that he had to share his findings before he even entered school. A teacher at another school observed that children with SEN were able to think 'outside the box' and thrived in the openness of the activities, whereas higher-attaining children who were used to following directions found the task more difficult. This opened up her eyes to different ways of working with children that might expose their talents. The creative way the Momentum project explored scientific ideas was also the starting point for the Bristol Gifted and Talented group, which used many of the project ideas and resources as starting points for their own creative explorations. For these reasons it is important for science subject leaders to work closely with school SENCOs to introduce creative approaches to science which can also be more inclusive of all learners.

Mainstream schools often have much to learn from special schools in developing inclusive practices through creative approaches. For example, Lynne Gould, a teacher at Exeter House School, Salisbury, worked closely with local artist Catherine Lamont Robinson as part of the *5x5x5=creativity* project (see Chapters 4 and 8) to develop approaches to individualised learning through the scientific context of light. The school caters for children and young people of all ages (up to 19) who have special needs and severe learning difficulties; one severely visually impaired child who had recently 'discovered' his own shadow was led into dance through first mirroring an adult's body movements, then quickly taking the lead. The artist and educator built upon the child's interest in shadows and reflections using mirrors, coloured gels, torches and projections. It involved him in 'drawing' with shadows, repositioning slatted plastic chairs or an upturned car tyre so that the sun created dramatic patterns on the ground, or tracing a pattern with his finger down the damp surface of a slide on a winter's day. The publicising of this case study through the *5x5x5=creativity* network led other mainstream schools to develop similar approaches with children for whom verbal communication was difficult.

Working with 'real scientists'

One type of collaboration which can enhance the status of science within the school and bring a new dimension to classroom practice is to work with practising scientists. However, unless the school has scientist parents or existing links with a local university science department, it can be difficult for the science subject leader to make contact with likely candidates who work in a field which is intelligible to children, who are available to come into school and who can communicate effectively. In England, the Creative Partnerships scheme (Sharp *et al.* 2006) has included some examples of schools working with scientists, for example the Momentum project (see above), though most collaborations have been with artists. However, there are ways for enterprising science subject leaders to make effective links. For example, E. Towner, science coordinator at Grove Primary School in Romford, made contact with scientists through links with the Science and Technology Facilities Council, the Medical Research Council, local pharmaceutical companies, a local space company and also through the British Interplanetary Society. These scientists were invited in to support the school's project for the Rolls-Royce Science Prize in 2008, which involved children aged 7 to 11 in designing experiments that British-born private space traveller Richard Garriott could conduct in the zero-gravity environment of the International Space Station. The scientists invited into the school included:

- a materials scientist to talk about properties of materials used in spacecraft;
- a proteins crystal scientist to talk about how protein crystals are used;
- a climate scientist to discuss how Earth observation is conducted from space;
- a physiologist to talk about the effects of zero gravity on body mass;
- a dietician to consider aspects of space food;
- a solar weather expert to help students consider the effects of radiation and solar weather on their activities.

A further link was made with the National Space Centre in Leicester (www. spacecentre.co.uk) which allows children to carry out simulated space missions in its Challenger Learning Centre. The opportunity to design experiments for the International Space Station provided a wonderful way of exciting the pupils' interest in science, as experienced by children at Neston Primary School in Wiltshire who communicated live with astronauts on the station as it passed overhead (see Chapters 8 and 9). The Grove Primary School project provided an excellent opportunity to involve scientists in leading lessons, which helped to develop teachers' professional knowledge across the school.

CONTRIBUTING TO THE WIDER DEBATE

Teaching in a primary school is such a busy and involving task that it is sometimes difficult to look beyond the classroom to the wider world and the new scientific ideas which are profoundly influencing the way humans see the universe and themselves. As science educators, we tend to restrict our horizons to the science curriculum, but there is so much more science out there, the implications of which will directly impact upon the lives of our pupils, some of whom will live into the twenty-second century! For example, the Large Hadron Collider – a 17-kilometre circular tunnel under the Swiss–French border – is seeking to find the Higgs Boson, the so-called 'God particle' which can unite gravity with the other fundamental forces of the universe. The high-energy collisions of protons travelling at nearly the speed of light in the collider could also potentially provide evidence in support of string theory, which posits that all matter is composed of ultra-tiny vibrating strands of energy in up to 11 dimensions. This theory even suggests that there may be many parallel universes coiled up in the minuscule gaps in our own! In biology we have mapped the human genome, are capable of synthesising proteins (the building blocks of life) and probably have the capability to clone human beings or create human–animal hybrids. In materials science we are able to engineer new substances – such as carbon nanotubes – by moving individual atoms into place.

Yet all of these new ideas have their moral dimensions, and as concerned and informed citizens we have a duty to contribute to the debates about how they should be used, because the misapplication of science in the past has placed the world in a perilous state. Despite (or maybe because of) the creativity of our great minds we have succeeded in profoundly altering the Earth's biosphere and upsetting its climatic balance within the comparatively brief period of two centuries, such that the very survival of life on the planet is under threat. We have engineered a revolution in agricultural production, yet a billion people go hungry. Medical science has developed inoculations and cures for many diseases, yet the poor are still ravaged by pandemics. And despite the huge expansion in scientific knowledge, there is still so much we do not know. In cosmology, we have no idea what 90 per cent of the universe is made from – we call it 'dark matter' – and have no understanding of what is driving the galaxies ever further apart (we call it 'dark energy'). We understand the movements of plate tectonics but cannot predict earthquakes. In neuroscience, we have no mechanism to explain how the firing of neurons creates our subjective experience of consciousness. And perhaps most relevant to this book, we still cannot define creativity with any certainty or link it to specific neural activity. These are some of what former US Defense Secretary Donald

Rumsfeld called the 'known unknowns'. Yet there are almost certainly plenty of 'unknown unknowns' – the things that we are not yet aware that we don't know. The children sitting in our classrooms will provide some of the answers to these questions, but they will need to do so in ways that break with the old patterns of thinking. If we carry on the way we are, their future could be bleak or catastrophic; only through radical and ethical creativity will they find a way out.

SUMMARY OF CHAPTER 10

The final chapter has reviewed some of the sources of support to sustain the creativity of primary science educators, including the professional networks, CPD opportunities and award schemes which constitute a national 'creative ecosystem'. Since many creative science teachers will become curriculum leaders within their school we have examined some of the ways in which they can foster a 'dialogic culture' which supports individual and school-wide change. Science subject leaders can also make a difference to how science is perceived within the school and community by mounting events such as science fairs or inviting 'real' scientists to be involved in classroom work. Children with special needs should also be of particular importance to a coordinator seeking to implement more creative approaches to science, in collaboration with the school SENCO. Finally, I have urged all creative primary science teachers to look out at the wider world of science in all its fast-changing complexity and confusion, and to be willing to enter into national debates as informed citizens who just happen to be teaching the generations for whom these ideas will make the greatest impact, for good or ill. However, we also need to remember that the children in our classrooms have the potential to become the creative scientists who solve the problems of sustainability. Through creativity, ethically applied, science just might hold the key to its own redemption.

CONCLUSION

Change is coming to the primary curriculum. In England, the future direction is not clear. I write this on the day of a UK general election in which there is likely to be a change of government, so that the proposed *Independent Review of the Primary Curriculum* (Rose 2009) may be abandoned in favour of something more traditional. However, following the many criticisms of primary education levelled by the *Cambridge Review* (Alexander 2009) the high-stakes testing regime at the end of Key Stage 2 has already been discontinued for science, and a proposed boycott of tests in English and mathematics may hasten its demise altogether. Few primary educators would disagree that this should benefit children's creativity. There is already evidence that following the abandonment of national science tests at age 11 in Wales, teachers are incorporating more hands-on, investigative approaches in Year 6 than previously (Collins *et al.* 2008). Freedom from the pressure to prepare for external assessment has the potential to release a flowering of creative approaches to science pedagogy, such as those I have outlined in this book.

Yet there are clouds on the horizon. First, what is to replace the testing regime? The current answer comes in the form of *Assessing Pupils Progress* (APP), produced by the Primary National Strategy as a means of improving the accuracy and reliability of teacher assessment against National Curriculum levels. The APP materials for science have been available on government websites since January 2010 and consist of a bewildering array of level statements which divide scientific enquiry into five 'assessment focuses'. Unlike the level descriptors in the National Curriculum (DfEE/QCA 1999) which were designed for use 'holistically' using the notion of a 'best fit', the recommended approach to making level judgements using APP statements is 'atomistic'; pupils' work must demonstrate evidence for all components in order to be awarded a particular level. This is likely to place a great administrative burden on teachers to collect large quantities of mainly written assessment evidence for each child, resulting in further assessment-driven teaching and less time for creative approaches. Since the whole APP framework is non-statutory, there is even the danger that schools will revert to internal testing in science simply because it is easier to administer and mark. Unless we are able to develop an assessment regime which rewards creativity and is less demanding of teachers' time and energy, the prospects for developing creative pedagogies in science are not good.

The other threat to creative teaching in science comes in the form of a possible return to a more subject-bound primary curriculum, in which the potential for cross-curricular links – in the form of scientific and technological understanding, but also with language, mathematics and other areas – is much reduced. It seems unlikely that science would retain its supposed 'core' status in any such curriculum, with the continuing pressure on literacy and numeracy skills. We must trust that the momentum towards school-specific creative curricula in primary education, built up over the past decade, is strong enough to withstand such a traditionalist onslaught. Surely one of the lessons of government-imposed curriculum change over the past 20 years is that we ignore creativity at our peril. In this book I have argued that scientific learning could and should be at the heart of any curriculum for creativity in the primary school, and that creative teachers are best placed to make this a reality.

BIBLIOGRAPHY

Aikenhead, G.S. (1996) 'Science education: border crossing into the subculture of science', *Studies in Science Education* 27 (1): 1–52.

Alexander, R. (ed.) (2001) *Culture and Pedagogy: International Comparisons in Primary Education*, Oxford and Boston: Blackwell.

—— (2004) *Towards Dialogic Teaching – Rethinking Classroom Talk*, Cambridge: Dialogos.

—— (2009) *Children, Their World, Their Education: Final Report and Recommendations of the Cambridge Primary Review*, London: Routledge.

Alexander, R., Rose, J. and Woodhead, C. (eds) (1992) *Curriculum Organisation and Classroom Practice in Primary Schools – A Discussion Paper*, London: Department of Education and Science.

Anderson, C.W. (2007) 'Perspectives on science learning', in S.K. Abell and N.G. Lederman (eds) *Handbook of Research on Science Education*, New Jersey: Lawrence Erlbaum Associates, pp. 3–30.

Association for Science Education (2002) *ASE Science Year Primary CD ROM*, Hatfield: Association for Science Education–*Teacher Partnership*, London: Paul Chapman.

Bakhtin, M. (1986) *Speech Genres and Other Late Essays*, Austin, Tex.: University of Texas Press.

Bancroft, S., Fawcett, M. and Hay, P. (eds) (2008) *Researching Children Researching the World: 5x5x5=Creativity*, Stoke on Trent: Trentham Books.

Bell, D. and Ritchie, R. (1999) *Towards Effective Subject Leadership in the Primary School*, Buckingham: Open University Press.

Bianchi, L. (2002) 'Teacher's perceptions of the teaching of personal capabilities through the science curriculum', unpublished PhD thesis, Sheffield Hallam University.

Bianchi, L. and Barnett, R. (2006) *Smart Science: Activating Personal Capabilities in Science*, Sheffield: Centre for Science Education, Sheffield Hallam University.

Black, P. and Hughes, S. (2003) 'Using narrative to support young children's learning in science and D&T', in D. Davies and A. Howe (eds) *Teaching Science and Design & Technology in the Early Years*, London: David Fulton, pp. 38–50.

Bore, A. (2006) 'Creativity, continuity and context in teacher education: lessons from the field', *Australian Journal of Environmental Education* 22 (1): 31–38.

Boyle, B. and Bragg, J. (2005) 'No science today – the demise of primary science', *Curriculum Journal* 16 (4): 423–437.

Braund, M., Hall, A. and Holloway, K. (2007) 'Talking science in the primary school', in G. Venville and V. Dawson (eds) *Proceedings of CONASTA 56 and ICASE 2007 World Conference on Science and Technology Education*, Perth: Science Teachers' Association of Western Australia, pp. 78–84.

Briten, E. (2006) 'Sowing the seeds of creativity', *Primary Science Review* 91: 22–25.

Broadhead, P. and English, C. (2005) 'Open-ended role play: supporting creativity and developing identity', in J. Moyles (ed.) *The Excellence of Play*, 2nd edn, Maidenhead: Open University Press, pp. 72–85.

Bruce, T. (1994) 'Play, the universe and everything!', in J. Moyles (ed.) *The Excellence of Play*, 1st edn, Buckingham: Open University Press, pp. 189–198.

Bruner, J.S. (1996) *The Culture of Education*, Harvard, Mass.: Harvard University Press.

Bruner, J.S., Jolly, A. and Slyva, K. (1976) *Play: Its Role in Development and Evolution*, Harmondsworth: Penguin.

Carson, R. (1956) *The Sense of Wonder*, New York: HarperCollins.

Cassidy, S. (2004) 'Learning styles: An overview of theories, models, and measures', *Educational Psychology* 24 (4): 419–444.

Central Advisory Council for Education (England) (ed.) (1967) *Children and their Primary Schools – the Plowden Report*, London: Her Majesty's Stationery Office.

Childwise (ed.) (2008) *Benchmarking the Views of Young Children Aged 7–10, on Food, Farming and Countryside Issues*, Norwich: Childwise.

Claxton, G. (2002) *Building Learning Power*, Bristol: TLO Publishing.

Collier, C. (2006) 'Creativity in materials and their properties', in A. Oliver (ed.) *Creative Teaching: Science in the Early Years and Primary Classroom*, London: David Fulton, pp. 143–160.

Collins, S., Reiss, M. and Stobart, G. (eds) (2008) *The Effects of National Testing in Science at KS2 in England and Wales*, London: Wellcome Trust.

Cox, M. and Web, M. (2004) 'A review of pedagogy related to information and communications technology', *Technology, Pedagogy and Education* 13 (3): 235–284.

Craft, A. (2000) *Creativity Across the Primary Curriculum: Framing and Developing Practice*, London: Routledge.

—— (2002) *Creativity and Early Years Education*, London: Continuum.

—— (2005) *Creativity in Schools: Tensions and Dilemmas*, London: RoutledgeFalmer.

—— (2008) 'Studying collaborative creativity: implications for education', *Thinking Skills and Creativity* 3 (3): 241–245.

Cremin, T., Barnes, J. and Scoffam, S. (eds) (2006) *Creativity Teaching for Tomorrow: Fostering a Creative State of Mind*, Margate: Creative Partnerships.

Crooks, T., Smith, J. and Flockton, L. (eds) (2008) *National Education Monitoring Project Science Assessment Results 2007*, Dunedin: University of Otago Educational Assessment Research Unit.

Csikszentmihalyi, M. (1990) 'The domains of creativity', in M.A. Runco and R.S. Albert (eds) *Theories of Creativity*, Newbury Park, Calif.: Sage, pp. 190–212.

—— (2002) *Flow*, London: Rider.

Dahlin, B. (2001) 'The primacy of cognition – or of perception? A phenomenological critique of the theoretical bases of science education', in F. Bevilacqua, E. Giannetto and M. Matthews (eds) *Science Education and Culture*, London: Kluwer, pp. 129–151.

Davies, D. (1997) 'The relationship between science and technology in the primary curriculum – alternative perspectives', *The Journal of Design and Technology Education* 2 (2): 101–111.

—— (2006) 'Creative teaching and learning in physical processes', in A. Oliver (ed.) *Creative Teaching: Science in the Early Years and Primary Classroom*, London: David Fulton, pp. 161–181.

Davies, D. and Howe, A. (2007) 'Exploration, investigation and enquiry', in J. Moyles (ed.) *Beginning Teaching, Beginning Learning*, 3rd edn, Maidenhead: McGraw Hill, pp. 74–85.

—— (2003) *Teaching Science and Design & Technology in the Early Years*, London: David Fulton.

Davies, D. and McMahon, K. (2004) 'A smooth trajectory: developing continuity and progression between primary and secondary science education through a jointly-planned projectiles project', *International Journal of Science Education* 26 (8): 1009–1021.

Davies, D., Howe, A. and Haywood, S. (2004a) 'Building a creative ecosystem – the Young Designers on Location Project', *International Journal of Art and Design Education* 23 (3): 278–289.

Davies, D., Howe, A. and McMahon, K. (2004b) 'Challenging primary trainees' views of creativity in the curriculum through a school-based directed task', *Science Teacher Education* (41): 2–4.

—— (2004c) 'Trainee primary teachers and creativity in the curriculum', paper presented at Association of Tutors in Science Education Annual Conference, Northampton, September 2004.

Davies, D., Howe, A., Rogers, M. and Fasciato, M. (2004d) 'How do trainee primary teachers understand creativity?', in E. Norman, D. Spendlove, P. Grover and A. Mitchell (eds) *Creativity and Innovation – DATA International Research Conference 2004*, Wellesbourne: DATA, pp. 41–54.

Department for Children, Schools and Families (DCSF) (2005) *Social and Emotional Aspects of Learning: Improving Behaviour, Improving Learning*, London: DCSF.

—— (2007) *The Children's Plan: Building Brighter Futures*, London: DCSF.

—— (2008) *Statutory Framework for the Early Years Foundation Stage*, London: DCSF.

Department for Culture, Media and Sport and Department for Education and Skills (2006) *Government Response to Paul Roberts' Report on Nurturing Creativity in Young People*, London: DCMS/DfES. Online. Available www.culture.gov.uk/reference_library/publications/3510.aspx (accessed 18 May 2009).

DfEE/QCA (1999) *The National Curriculum Handbook for Primary Teachers in England*, 1st edn, London: HMSO.

—— (1999a) *The National Curriculum for Science*, London: DfEE/QCA.

Department of Education Northern Ireland (DENI) (2007) *The Education (Other Skills) Order (Northern Ireland) 2007*, Belfast: DENI.

Department of Education and Science (1987) *The National Curriculum 5–16: a Consultation Document*, London: Her Majesty's Stationery Office.

Department for Education and Skills (DfES) (2003) *Excellence and Enjoyment – the Primary National Strategy*, London: DfES.

Dickey, B. (1995) *Making Sense of Science: Making Sense of Materials*, London: Software Production Enterprises.

Dillon, J. (2006) 'Education! Education! Out! Out! Out!', *Primary Science Review* (91): 4–6.

Dillon, J., Rickinson, M., Teamey, K., Morris, M., Choi, M.Y., Sanders, D. and Benefield, P. (2006) 'The value of outdoor learning: evidence from research in the UK and elsewhere', *School Science Review* 87 (320): 107–111.

Donaldson, P. (1978) *Children's Minds*, Glasgow: Fontana Press.

Driver, R. (1983) *The Pupil as Scientist?*, Milton Keynes: Open University Press.

Dust, K. (ed.) (1999) *Motive, Means and Opportunity: Creativity Research Review*, London: NESTA.

Edens, K.M. and Potter, E. (2003) 'Using descriptive drawings as a conceptual change strategy in elementary science', *School Science and Mathematics* 103 (3): 135–144.

Edgington, M. (1998) *The Nursery Teacher in Action: Teaching 3, 4 and 5-Year-Olds*, London: Paul Chapman.

Egan, K. (2005) *An Imaginative Approach to Teaching*, San Francisco: Jossey-Bass.

Elliot, R.K. (1975) *'Imagination, a Kind of Magical Faculty'*, Inaugural Lecture, University of Birmingham.

Epstein, D. (1995) '"Girls don't do bricks": gender and sexuality in the primary classroom', in J.

Siraj Blatchford and I. Siraj Blatchford (eds) *Educating the Whole Child – Cross Curricular Skills, Themes and Dimensions*, Buckingham: Open University Press.

Feasey, R. (2005) *Creative Science: Achieving the WOW Factor with 5–11 Year Olds*, London: David Fulton.

Feasey, R., Goldsworthy, A., Phipps, R. and Stringer, J. (2003) *New Star Science*, Oxford: Ginn.

Feyerabend, P. (1994) *Against Method: Outline of an Anarchist Theory of Knowledge*, London: Verso.

Fradley, C. (2006) 'Welly walks for science learning', *Primary Science Review* 91: 14–16.

Fullan, M. (2007) *Planning, Doing and Coping with Change: The New Meaning of Educational Change*, Oxford: Routledge.

Gardner, H. (1983) *Frames of Mind: The Theory of Multiple Intelligences*, London: Fontana.

—— (1999) *The Disciplined Mind*, London: Simon and Schuster.

Gaver, W. (1991) 'Affordances of technology', in S. Robertson, G. Olson and J. Olson (eds) *Proceedings of the SIGCHI Conference on Human Factors in Computing Systems: Reaching through Technology*, New York: Association for Computing Machinery, pp. 79–84.

George, R. (2000) 'Measuring change in students' attitude toward science over time: an application of latent variable growth model', *Journal of Science Education and Technology* 9 (1): 213–225.

Girod, M. and Wong, D. (2002) 'An aesthetic (Dewyan) perspective on science learning: case studies of three fourth graders', *The Elementary School Journal* 102 (3): 199–226.

Godlovitch, S. (1998) *Musical Performance*, London: Routledge.

Goldsworthy, A. and Feasey, R. (1997) *Making Sense of Primary Science Investigations*, Hatfield: Association for Science Education.

Goldsworthy, A. and Ponchaud, B. (2007) *Science Enquiry Games*, Sandbach, Cheshire: Millgate House Publishing.

Goldsworthy, A., Watson, R. and Wood-Robinson, V. (2000a) *The AKSIS Project: Getting to Grips with Graphs*, Hatfield: Association for Science Education (ASE).

—— (2000b) *Developing Understanding (AKSIS Project)*, Hatfield: Association for Science Education (ASE).

Goleman, D. (1996) *Emotional Intelligence: Why It Can Matter More Than IQ*, New York: Bantam Books.

Goodwin, A. (2001) 'Wonder in science teaching and learning: an update', *School Science Review* 83 (302): 69–73.

Greenfield, S. (2000) *Brain Story*, London: BBC Books.

Grimshaw, M. (2009) 'Interactive tools "voted" a success', *Primary Science* 110: 28–29.

Gura, P. (ed.) (1992) *Exploring Learning: Young Children and Block Play*, London: Paul Chapman.

Haigh, M. (2007) 'Can investigative practical work in high school biology foster creativity?', *Research in Science Education* 37: 123–140.

Harlen, W. (ed.) (2000) *The Teaching of Science in Primary Schools*, 2nd edn, London: David Fulton.

—— (2008) *Science as a Key Component of the Primary Curriculum: A Rationale with Policy Implications. Perspectives on Education 1 (Primary Science)*, London: Wellcome Trust.

Harrington, D.M. (1990) 'The ecology of human creativity: a psychological perspective', in M.A. Runco and R.S. Albert (eds) *Theories of Creativity*, London: Sage, pp. 134–169.

Hawking, S. (1988) *A Brief History of Time: From the Big Bang to Black Holes*, London: Bantam Press.

Hoath, L. (2009) 'Asking questions', *Science Teacher Education* 56: 22–26.

Howe, A. and Davies, D. (2005) 'Science and play', in J. Moyles (ed.) *The Excellence of Play*, 2nd edn, Maidenhead: Open University Press, pp. 154–169.

Howe, A., Davies, D., McMahon, K., Towler, L., Collier, C. and Scott, T. (2009) *Science 5–11: a Guide for Teachers*, 2nd edn, London: Routledge.

Hurley, M.M. (2001) 'Reviewing integrated science and mathematics: the search for evidence and definitions from new perspectives', *School Science & Mathematics* 101 (5): 259.

Hutt, C. (1979) 'Play in the under-fives: form, development and function', in J.G. Howells (ed.) *Modern Perspectives in the Psychiatry of Infancy*, New York: Brunner/Marcel, pp. 94–144.

Hutt, S.J., Tyler, S., Hutt, C. and Christopherson, H. (1989) *Play, Exploration and Learning: A Natural History of the Preschool*, London: Routledge.

Jane, B. and Jobling, W. (1995) 'Children linking science and technology in the primary classroom', *Research in Science Education* 25 (2): 191–201.

Jeffrey, B. (2006) 'Creative teaching and learning: towards a common discourse and practice', *Cambridge Journal of Education* 36 (3): 399–414.

Johnston, J. (1996) *Early Explorations in Science*, Buckingham: Open University Press.

—— (2005) 'What is creativity in science education?', in A. Wilson (ed.) *Creativity in Primary Education*, Exeter: Learning Matters, pp. 88–101.

—— (2008) 'Emergent science', *Education in Science* 227: 26.

Kaufman, J. and Baer, J. (1998) 'The role of domains in creative thinking in the USA', in A. Craft, T. Cremin and P. Burnard (eds) *Creative Learning 3–11 and How We Document it*, Stoke-on-Trent: Trentham Books, pp. 27–33.

Koballa, T.R. and Glynn, S.M. (2007) 'Attitudinal and motivational constructs in science learning', in S.K. Abell and N.G. Lederman (eds) *Handbook of Research on Science Education*, Mahwah, NJ: Lawrence Erlbaum Associates, pp. 75–102.

Koestler, A. (1964) *The Act of Creation*, London: Hutchinson.

Kuhn, T. (1970) *The Structure of Scientific Revolutions*, Chicago: University of Chicago Press.

Learning Through Landscapes (2003) *National School Grounds Survey*, Winchester: Learning Through Landscapes.

Lemke, J.L. (1990) *Talking Science: Language, Learning and Values*, Norwood: Ablex Publishing Company.

Leslie, A. (1987) 'Pretense and representation: the origins of "Theory of Mind"', *Psychological Review* 94: 412–422.

Lewisham Education and Culture (1999) *Find That Book: Making Links Between Literacy and the Broader Curriculum*, London: LB Lewisham.

Loveless, A. (2003) *The Role of ICT*, London: Continuum.

Loveless, A. and Wegerif, R. (2004) 'Unlocking creativity with ICT', in R. Fisher and M. Williams (eds) *Unlocking Creativity: Teaching Across the Curriculum*, London: David Fulton, pp. 92–100.

Maine, F. (2009) 'In pursuit of meaning: exploring the language of critical and creative thinking in text comprehension', unpublished PhD thesis, Bath Spa University.

Malaguzzi, L. (1998) 'History, ideas and basic philosophy', in C. Edwards, L. Gandini and G. Forman (eds) *The Hundred Languages of Children*, 2nd edn, Greenwich, Conn.: Ablex, pp. 49–97.

Malone, K. (ed.) (2008) *An Evidence-based Research Report on the Role of Learning Outside the Classroom for Children's Whole Development from Birth to Eighteen Years*, Wollongong, Australia: Farming and Countryside Education.

Mardell, B., Otami, S. and Turner, T. (2008) 'Metacognition and creative learning with American 3–8 year-olds', in A. Craft, T. Cremin and P. Burnard (eds) *Creative Learning 3–11 and How We Document It*, Stoke-on-Trent: Trentham Books, pp. 113–121.

Marshall, S. (2006) *Talk, Talk, Science and Talk: Support Materials for Presentation at ASE Conference 2006*. CD-ROM.

Martin, M.O., Mullis, I.V.S. and Foy, P. (eds) (2008) *TIMSS 2007 International Science Report: Findings from IEA's Trends in International Mathematics and Science Study at the Fourth and Eighth Grades*, Boston: TIMSS & PIRLS International Study Center.

McKinley, E. (2007) 'Postcolonialism, indigenous students and science education', in S.K. Abell and N.G. Lederman (eds) *Handbook of Research on Science Education*, Mahwah, NJ: Lawrence Erlbaum Associates.

McMahon, K. (2006) 'Creativity in life processes and living things', in A. Oliver (ed.) *Creative Teaching: Science in the Early Years and Primary Classroom*, London: David Fulton, pp. 119–142.

—— (2009) 'Interactive whole-class teaching in science lessons in Key Stage 2 classes', unpublished PhD thesis, Bath Spa University.

McMahon, K. and Davies, D. (2001) 'Literacy and numeracy in science', in S. Alsop and K. Hicks (eds) *Teaching Science: a Handbook for Primary and Secondary School Teachers*, London: Kogan Page, pp. 169–182.

—— (2003) 'Assessment for enquiry: supporting teaching and learning in primary science', *Science Education International* 14 (4): 29–39.

Mercer, N. and Littleton, K. (2007) *Dialogue and the Development of Children's Thinking*, London: Routledge.

Mercer, N., Dawes, L. and Staarman, J.K. (2009) 'Dialogic teaching in the primary science classroom', *Language and Education* 23 (4): 353–369.

Meredith, P. (2009) 'Matariki – Maori New Year – heralding the new year', in New Zealand Ministry for Culture and Heritage (ed.) *Te Ara – the Encyclopedia of New Zealand*. Online. Available: www.teara.govt.nz/

Meyer, K. and Woodruff, E. (1997) 'Consensually driven explanation in science teaching', *Science Education* 81 (2): 173–192.

Millar, R. and Osborne, J. (1998) *Beyond 2000 – Science Education for the Future*, London: Kings College.

Montessori, M. (1917) *Spontaneous Activity in Education: the Advanced Montessori Method*, New York: Schocken Books.

Moran, J. (ed.) (1988) *Creativity in Young Children. ERIC Digest*, Urbana, Ill.: ERIC Clearinghouse on Elementary and Early Childhood Education.

Mortimer, H. (2001) *Special Needs and Early Years Provision*, London: Continuum.

Mortimore, E.F. and Scott, P.H. (2003) *Meaning Making in Secondary Science Classrooms*, Buckingham: Open University Press.

Moyles, J. (1989) *Just Playing? The Role and Status of Play in Early Childhood Education*, Milton Keynes: Open University Press.

Murphy, C. and Beggs, J. (eds) (2005) *Primary Horizons: Starting out in Science*, London: Wellcome Trust.

NACCCE (1999) *All Our Futures: Creativity, Culture and Education*, London: DfEE.

Naylor, S. and Keogh, B. (2009) 'Looking, thinking and talking in primary science', paper presented at NZASE Primary Science Conference, Dunedin, April.

Naylor, S., Keogh, B. and Downing, B. (2007) 'Argumentation and primary science', *Research in Science Education* 37 (1): 17–39.

New Zealand Ministry of Education (1993) *The New Zealand Curriculum Framework*, Wellington: New Zealand Ministry of Education.

—— (1996) *Te Whariki: Early Childhood Curriculum*, Wellington: Learning Media.

—— (1999a) *Building Science Concepts*, Wellington: Learning Media.

—— (1999b) *Making Better Sense of the Physical World – Levels 1 to 4*, Wellington: New Zealand Ministry of Education.

—— (2007) *The New Zealand Curriculum for English-medium Teaching and Learning in Years 1–13*, Wellington: New Zealand Ministry of Education.

Nicholls, G. (1999) 'Young children investigating: adopting a constructivist framework', in T. David (ed.) *Teaching Young Children*, London: Paul Chapman.

Nicol, J. (2007) *Bringing the Steiner Waldorf Approach to Your Early Years Practice*, Abingdon: Routledge.

O'Donnell, L., Morris, M. and Wilson, R. (eds) (2006) *Education Outside the Classroom: an Assessment of Activity and Practice in Schools and Local Authorities*, Slough: National Foundation for Educational Research (NFER).

Office for Standards in Education (OFSTED) (1999) *A Review of Primary Schools in England, 1994–1998*, London: The Stationery Office.

—— (2003) *Expecting the Unexpected: Developing Creativity in Primary and Secondary Schools*, London: OFSTED.

—— (2004) *Ofsted Subject Reports 2002/03: Science in Primary Schools*, London: OFSTED.

Oliver, A. (ed.) (2006) *Creative Teaching: Science in the Early Years and Primary Classroom*, London: David Fulton.

Oxfam (2001) *Photo Opportunities in Science*, Oxford: Oxfam.

Parnes, S.J. (1967) *Creative Behavior Guidebook*, New York: Charles Scribner's Sons.

Peacock, A. (2006) *Changing Minds: the Lasting Impact of School Trips*, Swindon: National Trust.

Piaget, J. (1929) *The Child's Conception of the World*, London: Harcourt Brace.

Polanyi, M. (1964) *Science, Faith and Society*, Chicago: University of Chicago Press.

Prensky, M. (2001) 'Digital natives, digital immigrants', *On the Horizon* 9 (5): 1–6.

Qualifications and Curriculum Authority (QCA) (2003) *Creativity: Find it, Promote it*, London: QCA.

Qualifications and Curriculum Authority (QCA)/Department for Education and Employment (DfEE) (1998) *Science – A Scheme of Work for Key Stages 1 and 2*, London: QCA.

—— (2000) *Curriculum Guidance for the Foundation Stage*, London: DfEE/QCA.

Real World Learning Partnership (2006) *Out of Classroom Learning: Practical Information and Guidance for Schools and Teachers*, Sandy, Bedfordshire: RSPB.

Rennie, L. (2007) 'Learning science outside of school', in S.K. Abell and N.G. Lederman (eds) *Handbook of Research on Science Education*, Mahwah, NJ: Lawrence Erlbaum Associates, pp. 125–169.

Rennie, L. and McClafferty, T.P. (1998) 'Young children's interactions with science exhibits', *Visitor Behaviour* 12 (3): 26.

Rivett, A., Harrison, T. and Shallcross, D. (2009) 'The art of chemistry', *Primary Science* Nov./ Dec. (110): 9–13.

Roach, J. (2010) 'Sowing the seeds of scientific understanding in the early years', *Primary Science Review* 111: 16–19.

Robinson, K. (2000) *Out of Our Minds: Learning To Be Creative*, Oxford: Capstone.

Rogers, M., Fasciato, M., Davies, D. and Howe, A. (2005) 'Trainee primary teachers' understanding of the assessment of creativity', paper presented at BERA 2005, University of Glamorgan, September.

Rojas-Drummond, S. and Mercer, N. (2004) 'Scaffolding the development of effective collaboration and learning', *International Journal of Educational Research* 39: 99–111.

Rose, J. (ed.) (2009) *Independent Review of the Primary Curriculum: Final Report*, Nottingham: DCSF Publications.

Rosenblatt, E. and Winner, E. (1988) 'The art of children's drawing', *Journal of Aesthetic Education* 22: 3–15.

Russ, S.W. (2003) 'Play and creativity: developmental issues', *Scandinavian Journal of Educational Research* 47 (3): 291.

Russell, T., Longden, K. and McGuigan, L. (eds) (1991) *Materials: Primary SPACE Research Report*, Liverpool: Liverpool University Press.

Sefton-Green, J. and Sinker, R. (2000) *Evaluating Creativity: Making and Learning by Young People*, London: Routledge.

Sharp, C., Pye, D., Blackmore, J., Brown, E., Eames, A., Easton, C., Filmer-Sankey, C., Tabary, A., Whitby, K., Wilson, R. and Benton, T. (2006) *National Evaluation of Creative Partnerships: Final Report*, London: Creative Partnerships.

Shayer, M., Ginsburg, D. and Coe, R. (2007) 'Thirty years on a large anti-Flynn effect? The Piagetian test volume heaviness norms 1975–2003', *British Journal of Educational Psychology* 77: 25–41.

Shepardson, D.P. (1997) 'The nature of student thinking in life science laboratories', *School Science & Mathematics* 97 (1): 37.

Sigel, I.E. (1993) 'Educating the young thinker: a distancing model of preschool education', in J. Roopnarine and J. Johnson (eds) *Approaches to Early Childhood Education*, New York: Macmillan, pp. 179–194.

Simon, S., Naylor, S., Keogh, B., Maloney, J. and Downing, B. (2008) 'Puppets promoting engagement and talk in science', *International Journal of Science Education* 30 (9): 1229–1248.

Sinclair, J. and Coulthard, M. (1975) *Towards an Analysis of Discourse*, Oxford: Oxford University Press.

Singer, J. (1994) 'Imaginative play and adaptive development', in J. Goldstein (ed.) *Toys, Play and Child Development*, Cambridge: Cambridge University Press, pp. 6–26.

Smythe, K. (2009) 'Getting the best out of the new curriculum', talk given to Tokoroa schools, Developmental Publications Ltd. Online. Available: www.networkonnet.co.nz/index.php?section=latest&id=121 (accessed 12 March 2009).

Spendlove, D. and Wyse, D. (2008) 'Creative learning: definitions and barriers', in A. Craft, T. Cremin and P. Burnard (eds) *Creative Learning 3–11 and How We Document it*, Stoke-on-Trent: Trentham Books, pp. 11–18.

Sylva, K., Melhuish, E., Sammons, P., Siraj-Blatchford, I., Taggart, B. and Elliot, K. (eds) (2003) *The Effective Provision of Pre-school Education (EPPE) Project: Findings from the Pre-school Period*, London: Institute of Education.

Tymms, P., Bolden, D. and Merrell, C. (eds) (2008) *Science in English Primary Schools: Trends in Attainment, Attitudes and Approaches*, London: Wellcome Trust.

Vygotsky, L.S. (1986) 'The genetic roots of thought and speech', in A. Kozulin (ed. and trans.) *Thought and Language*, Cambridge, Mass.: MIT Press.

Wadsworth, P. (1993) *Nuffield Primary Science – SPACE*, London: Collins Educational.

Wegerif, R. and Dawes, L. (2004) *Thinking and Learning with ICT: Raising Achievement in Primary Classrooms*, London: RoutledgeFalmer.

Wertsch, J. (1998) *Mind as Action*, New York: Oxford University Press.

Whetton, C., Ruddock, G. and Twist, E. (eds) (2007) *Standards in English Primary Education: the International Evidence (Primary Review Research Survey 4/2)*, Cambridge: University of Cambridge Faculty of Education.

Wickman, P. (2006) *Aesthetic Experience in Science Education*, Mahwah, NJ: Lawrence Erlbaum Associates.

Wolpert, L. (1992) *The Unnatural Nature of Science*, London: Falmer.

Wragg, E.C. and Brown, G. (2002) *Questioning in the Primary School*, 1st edn, London: Routledge.

Yanowitz, K.L. (2001) 'Using analogies to improve elementary school students' inferential reasoning about scientific concepts', *School Science and Mathematics* 101 (3): 133–142.

Yelland, N. (2003) 'Young children learning with Logo: an analysis of strategies and interactions', *Journal of Educational Computing Research* 9: 465–486.

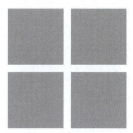

INDEX